Popular Media Cultures

Also by

AMERICAN SCIENCE FICTION FILM AND TELEVISION

CULT COLLECTORS: Nostalgia, Fandom and Collecting Popular Culture

LIVING WITH STAR TREK: American Culture and the Star Trek Universe

Popular Media Cultures
Fans, Audiences and Paratexts

Edited by

Lincoln Geraghty
University of Portsmouth, UK

First published 2015 by
PALGRAVE MACMILLAN

Palgrave Macmillan in the UK is an imprint of Macmillan Publishers Limited, registered in England, company number 785998, of Houndmills, Basingstoke, Hampshire RG21 6XS.

Palgrave Macmillan in the US is a division of St Martin's Press LLC, 175 Fifth Avenue, New York, NY 10010.

Palgrave Macmillan is the global academic imprint of the above companies and has companies and representatives throughout the world.

Palgrave® and Macmillan® are registered trademarks in the United States, the United Kingdom, Europe and other countries.

ISBN 978–1–137–35036–7

This book is printed on paper suitable for recycling and made from fully managed and sustained forest sources. Logging, pulping and manufacturing processes are expected to conform to the environmental regulations of the country of origin.

A catalogue record for this book is available from the British Library.

Library of Congress Cataloging-in-Publication Data
Popular media cultures : fans, audiences and paratexts / edited by Lincoln
   Geraghty, University of Portsmouth, UK.
      pages cm
   Consists of papers delivered at a symposium, Popular Media Cultures:
   Writing in the Margins and Reading Between the Lines, held at the Odeon
   Cinema Covent Garden in London in May 2012.
   Includes bibliographical references and index.
   ISBN 978–1–137–35036–7 (hardback)
   1. Subculture—Congresses.   2. Fans (Persons)—Congresses.
   3. Digital media—Social aspeccts—Congresses.   4. Mass media
   and culture—Congresses.   5. Popular culture—Social aspects—
   Congresses.   I. Geraghty, Lincoln, 1977– editor.
   HM646.P88 2015
   302.23—dc23   2014049953

Contents

List of Tables   vii

Acknowledgements   viii

Notes on Contributors   x

Introduction: Fans and Paratexts   1
Lincoln Geraghty

Part I   Writing in the Margins

1   "We Put the Media in (Anti)social Media": Channel 4's
    Youth Audiences, Unofficial Archives and the Promotion
    of Second-Screen Viewing   17
    Michael O'Neill

2   Television Fandom in the Age of Narrowcasting: The
    Politics of Proximity in Regional Scripted Reality Dramas
    The Only Way Is Essex and *Made in Chelsea*   39
    Cornel Sandvoss, Kelly Youngs and Joanne Hobbs

3   "A Reason to Live": Utopia and Social Change in *Star Trek*
    Fan Letters   73
    Lincoln Geraghty

Part II   Reading between the Lines

4   Victims and Villains: Psychological Themes, Male Stars
    and Horror Films in the 1940s   91
    Mark Jancovich

5   "I Want to Do Bad Things with You": The Television
    Horror Title Sequence   110
    Stacey Abbott

6   *Cannibal Holocaust*: The Paratextual (Re)construction of
    History   127
    Simon Hobbs

Part III   From Spoiler to Fan Activist

7   From *Angel* to *Much Ado*: Cross-Textual Catharsis,
Kinesthetic Empathy and Whedonverse
Fandom   149
Tanya R. Cochran

8   Location, Location, Location: Citizen-Fan Journalists' "Set
Reporting" and Info-War in the Digital Age   164
Matt Hills

9   Sherlock Holmes, the *De Facto* Franchise   186
Roberta Pearson

10 "Cultural Acupuncture": Fan Activism and the Harry
Potter Alliance   206
Henry Jenkins

Afterword: Studying Media with and without Paratexts   230
Jonathan Gray

Index   238

Tables

3.1 Summary of the five social problems and utopian
   solutions presented in the US musical   78

Acknowledgements

This volume is the result of "Popular Media Cultures: Writing in the Margins and Reading between the Lines", a symposium held at the Odeon Cinema Covent Garden in London in May 2012. That event proved to be popular and brought people together from around the UK to listen to some of the world's leading scholars in film, television and media studies. My thanks must go to a number of people involved in the success of the symposium. From the start, the event would not have been possible without the funding awarded by the Centre for Cultural and Creative Research based at the University of Portsmouth. The committee was wholly supportive of running the symposium in London, and because of that decision the event proved to be a great draw for delegates wishing to attend. I am indebted to my colleagues at Portsmouth, past and present, who served on the research committee, helped to prepare for the day and produced all of the publicity that contributed to its success: Justin Smith, Graham Spencer, Paul McDonald, Dominic Symonds, Esther Sonnet, Alison Habens, Steve O'Brien, Christine Etherington-Wright, Deborah Shaw, Laurel Forster, George Burrows, Sarah Eaton, Jackie Walker, Theresa Bassey-Effiok, Emma Austin, Trudy Barber and Rebecca Janicker. To the staff of the Odeon Cinema and Forbidden Planet, who supported the event with promotional material and a symposium discount, I must also give my thanks.

Of course, the symposium would not have been what it was without the great line-up of speakers. Therefore, I must offer my sincere gratitude to all of those who presented on the day: Henry Jenkins, Stacey Abbott, Joanne Garde-Hansen, Kristyn Gorton, Matt Hills, Mark Jancovich, Roberta Pearson, Will Brooker and Cornel Sandvoss. I must also thank the speakers for wanting to be involved in developing their papers into chapters for this volume. As the project progressed, some of the contributions could not be included but I wish to thank those who came on board and whose work adds so much to the quality and depth of the collection as a whole: Michael O'Neill, Simon Hobbs and Tanya R. Cochran. I must also acknowledge the editors of *Transformative Works and Cultures* who agreed for Jenkins' chapter to be reprinted. And to Jonathan Gray, who agreed to write the Afterword, I extend special thanks for all of his patience while the manuscript was being put together so that he could offer his response. Finally, my thanks go to my editors at Palgrave – Felicity Plester, Chris Penfold, Sneha Kamat Bhavnani and Marie Felina Francois – who also had to wait patiently as the contributors and I worked to shape this volume into its completed form.

Contributors

Stacey Abbott is Reader in Film and Television Studies at the University of Roehampton, London, UK, where she teaches courses on animation, film genres, the vampire in film and cult television. She is the author of *Celluloid Vampires* (2007) and *Angel: TV Milestone* (2009), and co-author of *TV Horror: The Dark Side of the Small Screen*, with Lorna Jowett (2013). She is the editor of *The Cult TV Book* (2010) and *Reading Angel* (2005), and co-editor of *TV Goes to Hell: The Unofficial Road Map of Supernatural*, with David Lavery (2011) and *Investigating Alias*, with Simon Brown (2007). She is the general editor of the Investigating Cult TV series and is currently writing a book on the vampire and zombie in 21st-century film and television.

Tanya R. Cochran is Associate Professor of English at Union College in Lincoln, Nebraska, USA, where she teaches first-year writing, upper-division rhetoric and honours composition and research methods. She is also the director of Union College's Studio for Writing and Speaking. Her interests are eclectic and include media and fandom studies, critical race theory, gender studies, narratology, cognitive psychology and the intersection of faith and learning. A past president (2012–2014) and co-founder of the Whedon Studies Association, she is an editorial board member for *Slayage: The Journal of the Whedon Studies Association* and its undergraduate partner, *Watcher Junior*. Additionally, she reviews for *The Journal of Fandom Studies*. Her work has appeared online in *PopMatters*, as well as in journals such as *Composition Studies* and *Transformative Works and Cultures*. Her publications include the coedited collections *Investigating Firefly and Serenity: Science Fiction on the Frontier* (2008), *The Multiple Worlds of Fringe: Essays on the J.J. Abrams Science Fiction Series* (2014) and *Reading Joss Whedon* (2014).

Lincoln Geraghty is Reader in Popular Media Cultures in the School of Media and Performing Arts at the University of Portsmouth, UK. He serves as Editorial Advisor for *The Journal of Popular Culture*, *Reconstruction*, *Journal of Fandom Studies* and *Journal of Popular Television*, with interests in science fiction film and television, fandom, merchandising and collecting in popular culture. He is the author of *Living with Star Trek: American Culture and the Star Trek Universe* (2007), *American Science*

Fiction Film and Television (2009) and *Cult Collectors: Nostalgia, Fandom and Collecting Popular Culture* (2014). He has edited *The Influence of Star Trek on Television, Film and Culture* (2008), *Channeling the Future: Essays on Science Fiction and Fantasy Television* (2009), *The Smallville Chronicles: Critical Essays on the Television Series* (2011) and, with Mark Jancovich, *The Shifting Definitions of Genre: Essays on Labeling Film, Television Shows and Media* (2008). He is currently serving as Editor of the *Directory of World Cinema: American Hollywood*, an online and print publication (2011, 2015).

Jonathan Gray is Professor of Media and Cultural Studies at University of Wisconsin-Madison, USA. He is the author of *Television Studies*, with Amanda D. Lotz (2007), *Show Sold Separately: Promos, Spoilers, and Other Media Paratexts* (2010), *Television Entertainment* and *Watching with The Simpsons: Television, Parody, and Intertextuality* (2006). He is the editor of *A Companion to Media Authorship*, with Derek Johnson (2013), *Satire TV: Politics and Comedy in the Post-Network Era*, with Jeffrey P. Jones and Ethan Thompson (2009) and *Fandom: Identities and Communities in a Mediated World*, with Cornel Sandvoss and C. Lee Harrington (2007).

Matt Hills is Professor of Film and TV Studies at Aberystwyth University. He is the author of five books including *Fan Cultures* (2002) and *Triumph of a Time Lord: Regenerating Doctor Who in the Twenty-first Century* (2010). He has published widely on cult film, TV and fandom, including recent contributions to Palgrave-Macmillan collections such as *Cult Film Stardom* and *Critical Approaches to the Films of M. Night Shyamalan*. He is currently working on a study of BBC Wales' *Torchwood*.

Joanne Hobbs studied media at the University of Surrey, UK, and is now working in the print industry.

Simon Hobbs is a PhD candidate at the University of Portsmouth, UK. His thesis, entitled "Extreme Art Cinema: Text, Paratext and Industry", explores the intersection between "high" and "low" culture within the marketing of transgressive art narratives.

Mark Jancovich is Professor of Film and Television Studies at the University of East Anglia, UK. He is the author of several books: *Horror* (1992), *The Cultural Politics of the New Criticism* (1993), *Rational Fears: American Horror in the 1950s* (1996) and *The Place of the Audience: Cultural Geographies of Film Consumption*, with Lucy Faire and Sarah Stubbings

(2003). He is also the editor of several collections: *Approaches to Popular Film*, with Joanne Hollows (1995), *The Film Studies Reader*, with Joanne Hollows and Peter Hutchings (2000), *Horror, The Film Reader* (2001), *Quality Popular Television: Cult TV, the Industry and Fans*, with James Lyons (2003), *Defining Cult Movies: The Cultural Politics of Oppositional Taste*, with Antonio Lazaro-Reboll et al. (2003), *Film Histories: An Introduction and Reader*, with Paul Grainge and Sharon Monteith (2006), *Film and Comic Books*, with Ian Gordon and Matthew P. McAllister (2007), and *The Shifting Definitions of Genre: Essays on Labeling Films, Television Shows and Media*, with Lincoln Geraghty (2008). He was also the founder of *Scope: An Online Journal of Film Studies*. He is the series editor, with Eric Schaefer, of the book series *Inside Popular Film*, and he is the series editor, with Charles Acland, of the book series *Film Genres*. He is currently writing a history of horror in the 1940s.

Henry Jenkins is currently the Provost's Professor of Communication, Journalism, Cinematic Art and Education at the University of Southern California and was formerly the co-director of the Comparative Media Studies Program at MIT, USA. He is the author or editor of 17 books, including *Textual Poachers: Television Fans and Participatory Culture* (1992), *Fans, Bloggers, and Gamers* (2008), *Convergence Culture: Where Old and New Media Collide* (2008), *Spreadable Media: Creating Meaning and Value in a Networked Culture*, with Sam Ford and Joshua Green (2013), *Reading in a Participatory Culture*, with Wyn Kelley et al. (2013) and the forthcoming *By Any Media Necessary: Mapping Youth and Participatory Politics*, with Sangita Shresthova, Neta Kligler-Vilenchik, Liana Gamber-Thompson and Arely Zimmerman. He blogs regularly about media and cultural studies related topics at henryjenkins.org.

Michael O'Neill completed his PhD in the School of Creative Arts, Film and Media at the University of Portsmouth, UK. His thesis, entitled "Digital Spray: Channel 4, Innovation and Youth Programming in the Age of New Technologies", examines both the historical and contemporary usage and promotion of youth-oriented television by Channel 4 in the UK.

Roberta Pearson is Professor of Film and Television Studies at the University of Nottingham, UK. She is the co-author of *Star Trek and American Television* (2014), and the editor or co-editor of *Many More Lives of the Batman* (2015), *Storytelling in the Media Convergence Age: Exploring Screen Narratives* (2015) and *Reading Lost* (2009). She has also published numerous book chapters and articles on topics that include Shakespeare, Sherlock Holmes, early US cinema and fan studies.

Cornel Sandvoss is Professor of Media and Journalism at the University of Huddersfield, UK. He has published widely on the interplay between media use, identity and globalisation, including *Bodies of Discourse: Sport Stars, Media and the Global Public*, with Michal Real and Alina Bernstein (2012), and *A Game of Two Halves: Football, Television and Globalization* (2003), as well as on fans and fan cultures: *Fans: The Mirror of Consumption* (2005) and *Fandom: Identities and Communities in a Mediated World*, with Jonathan Gray and Lee Harrington (2007). He is a former Chair of the Popular Communication Division of the International Communication Association and recently completed two Arts and Humanities Research Council-funded projects on cultural value, participatory culture and popular media.

Kelly Youngs studied media at the University of Surrey, UK. She also holds a master's from the University of Westminster, UK and is working as an events manager.

Introduction: Fans and Paratexts

Lincoln Geraghty

The first step towards a wider consideration of popular media cultures surrounding music, comics, film, television and the Internet, and the relationship between fans and their object of fandom, is to acknowledge the prominent position of what Jonathan Gray (2010) calls media "paratexts" as opposed to the centrality of specific films or television series as the "text". Indeed, we are now accustomed in fan studies to stating that the productivity of fans and their related fan practices represents an appropriate and worthy text to study just as much as the media text to which they are related or inspired by. So, rather than studying *Star Trek* as cult text, we might study fan-produced videos on YouTube as important texts of fan activity that carry inherent meaning and significance in and of themselves. Or, for example, *Star Wars* carries with it meaning within and outside the narrative – from an analysis of its mythic story structure using the work of Joseph Campbell, to studies of its fans who actively engage in their own meaning-making by dressing up, making videos and writing fan fiction. However, the peripheral texts – those associated with the commercialisation of the franchise, such as the lunchboxes, toys, video games and websites – are so much a part of the meaning-making process that they become texts to study in their own right.

Popular Media Cultures seeks to explore the relationship between audiences and media texts, their paratexts and interconnected ephemera, and the related cultural practices that add to and expand the narrative worlds with which fans engage. How audiences make meaning out of established media texts will be discussed in connection with the new texts produced by fans. The collection will focus on the cultural work done by media audiences, how they engage with new technologies, and how convergence culture impacts on the strategies and activities of

1

popular media fans. If, Ken Gelder argues, "Subcultures are brought into being through narration and narrative: told by the participants themselves, as well as by those who document them, monitor them, 'label' them, outlaw them, and so on" (2007: 66), then this collection will pay attention to what media audiences add to a text, what gets written in the margins of a text and what new meanings fans read between the lines. This collection brings together leading academics in the fields of film, television, and fan and cultural studies to open up and take further the debates surrounding popular media, its producers, its audiences and the cultures in which they are ultimately located.

Making paratexts: Brick by brick

Previous studies of why film and television have attracted devoted fan followings have focused on the texts themselves – specifically, how their narratives and the ever-expanding fictional worlds in which they are set allow for interaction and offer the possibility for fans to create their own meaning from and within the text, illustrated by such practices as slash fiction, fan-made videos and fantasy role-playing. Gwenllian-Jones and Pearson (2004: xvii) describe how "the potentially infinitely large metatext" of media franchises "create the space for fans to revel". Likewise, Matt Hills (2002) describes how cult television series, from *The Prisoner* (1967–1968) to *The X-Files* (1993–2002), offer a "perpetuated hermeneutic" (central mystery) that draws viewers into their "hyper-diegesis" (unfinished worlds) that fans can then add to and make use of in their own creative lives. My own previous work on *Star Trek* also draws attention to the importance of narrative in the popularity of media texts, stating that the series "reproduces a historical narrative" providing "fans a framework" for their own understanding of history, morality and social interaction (Geraghty, 2007: 29). But what about the paratextual elements of fandom – how and where are these fictional worlds and narratives used within the paratextual play of fans? If these fantastic film and television texts offer multiple universes that express concerns within contemporary culture, how is this reflected in the rituals of fan paratextual production?

A brief look at the ever-expanding world of Lego might shed some light on the answers to these questions and go some way to foregrounding the issues and concerns relating to fans and paratexts found in the chapters of this volume. Lego, a children's toy originally based on the physicality of construction, has taken on new significance in contemporary media culture because it allows adult collectors/fans to reconnect with their childhood and define a fan identity through more ephemeral and digital interaction, such as making stop-motion videos and uploading them to YouTube and the official Lego website. Fans are actively encouraged to make videos, using all manner of Lego products to create increasingly ingenious and humorous short films that both extend the narrative worlds of the Lego characters involved and promote the Lego brand across various media platforms. The creation of such paratextual entertainment is in part due to wider changes in toy culture and media franchising. Following developments in the US toy industry in the 1970s and 1980s, where fantasy and action toys became central components of movie merchandise and licensing agreements (see Cross, 1997), Lego turned to creating its own ranges of themed building sets and minifigure characters; where before children built what they wanted (limited only by their own imagination), they now followed plans and built within prescribed "systems": city, space, medieval, pirates, etc. (see Kline, 1993). Lego would buy into the merchandising market with its range of very popular *Star Wars*, *Harry Potter* and *Pirates of the Caribbean* sets that allowed children to rebuild and reconstruct artefacts from famous film franchises.

Lego's shift to producing product tie-ins has been supported by a popular range of video games (e.g. *Lego Star Wars*) and the creation of online fan clubs aimed at both children and adults. These games and websites encourage multimedia play: use your Lego sets to recreate the Death Star or imagine what Imperial Stormtroopers get up to when they are on a lunch break. Indeed, the animated Lego films inspired by the video games are often sold on DVDs which also include winning fan-made videos entered into official Lego competitions. Now that the Lego "system" incorporates global franchises such as *Star Wars*, it means that collectors/fans of one brand cross over to become collectors/fans of another. The Lego *Star Wars* universe develops a fandom of its own with the minifigure versions of Han Solo and Darth Vader (animated with comic effect in the video games, fan videos and Lego films) becoming just as iconic and desirable among fans as the "real" originals. Moreover, what started as a paratext, based on the original narrative of *Star Wars*, has evolved to become a text in itself that produces further meaning as the fan-made narrative universe expands with each video made and uploaded. In these web spaces, personal memories and official histories of global media franchises are constantly negotiated and reshaped, taking on new meanings. These negotiations impact on the construction of a fan identity and the production of culturally important paratexts that require scholarly attention in their own right.

For example, in the seven-minute video "Tales of the Savage, Blood-Thirsty, Rampaging, Out-of-Control Wampa!" by alnickelsfilms, we are introduced to a Lego wampa (a monster seen in *The Empire Strikes Back* [1980]) who walks into a fan re-creation of Jabba's Palace with a Lego Jabba the Hutt trying to eat from a dinner table. In comedy accents they converse, with the wampa moaning that he is misunderstood in the *Star Wars* universe and is therefore ostracised, and Jabba grumbling that the height of Lego furniture is stopping him from feeding. Meant as an extratextual joke for fans, Jabba would never come face to face in a bar with a wampa, and, containing intertextual references to the physical limitations of Lego minifigures (lack of poseability, etc.), this video plays with convention and subverts the *Star Wars* narrative. Relying on fan knowledge and memory, it uses comedy to emphasise the constructed nature of the films, the fantasy worlds of Lucas' imagination and the malleability of Lego-building and creativity. As with many fan videos on YouTube, it combines pre-established textual elements (in this case the Lego *Star Wars* figures and the characters themselves) with original contributions (the fan story and dialogue) to create a mashup that speaks to fans (of both Lego and *Star Wars*). Both playful and intuitive, fan videos such as this one do not simply add one element to another to make a new whole but form what Shaun Wilson calls "a rupture of narrative" where "the weighted memory" of the original characters from the *Star Wars* universe are "repositioned through its facsimile" (2009: 192). For Garde-Hansen (2011: 116), the "repositioning of the memory of the original is important because we see the mediated past in a new light" (and in this case a totally new form: Lego). Therefore this video, like many others on YouTube, plays, an important part in the retelling of the *Star Wars* story, which has already been transformed through Lego. Barbara Klinger (2011: 210) argues that "once ephemeral productions are given exposure through mediatisation, their status as texts with some endurance amplifies their capacity to signify", therefore they create new meanings and new beginnings for future fan stories. Indeed, online videos give fans "more autonomy over their (multi)mediated portrayals" of personal identity, cultural capital and the text (van Dijck, 2007: 140). They are evidence of hard work and enjoyable play, visual reminders of the world-building potential that using Lego in reconstructing media narratives and texts offers fans in the production of new paratexts.

Similarly, Lego video games offer fans the opportunity to make new texts from old. In 2005 the company released the first *Star Wars* tie-in game, *Lego Star Wars: The Video Game*, closely followed by *Lego Star Wars II: The Original Trilogy* in 2006, *Star Wars: The Complete Saga* in 2007 and finally *Star Wars III: The Clone Wars* in 2011. Clearly, part of the attraction of these games is that gameplay is tied directly to the overarching narrative of the original source text. So, for example, gamers can play through scenes from all three original films and three prequels, and play as all the important and well-known characters to achieve the ultimate goal of finding Princess Leia, destroying the Death Star or defeating the Emperor. In addition to this narrative play, gamers can enjoy extra missions and tasks that are linked to the overall theme of the game/movie but are driven more by adventure than the limits of the original story. Across all Lego games this adventurous play, or "free play" as it is called, allows for greater experimentation. This freedom is greatly enhanced by the fact that while gamers play the story they earn points so that they can buy access to extra levels, new characters and other abilities. Once all levels and abilities are open, gamers can then create their own characters and play as them within the story and "free play". Narrative and digital play thus become more personalised, with the gamer's own Lego character (designed and named by them) engaging with the famous Lego versions of Luke Skywalker or Yoda. The creative element of the games allows for the convergence of fan identity and fictional narrative, making the experience more individual, more real and more affective.

Fandom has been described by Matt Hills as a form of "affective play" in that fans "play" within and outside their favourite films or television series by dressing up and performing, writing their own fan fiction or simply attending conventions. What distinguishes any and all of these activities as "play" is that they deal "with the emotional attachment of the fan" and they suggest "that play is not always caught up in a pre-established 'boundedness' or set of cultural boundaries, but may instead imaginatively create its own set of boundaries and its own auto-'context'" (Hills, 2002: 112). Thus we can see the use of self-created minifigures in the playing of *Lego Star Wars* as part of this fan "affective play" in that gamers can transform and go beyond the boundaries of the original game and story, and insert their own self into the narrative. The software in all themed games also presents fans and gamers with the opportunity to transfer their physical self into the digital world. So fans can create a minifigure identity from the head of Chewbacca and the torso of Princess Leia if they so wish. In the games, these body parts exist in the game hub and so gamers can recreate their figures, therefore themselves, and insert them into the context of the game world and thus create their own context for interacting with established characters, scenarios and gaming levels.

The transference of characters and narrative across different media platforms is emblematic of what media scholars call "transmediality" or "transmedia storytelling". Henry Jenkins (2006: 334) defines the latter as "stories that unfold across multiple media platforms, with each medium making distinctive contributions to our understanding of the world". In the context of the Lego games, each game version of the movie adds another level of meaning and story to the original. With fan-created minifigures also part of this transmedia process, gamers can move the story from the real world (physical toy) to the fictional world (virtual avatar) – and back again – playing through the narrative in ways that are not achievable simply by watching and rewatching the film, building the toy or even being one of the main characters in the game. As gamers play through the levels as their Lego self they can interact with original characters from the movies and literally place themselves on board the Death Star or Hoth and take part in the *Star Wars* universe. Dan Fleming recognises this shift in toy culture stating that toys "are not the only mediatory objects in our lives; not the only objects to function transitionally for us", going on to argue that technological objects like video consoles are not so much "toys for big boys and girls" but "generate a safe feeling when we give ourselves over to them" (1996: 195). Building on this, I would argue that *Lego Star Wars* is now as much a transmedia narrative as it is a toy brand or video game, and that the "affective play" of fan gaming (making and collecting, playing with and as Lego characters) brings that narrative to life in a paratextual world that extends beyond the boundaries that were established by the original text.

The examples from the world of Lego *Star Wars* discussed above illustrate the continued importance and centrality of paratexts in fan communities as well as highlight the increasing significance that media companies place on fan-created texts in the promotion and circulation of popular culture brands. Thus, while a collection such as *Popular Media Cultures* addresses fan activity and the creation of fan paratexts it also has to attend to how broadcasters, producers, writers and journalists contribute to the paratextual meaning-making process. How do the creators of television series such as *Utopia* or *Doctor Who* engage fans through social media, and to what extent can their interactions and content online be considered just as important to the fan experience and community? What about the production of textual meaning through film reviews and DVD packaging – how might these works of critical reception and physical objects of marketing help to construct new meanings in and outside the originating text? This volume attempts to answer these types of question, as well as proposing more, as we continue to understand the popularity and power of the media in which we immerse ourselves.

Contents

This collection is in part made up by essays written by those who presented at Popular Media Cultures: Writing in the Margins and Reading Between the Lines, a symposium held at the Odeon Cinema Covent Garden in London in May 2012 (http://popularmediacultures.port.ac.uk/). However, with the luxury of space and time to put together this volume, I have been able to include current work from other scholars who also make valuable contributions to the field of fan and paratextual studies. The book is split into three parts: the first discusses the virtual and ephemeral activities and spaces of media fans and the responses that they articulate towards their particular objects of affection (youth-orientated drama, scripted reality television and science fiction); the second part focuses on the paratextual elements that surround, inform and create popular media culture texts (such as the critical reception of horror film stars and their personas, the appeal of television horror opening credit sequences, and the marketing of a cult horror film on DVD); and the third focuses on the activities of specific fan communities and the personalised narratives formed in and around popular media (fan responses to the authorship of Joss Whedon texts, *Doctor Who* Internet spoilers and set reports, contested ownership of the Sherlock Holmes franchise, and Harry Potter political fan activism). What all of the chapters highlight is the ongoing engagement of fans with popular media texts and the shifting levels of meaning that are brought to those texts through the proliferation of official and unofficial paratexts. Jonathan Gray says in the Afterword to the volume that to ignore the paratextual elements to any popular media form that attracts fan affection and productivity "and yet still feel comfortable to make a declaration about a text's meaning, impact, power, effects, or value, would be an act akin to reading only the third and fourth chapters of a book and feeling that this suffices for a full analysis". Therefore, as the following essays demonstrate, scholars of fans and popular media must cast their net wider and look to investigate the cultures of meaning and textual production that inform the television series that we watch or the films that we go to see. Furthermore, in an age of convergence and social media, the various technologies of interaction shared by producers and audiences must also be considered as valuable sources of information. Fan commentaries online are paratexts in and of themselves and thus serve as constant reminders that there is another level of meaning-making away from the textual spotlight that shines on every media franchise, producer or text, large or small.

Michael O'Neill (Chapter 1) provides the volume's first analysis of fan/producer relations, focusing on Channel 4's recent provision and strategy in terms of social media and multiplatform commissioning, and its dealings with changing user-consumption practices within a variety of spaces and platforms. Alternative, "unofficial" spaces and archives of television content (e.g. YouTube) have become sites where users not only consume difficult-to-locate content but can contribute towards alternative repositories of ephemeral content. This, O'Neill argues, contributes to the processes of fandom of specific youth-oriented texts, as well as the paratextual content pertaining to them, and leads to an increased policing of content and shaping of experiences within these spaces by Channel 4. He also refers to "second-screen" viewing – a practice whereupon the longstanding primacy of the television screen is reduced due to mobile technologies and social media both supplementing and supplanting the televisual experience. These practices and strategies are discussed using examples of their implementation through increasingly popular factual and drama commissions that are targeted at youth audiences: the campaigning series *Battlefront* (2008), the E4 drama series *Skins* (2007–2013) and Channel 4's "first multiplatform commission" *Utopia* (first broadcast in 2013).

Similarly, regional part-scripted reality dramas have become unexpected successes for non-terrestrial channels such as ITV2, E4 and MTV. At the same time, their popularity remains confined to particular demographics. Sandvoss, Youngs and Hobbs (Chapter 2) examine the success of two of these shows in the post-network era: *The Only Way Is Essex* (2010–present) and *Made in Chelsea* (2011–present). Through the study of the fan cultures surrounding these programmes, the different forms of textuality resulting from *The Only Way Is Essex* and *Made in Chelsea* fandom across different media platforms, fans' varying levels of productivity, and the individual readings and appropriations through which the affective bond between fans and the programmes is maintained, they examine forms of reciprocality and proximity of celebrity in the convergent era, the changing relationship between place and objects of fandom, and the role of engagements with forms of Otherness in fandom as a practice of transmedia reading and meaning construction. Their chapter also evaluates the impact of fandom on both texts and technologies on contemporary television drama.

While the first two chapters examine online sites for fan interaction and feedback, my own contribution (Chapter 3) examines to what extent *Star Trek* fan letters can be seen as evidence for a supportive community, where fans' hopes, desires and traumatic experiences can be expressed, shared and utilised. This community, or what I term "network of support", relies on the fictional television text as a common frame of reference. Relevant *Star Trek* episodes and characters are used as markers for specific emotional and physical experiences. If mass communications mediate the boundaries between the public and the private, then they not only provide images of the world around us and places with which we are not familiar but also provide us with the practices and beliefs for a sense of community. These letters describe Gene Roddenberry's depiction of utopia and how fans feel that his vision was, and still is, an attainable goal in their own lifetime. Fans define the series as a blueprint for solving existing social problems in the USA, such as racism, poverty and war. In their letters, fans see the series as representing a utopian future that exists in contrast with the dystopian future to which existing social problems will lead. Thus, as forms of paratextual meaning-making, fan correspondence provides crucial evidence of how fans talk about and through the original text. Without acknowledging such paratextual talk we risk losing sight of what keeps fans motivated and entertained.

Science fiction is a popular genre; so too horror and the stars that embody famous monstrous characters. Icons of horror cinema have become firm favourites with fans, and their images last long in the memory of cinema history. Consequently, Mark Jancovich (Chapter 4) explores horror stars and their critical reception in the trade press as paratexts. Although Boris Karloff, Bela Lugosi and Lon Chaney Jr are seen as the key horror stars of the 1940s, along with lesser figures such as Lionel Atwill and George Zucco, the period was one in which the horror film was not limited to the low-budget productions of Universal, Columbia and others but, on the contrary, one in which many horror films emphasised large budgets and stellar casts in their marketing. Consequently, a number of romantic male leads became closely associated with the genre – stars such as Ray Milland, Joseph Cotton, Cary Grant and George Sanders. If these stars are hardly remembered in this way today, that is largely because many of their key horror films are no longer associated with the genre, although they were understood as horror films at the time of their original release. For example, the figure of the gangster and the spy were no strangers to the horror film during the 1940s, and many films that would commonly be understood as thrillers today were clearly seen as horror films at the time. Therefore, in this chapter, Jancovich examines the ways in which Milland, Cotton, Grant and Sanders were discussed in contemporary commentary in order to explore how they and their films were understood. The intention is not to suggest that these "original" meanings are the only legitimate meanings but only to clarify how they were understood within a specific historical context and, in so doing, to demonstrate that understandings of them today are neither necessary nor inevitable but a product of our own historical context. In the process, he looks at the cultural politics underlying the paratextual critical reception of their films, before moving on to examine the various stages through which their reputation as horror stars developed during the period.

Following this focus on horror film paratexts such as film reviews, Stacey Abbott (Chapter 5) examines how the opening credit sequence of recent television horror plays an interesting role within contemporary cult television audiences. Credits are part of the television series, establishing atmosphere, theme and occasionally providing clues to the show's mysteries, but they are also separate from the show, often made by a different company than the one that produces the television series. The credit sequence for *True Blood* (2008–2014) situates the show within the sultry traditions of southern gothic, while also establishing a harder, more violent edge that is a key element of the show. The credits for *American Horror Story* (2011–present) clearly establish the show's pedigree as contemporary horror because they are made by the same company that produced the credits to the film *Se7en* (1995). Credit sequences also have a particular attraction to fans as they analyse the meaning behind the credits and often rework credits to suit their own interpretation of the series. Therefore Abbott considers the television horror credit sequence to be an example of paratextuality, in which a puzzle and game are being played between the creators of the show and their fans.

Simon Hobbs (Chapter 6) extends this study of the horror genre by focusing on the extreme example of the "video nasty" *Cannibal Holocaust* (1980), and how its public meaning has changed over time. Its paratextual elements (critical reviews, DVD packaging, production interviews, fan collections, etc.) have worked to alter perceptions of its standing as a culturally important film text and subculturally valued fan object. Hobbs argues that film ephemera, such as the DVD and its associated packaging, can be addressed as an independently functioning bearer of meaning. He asserts the importance of paratextual remediation in reshaping the histories of seminal exploitation narratives such as *Cannibal Holocaust*, and more generally the worthiness of exploring media texts and their fans through their differing proliferations. This chapter highlights the significant themes of the collection in total: that paratexts are important markers of the media's textual presence in popular culture; that fans work to promote their favoured texts through the preservation of its incarnations in collections and new technologies; that fans and producers seek to raise up their valued texts through the proliferation of official and unofficial paratexts; and that the subcultural value of fan-related media is inherently linked to the paratextual play that is encouraged by audiences, critics and producers.

Play is at the heart of Tanya R. Cochran's contribution (Chapter 7) about Joss Whedon fans. She discusses how fans of specific actors playing characters that are killed off in one Whedon series or film enjoy seeing them reappear in another, playing strangely similar roles, in the process transferring narrative meaning and intertextual significance across media texts. She highlights the deep emotional impact of narratives, fans' desire and even a need for catharsis, the convergent nature of storytelling in our time, and the role of the human body – the actor's as well as the spectator's body – in enabling the existence of endlessly deferred narratives. The actor's body becomes the site for paratextual play as fans produce fan fiction that ships characters and actors in order to rewrite and extend stories and characters' lives that were previously cut short by primary author Whedon. Cochran's chapter acknowledges that fans are creative and driven to respond to the changes produced by writers that originate popular television series. The paratexts of fan fiction and the actors who themselves come to embody favourite characters are sites for active meaning-making, suggesting that while fans play within and around the boundaries of the text, they are deadly serious when it comes to the emotional attachments that they have with certain media.

For Matt Hills (Chapter 8), perhaps one of the key shifts affecting recent popular media culture has been a move from the "reactive audience" – responding to media texts – to anticipatory, proactive fandoms who seek information about new products far in advance of official release, and even ahead of industry public relations. For him the development of "pre-reading" and paratextual sifting by online fans means that within convergence culture, media-savvy fan audiences can be thought of not so much as textual poachers but rather as "pretextual poachers". Fans challenge the informational, brand control of media producers by discovering and circulating unofficial news, gossip, rumours and photos of on-set filming. Hills discusses the phenomenon of fan "set reporting", whereby audiences tweet, blog and upload their photos and videos of location filming. In discussing franchises such as *Twilight, Doctor Who* and *Sherlock*, which have all had to contend with this new digital mode of fan productivity, he argues that far from dematerialising the importance of location, this new fan practice combines immediacy with hypermediation, granting authenticity and status to "being there" and to documenting activities of media production. Socially networked fandom thus both reinforces the symbolic centrality of filming sites (e.g. Cardiff for *Doctor Who*) and brings fans into conflict with producers in novel, pre-textual ways. Hills contends that, far from being a mysterious, shut-away process, location filming has become an increasingly transparent, fan-mediated event, with "citizen-fans" placing the elite activities of popular media production into the subcultural public spheres of fan knowledge, debate and speculation, somewhat akin to the activities of citizen-journalists.

Roberta Pearson (Chapter 9) addresses larger questions of franchising and paratextual production, particularly that of the fictional detective Sherlock Holmes. In addition to the novels from Sir Arthur Conan Doyle, the great detective stars in a Warner's film series, a BBC television series and a bestselling novel, *The House of Silk* (2011) by Anthony Horowitz, authorised by the Conan Doyle estate, and his fans can be found all over the web. Pearson assesses Sherlockian fandoms' relationship to the franchise, extended across film, television and literature. She argues that Holmes' current multimedia incarnations exhibit some of the characteristics of a franchise engaged in transmedia storytelling, but, uniquely among current media franchises, intellectual property is not vested in a single corporate entity. In fact, intellectual property isn't vested anywhere since Holmes is out of copyright. As a result, the lines between fanfic and profic are more blurry in Sherlockian fandom than in any other. At the top of the profic ladder are Steven Moffat and Mark Gatiss, hardcore Sherlockians as evidenced both by their *Sherlock* series and by their interviews. At the bottom of the fanfic ladder are those turning out stories for the myriad Sherlockian Internet sites. In between are those creating Holmes novels and short stories, primarily for distribution by Amazon. In looking at the multiplicity of Sherlock Holmes stories across public and private domains, Pearson also explores the legal claims and counterclaims of authorship. In examining the case of the Conan Doyle estate's legal attempts to wrestle control over the exclusive right to make paratexts, Pearson shows just how important courts and policy will be in determining the future of paratexts that are created by fans and official producers alike.

In what was the keynote presentation at the original London symposium, Henry Jenkins (Chapter 10) examines how powerful and important fans have become in contemporary media culture. For example, fan activists have struggled to defend series from cancellation, defend themselves from cease and desist orders, promote alternative representations and raise money for charity. Building on this background, he examines how the Harry Potter Alliance encourages young people to speak out as fans on a range of human rights and social justice issues through what the group's leader, Andrew Slack, calls "cultural acupuncture". The group's practice of mapping the fictional content world onto real-world concerns helps to empower young people to become civically engaged and politically active. Thus the paratextual production of websites, adverts, poster campaigns and Internet memes based on corporate brands such as Harry Potter highlights how fans can take part in the process of active political engagement, contesting at the same time the dominance of the pre-existing text – writing new stories and creating new meanings that no longer serve the profit-making strategies of the companies that originally created them. Fans are activists, and their reworkings of established media franchises are prime examples of how integral paratexts have materialised in trying to understand the motivations of producers and fans as they continue to struggle with issues of ownership and creative freedom.

References

Cross, G. (1997), *Kid's Stuff: Toys and the Changing World of American Childhood*. Cambridge: Harvard University Press.

Fleming, D. (1996), *Powerplay: Toys as Popular Culture*. Manchester: Manchester University Press.

Garde-Hansen, J. (2011), *Media and Memory*. Edinburgh: Edinburgh University Press.

Gelder, K. (2007), *Subcultures: Cultural Histories and Social Practice*. London: Routledge.

Gray, J. (2010), *Show Sold Separately: Promos, Spoilers, and Other Media Paratexts*. New York: New York University Press.

Gwenllian-Jones, S. and Pearson, R.E. (2004), "Introduction." In S. Gwenllian-Jones and R.E. Pearson, eds., *Cult Television*. Minneapolis, MN: University of Minnesota Press, pp. ix–xx.

Hills, M. (2002), *Fan Cultures*. London: Routledge.

Jenkins, H. (2006), *Convergence Culture: Where Old and New Media Collide*. New York: New York University Press.

Kline, S. (1993), *Out of the Garden: Toys and Children's Culture in the Age of TV Marketing*. London: Verso.

Klinger, B. (2011), "Re-enactment: Fans Performing Movie Scenes from the Stage to YouTube." In P. Grainge, ed., *Ephemeral Media: Transitory Screen Culture from Television to YouTube*. London: BFI, pp. 195–213.

van Dijck, J. (2007), *Mediated Memories in the Digital Age*. Stanford: Stanford University Press.

Wilson, S. (2009), "Remixing Memory in Digital Media." In J. Garde-Hansen, A. Hoskins, and A. Reading, eds., *Save As...Digital Memories*. Basingstoke: Palgrave Macmillan, pp. 184–197.

Part I
Writing in the Margins

1
"We Put the Media in (Anti)social Media": Channel 4's Youth Audiences, Unofficial Archives and the Promotion of Second-Screen Viewing

Michael O'Neill

Fans, and the agency of media audiences, are a longstanding cultural phenomenon. Their increased visibility and the everydayness of fan practice and user production, on the other hand, are relatively recent and have been propagated by the empowering function and disseminating power of online spaces and social media. These groups and audiences have long been recognised and often ill-served by UK broadcasting. However, in the case of Channel 4, a publisher-broadcaster with the remit to represent minorities and niche audiences while championing innovation and experimental content, minority audiences (particularly youthful ones) have historically been catered for in a variety of ways, often through the use of bespoke stranding strategies created within its schedules, catering for these neglected groups (and fans) while fulfilling its remit.

Its late-night content in the 1990s acted as a harbinger for user empowerment, with "The Collective" (an online forum and fan space connecting to 4Later, one such bespoke strand) contributing to the shape and feel of interstitial content, providing supplementary material around various televisual texts. *The Adam & Joe Show* (1996–2001), produced at a similar point in Channel 4's history, was the culmination and evolution of public access-style programming such as *Takeover TV* (1995), displaying the power and appeal of user-generated content and amateur production, along with an active online fan community. Channel 4's embrace of online and the recognition of the usefulness of user agency (however illusory) spread to promotional (paratextual) content after the turn of the millennium, with its work on the teaser campaign for *Lost* (2004–2010) in 2005 acting as a precursor and template for how it would subsequently approach and address specific audiences and demographics.

Channel 4 subsequently sought to adapt to, and exploit, changing audience practices, brought about by digital spaces and social media platforms since the turn of the millennium. Indeed, there was a greater awareness of, and emphasis upon, user practices and content which is generated outside the televisual text itself, yet which is vital to broadcasters in terms of their understanding and commissioning of future media texts. The increased exploitation of digital platforms and online spaces allowed the broadcaster to partially fulfil its promises made within its *Next on 4* policy document in 2008 (championed by Andy Duncan, chief executive at the time, foreshadowing the *Digital Britain* report in 2009), to become a public service network, delivering varied types and shapes of content across a variety of platforms and spaces, both native to Channel 4 and external. This was in order to keep pace with rapidly mutating audience practices, as well as to allow itself the opportunity to draw upon alternative and untapped revenue streams. Channel 4's content, in short, needed to change along with audiences and the broadcaster itself, while coherent multiplatform programme brands required careful development through Channel 4's publishing-house-turned-digital-network. The aggregation of varied content across Channel 4's network of branded spaces was therefore necessary in order to retain the interest of its designated youthful "minority audiences", who themselves engaged with material across multiple platforms, not just the televisual.

This chapter aims to provide a snapshot of Channel 4's recent provision and strategy in terms of social media, multiplatform commissioning and, most importantly, its dealings with changing user-consumption practices within a variety of spaces and platforms. By that I refer to the alternative, "unofficial" spaces and archives of content (such as YouTube) where users can not only consume difficult-to-locate content but also contribute towards alternative repositories of ephemeral content. This, while contributing to the processes of fandom of specific youth-oriented texts, as well as a more varied selection of content pertaining to them, also leads to increased policing of content and shaping of experiences within these spaces by Channel 4. I also refer to "second-screen" viewing – a practice whereupon the longstanding primacy of the television screen is no more in terms of consuming televisual content, due to mobile technologies and social media both supplementing and supplanting the televisual experience. These practices and strategies will be illuminated with examples of their implementation via both youthful factual and drama commissions. The former is showcased through the campaigning series *Battlefront* (2008) while the latter is highlighted through the E4 drama series *Skins* (2007–2013) and Channel 4's "first multiplatform commission" *Utopia* (first broadcast in 2013).

However, before these texts can be discussed in terms of how Channel 4 deployed its multiplatform/paratextual strategies, an outlining of the struggles that it faced in order to address audiences and to ensure that they engaged with its content in a fashion commensurate with its goals, both commercial and public service, needs to take place. In this instance, YouTube, along with other "unofficial" spaces of consumption, proved to be a battleground between fan users and Channel 4.

Unofficial fan archives, ephemera and YouTube

> Patterns of audience usage are shifting dramatically, to the bewilderment of network executives who seem willing to embrace new models of viewership (and economic support), from iPods to streaming video, at the drop of a hat in the pursuit of the youth demographic. Viewing patterns that had been enshrined as laws, such as flow, now appear washed away with the click-accessibility of Internet TV.
>
> (Simon and Rose, 2010: 52)

> it is not enough to offer read-only access, the market demands to be able to read and rewrite. For the ability to read, hear or view stories at any point has led inevitably to the desire to annotate, comment and mark, alter and remix, the work ourselves.
>
> (Knight and Weedon, 2010: 149)

Whereas social networking spaces such as Myspace and, latterly, Facebook were deployed in aid of the officially sanctioned promotion of various youth-centred texts, such as *Skins*, via links within Channel 4/E4 programming webpages, the interrelationship between such programming, YouTube, (fan) audiences and broadcasters was considerably less straightforward. YouTube is a contrary entity, as Burgess and Green (2009) have illustrated, in that it operates as a corporate, commercialised concern that happens to enable "cultural citizenship" through its "communities of practice" (2009: 78). It can be seen as an alternative public sphere that allows its users to participate democratically, interacting with one another on a global scale through their submission of video content, which is often concerned with the personal politics of everyday life (Burgess and Green, 2009: 78–79). However, it has also acted as a somewhat disorganised but culturally vital repository of visual content, collating filmic and televisual ephemera, promotional material and historical footage as part of an "accidental archive", in that this was never its intended purpose (Burgess and Green, 2009: 87–90). Prelinger (2009: 270–272) outlines YouTube's appeal to audiences and those seeking alternatives to official (and limited) media archives in a succinct fashion:

> First, it was a complete collection – or at least appeared to be... Second, YouTube was open to user contributions... Third, YouTube offered instantaneous access with very few limitations other than reduced quality... Fourth, YouTube offered basic (if not overly sophisticated) social-networking features... Finally, though it takes some skill to download a video from YouTube, the videos were very easily embeddable.

As Wilson (2009: 190–191) points out in his work on ephemera and media history, the official, corporate system often favours the exploitation of finished products to consumers rather than showcasing entire archives that display "evidence of the process and supporting materials". He articulates a vision of media history that is shaped through commercial interests and corporate institutions, where success, quality and public value are emphasised. The utility of digital spaces such as YouTube is to potentially preserve moments of media history that would otherwise go unremarked upon or be supplanted in favour of official rhetoric and corporate narratives that showcase either media institutions or programming policy in the best possible light. As Garde-Hansen (2011: 75–76) suggests, "the logic that drives the archiving of content by major institutions has been less interested in what media means personally, emotionally and memorably to (fans and individuals)", meaning that tools that allow fan audiences to build their own archives are vital in the process of experiencing content in an idiosyncratic, rather than standardised, way. It is often left to those who are not affiliated with broadcasters or media companies to provide an accurate insight into modern televisual history, as Nelson and Cooke (2010: xviii) postulate:

> The role of fans and enthusiasts in caring about television history, and in sustaining the quest for as full an information retrieval as

possible, is clear when institutions, careless of television history in the past, now follow mainly commercial – or other institutional – interests.

Artefacts such as idents, interstitial promotions, music videos, trailers and fan-produced materials seemingly have little place within official discourses and histories concerned with televisual institutions such as the BBC and Channel 4. These ephemeral moments and artefacts "offer a snapshot of the past that seems to capture our forebears when they weren't looking" (Byerly, 2009: 1), uncovering patterns and revealing cultural preoccupations of the period (Byerly, 2009: 7). This ties into Jermyn and Holmes' (2006: 55) discussions regarding the rise of "telephilia" and the prominence of television fan practices, which are often stymied by broadcasters, suggesting that

> only certain kinds of television series typically make it to DVD in their entirety, so that the telephile does not quite have a free rein in choosing and building their television archive in this regard, but is instead hampered by institutionalised hierarchies. But these hierarchies are perhaps more fluid than they once were: the various spaces and forms of consumption open to the telephile, whether institutionally sanctioned or otherwise, are more diverse than they have ever been.

Indeed, this process has been aided by new technologies and new media spaces, such as YouTube and BitTorrent, to facilitate archives and collections of texts that broadcasters have not favoured with commercial DVD or digital releases, along with the promotional ephemera that surrounded the texts upon their initial broadcast.

The archiving function of YouTube, as well as its potential for democratic community, highlights its usefulness to fan cultures, who desire not only to post and share examples of fan work on the site (such as homemade music videos), but also to use the space to upload any material that is associated with their object of fandom. This includes the aforementioned ephemera, such as interviews and adverts, which fall into the "spirit" of YouTube archiving of miscellany. However, it also includes material ripped from DVD releases or recorded from broadcast television, in order to provide an extensive variety of material within a single site. It dwarfs the selective and incomplete collection made available by broadcasters such as Channel 4 within its own branded spaces and through its own bespoke video delivery systems (e.g. 4oD). Understandably, the latter material is often rapidly pulled from YouTube at the request of the broadcaster under the banner of copyright infringement. However, this situation may not be as clear-cut as it first appears. To provide a pertinent example with the E4 teen drama *Skins*, weeks prior to the broadcast of its third series in 2009, such copyrighted content had been hosted on YouTube via fan channels Skinsonline, Skinsmedia and Skinsissss. This material was subsequently pulled from these unofficial channels – and by association, the "accidental archive" that YouTube represented, impacting upon the utility and usefulness of the resource – upon the relaunch in 2009 of the E4 online *Skins* space, which made video materials available that were previously only accessible through unofficial channels. This was a foreshadowing of Channel 4's renewed push to digitise and exploit its televisual archives via its 4oD service, made accessible through digital television services and online through Channel 4/E4 hubs. The desired effect of closing off this unofficial digital avenue to fans was to push them towards Channel 4's proprietary technology and enclosed, branded online spaces, which is something that has subsequently been re-emphasised through the recent removal of full-length programming from Channel 4's 4oD YouTube channels. This would subsequently limit the alternatives to officially sanctioned viewing while promoting a more unified, less fragmentary fan user experience. As Marshall (2009: 44) confirms,

> [Both commercial and public] broadcasters have worked to make their own sites the portals for their own content through a partial embrace of the internet cacophony via multiple add-on videos to productions and extended capacities for viewers/users to write in or video in their own comments.

This suggests that broadcasters wish to control not only the delivery and consumption of the primary televisual text, but also all of the associated ephemera, "paratexts" (Gray, 2010) and "overflow" (Brooker, 2001) along with it, which served to make the relationship between users and producers antagonistic. However, complicating the situation further is the equally complex and uneasy relationship between "old" (broadcasters) and "new" (Internet-centric) media producers and institutions, which Ross (2008) discusses in depth in the context of US television.

This discouraging of unofficial or "illegal" practices of consumption, as Newman (2012) discusses regarding "peer-to-peer" distribution and the use of the BitTorrent protocol, can often be counterproductive in that this "closing down" of choice can alienate fan users, pushing them to utilise alternative methods of viewing as a means to countering overbearing institutional practices. These torrent communities also run counter to officially sanctioned, preferred modes of consumption (which within the online realm revolves around on-demand streaming) in a manner similar to YouTube. As Smith (2011: para. 10) highlights in relation to "bootleg archives" of film content, "these filesharing communities offer a makeshift archive of rare material that provides access to films that might otherwise be forgotten". It is the closing-down of choice and restrictions to access that cause unofficial and unsanctioned audience practices, while the broadcasters' attempts to control the televisual experience within non-televisual spaces leads to issues when it comes to either monetising or restricting access to it, given its previous position as "a public good, freely available to anyone" (Newman, 2012: 467). As Newman (2012: 466) again mentions,

> The ability of users to program their own viewing rather than being "slaves to the schedule" of broadcasters, and the possibility of watching television shows purged of commercials and promotions, function to legitimate television (Newman and Levine, 2011)...Thus the P2P distribution of television is one among a cluster of technologies of agency...

Mittell (2005: para. 10) also suggests that, relating to the online consumption of US television series, such "illicit practices" can often generate larger audiences and greater revenue thanks to the "try before you buy" logic of these practices. This allows audiences that may not have had access to (or a desire to access) the programming in question to enjoy it after it has been broadcast. However, it is this desire to control the way in which the text is enjoyed that is the driving force here. This was part of the increasing need of old media broadcasters such as Channel 4 to enforce their authority and control upon new media platforms and spaces, rather than fear of revenue loss by Channel 4, although the latter concern is certainly a driver of modern Channel 4 strategy. As Amanda Lotz (2007: 150–151) discusses in relation to the US "post-network" era of broadcasting,

> Viewers do, indeed, appear likely to benefit to some degree as the cultural institution of television evolves...New distribution methods allow more viewer choice...and have more ready access to content outside of that created by commercial conglomerates.... [However],

> although expanded viewer sovereignty still seems possible in this
> nascent stage of the post-network era, the history of distribution tells
> a different story... [with emergent technologies being] subsumed by
> dominant and controlling commercial interests as they become more
> established.

Lotz suggests that although these new technologies, and alternative
spaces and practices may allow for audience agency and rebellious
practices in the short term, media corporations and broadcasters will
eventually find ways to circumvent them and redeploy these spaces (or
reassert the primacy of their own preferred viewing practices and spaces)
in the longer term.

The key issues at work here for broadcasters then are getting audiences
consuming content in a manner that makes economic and strategic
sense to broadcasters and justifies their existence, while simultaneously exploiting new technologies and social media spaces that key
audiences dwell within. In the case of Channel 4, these were youth
audiences. A period of experimentation by Channel 4 and reconceptualisation of youth audiences and their practices, post *Next on 4*, bore
fruit when Channel 4 looked to fulfil its promises of moving beyond
the televisual and collaborated with new media companies and social
networks. It was within this period that Channel 4 began to consider
the potential of social networking spaces, new mobile technologies and
the agency of their audiences, which wanted to experience and rework
media content on their own terms rather than have their experiences
managed by broadcasters. *Battlefront*, also a multiplatform education
commission, was one of the more successful implementations of this
strategy.

Channel 4, social media and multiplatform commissions

> [Public service broadcasters] seem to have found a powerful rhetorical
> tool in the coupling of the classic ideal of serving the public as active
> citizens, and prospects of a digital, convergent media environment.
> The positive connotations of "participation", in contrast to "passive
> viewing", are employed rhetorically to renew the appeal of public
> service broadcasting.
>
> (Enli, 2008: 116)

> Scratch an activist and you're apt to find a fan.
>
> (Duncombe, 2012: para. 1)

Commissioned by Matt Locke (commissioning editor for education and new media at the time) and effectively displaying Channel 4's movement away from schools programming towards multiplatform projects, *Battlefront* was perhaps the most effective exemplar of this strategic shift, winning an International Digital Emmy in 2008 (Channel 4 Corporation, 2008: 5). The shift was part of a policy that targeted the engagement of youth audiences within informal social networking spaces, encouraging a form of informal or stealth learning that emphasised collaboration, creativity and the exchange of ideas, while highlighting the potential for gaining skills and knowledge relating to careers, business and politics, rather than pushing school-style learning (Monahan, 2008). Greenhow and Robelia's (2009: 122) work on informal learning provides further nuance, suggesting that "*Informal learning, as we define it, is spontaneous, experiential, and unplanned*", while comparing it to "non-formal" learning (students actively completing their own research, helped by peers or the media) and "formal" learning (classroom or other structured/directed learning environments). They go on to suggest that informal or non-formal learning spaces and social platforms,

> such as blogging, MySpace, and other Web 2.0 applications, have corresponded with discussions about how to prepare young people not only to become informed and watchful citizens, but also to promote their participation in civic life through internet-based volunteering, campaigning, and lobbying as well as through the creation of "youth media" (e.g. blog entries, e-zines, podcasts, videocasts, online communities) that present discussion and debate about political, social and cultural issues.
>
> (Greenhow and Robelia, 2009: 125)

Battlefront was an example of these productive practices in action, operating as a cross-media, multiplatform offering whose televisual content was secondary to the online space, with the first series being broadcast in two blocks (in 2008/2009) after the digital environment was well established. Described by Channel 4 as a project that gave teenagers the "tools and resources they needed to manage their own campaigns to change the world" (Channel 4 Corporation, 2008: 55), be they political, ethical or environmental (Parker, 2008), it was education project as digital activism. It offered up an example of crowdsourcing (as with Wikipedia) and collective intelligence (Jenkins, 2006) that allowed its youthful users the opportunity to operate in a democratic, politicised fashion, rather than being encouraged to behave as consumers of products and lifestyles. It provided a public-service counterpoint to more commercial and lifestyle-oriented strategies and spaces, such as 4Beauty, 4Homes and 4Food, which encouraged user participation with Channel 4 programme brands. Projects such as *Battlefront* were arguably designed to re-engage youth audiences with public service content outside the televisual space. Carter, in her brief editorial about children's news and youth audiences (citing BBC's *Newsround* (1972–present) as a key case study) postulates that

> Teenagers . . . are becoming increasingly disengaged from a political process that they believe largely ignores them and their interests . . . Media producers who appear only to want to appeal to young people as consumer citizens must now accept some responsibility for encouraging political citizenship by providing children and teenagers with critical and challenging news services . . .
>
> (Carter, 2009a: 35)

Carter, as well as Matthews (2009), surmises that there is a pressing need for youth provision that facilitates a sense of democratic action and citizenry, but highlights a crucial lack of provision for teen audiences in this area, at least televisually speaking. *Battlefront's* digitally oriented focus and user-driven community allowed for the production of a variety of public service content in an egalitarian fashion. As Mair (2009: para. 1) suggests, "*Battlefront* was a project that *needed* an integrated digital offering with an active online community to realise its full potential", and indeed this space (or variety of spaces) was key to the successful functioning of the project. Collaboration with other social networks, such as its partnership with Bebo, along with links to Myspace and Twitter, was vital in building brand awareness of the project. This was achieved primarily through campaigning and viral work through social networking sites, due to *Battlefront's* status as a multiplatform project which was lacking a prime-time scheduling presence (Willis, 2009). However, in the official documentation and press releases, the users are the ones who are considered to be most important in this promotional process: rather than operating as a top-down project, the rhetoric suggested a "bottom-up", grassroots ideal (Parker, 2008). They were involved in constructing a multiplatform corpus of shared knowledge for other users and campaigners to draw and learn from, while also allowing for a reconceptualisation of youth audiences as engaged and passionate, rather than as mere consumers.

Indeed, various campaigner-creators throughout various series of *Battlefront* exhort viewers to "get involved" and the notions of collaboration and teamwork through social networking, as well as face-to-face action, form the basis of what the *Battlefront* initiative was supposed to be for. Rather than having the debate shaped for them, *Battlefront* allowed its user-campaigners to engage in some agenda-setting and to operate as engaged citizens. This has not always happened, particularly in relation to youth news services such as BBC's *Newsround*, which often shaped the news agenda along populist/entertainment lines and negatively impacted upon the potential for youth audience engagement with key issues (Matthews, 2009: 561–562). However, *Battlefront* was an excellent example of educationally oriented multiplatform commissioning that leaned heavily on social media spaces as a means of pushing user agency, promoting innovation, while garnering a variety of user-generated content that would contribute to the overall aesthetic and tone of the brand.

However, to once again use E4's *Skins* as an example, as well as a counterpoint to the empowering practices evidenced within *Battlefront*, E4/Channel 4 also evolved increasingly enticing ways to encourage fan user involvement and productivity that was helpful to its aims, rather than potentially running counter to them (Jenkins, 1998; Gwenllian Jones, 2003). E4's invitation of a level of engagement which encouraged interactivity, through exhortations to "Get Involved" and "*Skins* Needs You!" via online and offline promotional campaigns in 2008 for series two, was to encourage the production and provision of officially sanctioned "fan work" (Andrejevic, 2008; Johnson, 2009; Santo, 2009) that would potentially enrich the online *Skins* universe.

The initial request for fan contributions came with the series two introduction of the "Skinscast", a short-lived weekly podcast that relied upon the fans submitting questions to the cast of *Skins* about elements concerning the episode of that week. The onus was thus placed on the audience to become producers of material that could be utilised for the benefit of the wider community and their understandings of the text. The subsequent agency of being allowed to ask questions that were pertinent to their fandom and the prospect of getting close to people involved in the making of *Skins* offset the fact that there was no economic recompense for their work. This invitation was an example of the growing (ostensible) democratisation of the televisual form that the Internet and social media have caused in their encouragements of audience interactivity (Jenkins, 2006; Russell et al., 2008), which Channel 4, with its mandate towards public service innovation, would wish to herald. These "organic invitations", in that the broadcasters and pro-ducers assumed that their youthful audiences were already currently engaged in such activities online within forums or social networks (Ross, 2008: 124–125), perhaps best displayed this fluidic power relation-ship between producers and consumers, as well as making broadcasters' intentions increasingly opaque.

Indeed, this institutional encouragement by Channel 4 and the programme-makers was potentially a cynical attempt to engender the misapprehension that all fan production was vital to the formation of the *Skins* text. In reality, only a fraction of the content generated by fan work was deployed, while the channel received a wealth of paratextual material that could be utilised across various platforms free of charge. Andrejevic (2008: 30) outlines these developments as part of an expec-tation of the "active consumer" to take on "work that used to be the province of producers" as part of a "duty of interaction", where it is the fans' responsibility within this "democratic" online space to bear the burden of production in order to make for a more pleasurable (read: active, rather than passive) fan experience, while adding "value" to the fan text (32). However, these examples of fan work and the agency of audiences were operating either pre- or post-broadcast, with consumption of the televisual text (as mentioned earlier) taking place asynchronously in a variety of spaces, with the importance of view-ing television-as-broadcast drastically lessened. New practices of viewing and modes of consumption were taking place, thanks to the increasing primacy of social media spaces and new technologies, which Channel 4 rapidly attempted to exploit and shape for its own ends.

Second screening and *Utopia*'s paratextual promotion

As was previously mentioned, Channel 4 championed versions of inno-vation and potential for audience agency since the "interactivity" that had been offered within the interactive television add-ons connected with *Big Brother*. As Jermyn and Holmes (2006: 52) surmised in relation to that brand, "both text and audience are dispersed across a range of media sites", while each of these sites has its "own temporal and spa-tial regimes, feeding off a live textual 'organism' in often divergent and contradictory ways", with online spaces operating both as a place of discussion as well as textual delivery.

E4, prior to the launch of the third series of *Skins* in 2009, attempted to harness its online users' behaviour and their televisual consump-tion practices by introducing the MSN "*Skins* Messenger" service. What

was essentially a bot (an automated program) that supplied information relating to *Skins* episodes as they were being broadcast to every user
who was on its friends list was also an encapsulation of the level of
institutional understanding by E4, developed over time, relating to how
youth audiences consumed televisual content. Specifically, how these
audiences often viewed distractedly or as part of a (convergent) process
of multitasking (Jenkins, 2006: 16), in which a variety of activities are
being engaged in simultaneously while the viewing takes place. By mim-
icking the synchronous activities of fans, or as Santo (2009: para. 4) puts
it the "co-opting (of) fan practice", who often discuss the fan text as they
view it, while providing insights and information relating to the content
of the episode as it is being broadcast, it brought the producers closer to
the fans and encouraged the latter to view at the time it was scheduled
on broadcast television, when the bot was active. This acted as a more
subtle example of E4 dissuading fan users from viewing the *Skins* text via
the alternative or illicit means mentioned earlier in this section, through
the suggestion that the experience will not be as fulfilling, interactive or
content rich. In short, the audience will miss out on vital paratextual
materials that enrich the fan experience if they do not engage in the
activities laid out for them within the official spaces and consume the
text in a manner that best suited E4's purposes. Although elements of
this strategy were valid (the provision of bonus content, opportunities
for increased knowledge and capital, the reassertion of the primacy of
live viewing), it was tricky to manage audience interactions through a
limited space, while it lacked elegance as a solution to the broadcaster's
attempts to garner greater awareness about their targeted demographic.

This use of a synchronous online messaging service in conjunction
with a teen television text displayed a growing appreciation by the channel of changing user practices. This had increasingly been picked up
on by staff within Channel 4's multiplatform department. They realised
that audiences were watching television "with their laptops open at the
same time", with programming like the innovative and multiplatform-
centric *Embarrassing Bodies* which "pioneered second screen watching
for factual programming" ("A nation of audience participation", 2012).
showing "that people multitask while watching factual programming"
(Carter, 2009b: 5). Second-screen operated as a strategy which emphasised the importance and primacy of "liveness" and immediacy of
viewing television-as-broadcast. It endeavoured to discourage viewing
practices such as timeshifting and downloading, which circumvented
and disrupted television's intentions regarding its intended delivery,
while also providing ostensible agency to audiences and users. Second

screen provided incentives and bonuses for viewing live (as demon-strated in the *Skins* MSN example), furnishing users with supplementary material and information, and allowing viewers to feel connected to a viewing community by ensuring that discussions about programming content occurred immediately after (or even during) broadcast. This allowed for the "watercooler" moments discussed by many television theorists in times past. Indeed, as Land (2012) suggests in relation to the contemporary situation,

> Second screen activity has become normal in many households, with viewers able to connect to, discuss and recommend the shows they are viewing through social networks like Facebook and Twitter. The experience of TV viewing is even more social and dynamic than ever before and we are now on the cusp of a significant shift in the way brands can connect with consumers through the medium of television, using social networks as the gateway.

He goes on to suggest that television, for youth audiences, operates as the second screen rather than the laptop or mobile phone, stating that television needs to reassert its relevance to this audience through the use of social media and apps, which are the contemporary drivers of interactivity. Indeed, these issues are also discussed in an editorial by Knight and Weedon (2010: 147), who suggest that new media tech-nologies and social networks are managing to bridge "the deep divide" between various "time-based media" (e.g. television), re-establishing the sense of liveness and "immediacy" that were key to the appeal of the televisual, as well as offering a solution to the potential loss of audi-ences and users. They highlight the potential for these technologies, devices and spaces to reunite fragmentary, disparate audience groups via these same spaces and technology, but potentially around key media: television texts. It therefore makes sense that practices and strategies involving an emphasis on immediate, synchronous communication and activity should be cultivated and encouraged.

Channel 4's early experimentation with the "social TV app" Zeebox, designed by Anthony Rose, who was also involved with the creation of BBC iPlayer, was one of many such apps being produced to cap-italise upon this shift towards social television (with Getglue being another that Channel 4 had collaborated with). Zeebox operates as a social media aggregator organised around the discussion of televisual content within social media spaces, while also supplying additional data pertaining to that content which facilitates additional discussion.

It is perhaps ironic that an aggregator of content (Channel 4) saw fit to collaborate with another aggregator, but the opportunity to receive information about viewing practices, feedback about content and the chance to produce bespoke content for the app (which it did with its *Desperate Scousewives* (2011–2012) commission) was one that was strategically useful (Davies, 2011), given Channel 4's contemporaneous shift towards mining data from individual youthful users. Indeed, Channel 4 subsequently developed its own bespoke app in 2013 (4Now) which continued further down this path. This early collaborative example was certainly instructive in articulating Channel 4's multiplatform commissioning intentions, with multiple-screen commissions, although placing the televisual at the forefront, certainly suggesting a greater flexibility and fluidity regarding what could be commissioned and where it might be deployed ("Louise Brown, multiplatform, Channel 4", 2011).

Tying into this shifting commissioning strategy was *Utopia*, whose commission was notable for being, in the words of Hilary Perkins (Channel 4 head of multiplatform drama), Channel 4's "first full multiplatform drama commission" (Davies, 2012). With *Utopia*, Channel 4 was following the success of similar commissions via E4, such as *Misfits* (2009–2013) and *Skins*, two programme brands which endeavoured to forge relationships with youth audiences across platforms with transmedia content. However, a different approach would have to be manufactured for Channel 4 audiences, which, unlike youth audiences, were assumed to have less time to investigate non-televisual spaces and content. Additionally, Perkins asserted that for *Utopia*, Channel 4 would

> not follow the template we have explored for Misfits and Skins, which is essentially building the world of the drama in social networks. There's always going to be an element of social networks in there as audiences use those platforms, but it is only a part of it – we are not building the world of the show there. We are more playing with the edges of where Utopia meets real life.
>
> (Perkins in Davies, 2012)

Utopia's promotional campaign arguably drew parallels with Channel 4's *Lost* teaser campaign, mentioned in the Introduction, particularly in its online elements, which were designed to provoke discussion and interaction from audiences while encouraging them to unravel clues and solve the mystery. However, it was the bespoke promotion utilising Twitter, particularly the tailored videos from "Wilson Wilson" to various prominent celebrity Twitter users, as well as the feed's use of mentions which detailed revealing information about other prominent Twitter users with a varied social media presence, which is particularly worthy of discussion here. Parks' (2004: 135) ideas regarding "flexible microcasting" and the increasing individualisation of user experience are pertinent here, where she suggests that

> computer and television technologies are combined to produce the effect of enhanced viewer choice in the form of a stream of programming carefully tailored to the viewer's preferences, tastes and desires. Flexible microcasting is organised around social distinctions... that are arranged to maximise profit for media producers, networks and advertisers. The personalisation of TV is ultimately about developing narrowly defined yet infinitely flexible content that commodifies layers of individual identity, desire, taste, and preference.

In this instance, *Utopia*'s Twitter interactions seized upon various individual users' tastes, identities and activity, and turned that information against them. Such manipulation of social media was part of a process of bringing users closer to the programme brand as well as deepening and furthering the key themes of paranoia and surveillance culture that were intrinsic to *Utopia*. This was an example of Channel 4 learning from its early social media experiments, displaying something which was coherent and consistent with *Utopia*'s narrative universe and characters, using the platform as a means of continuing the narrative and retaining the tone of the brand across various spaces. The Twitter feed, although performing the function of promotion, for the programme brand and for Channel 4 itself, was not primarily promotional in function but operated to extend the brand and narrative in a more integrated fashion than could be witnessed in previous Channel 4 attempts. Interestingly, the YouTube clips of Wilson Wilson that the Twitter feed linked to echoed earlier Channel 4 experiments with online video: namely "The Collective" fan-produced materials featured within the 4Later block mentioned at the start of this chapter. Wilson Wilson's videos were similarly effective in conveying the tone and feel of the primary *Utopia* brand while utilising Twitter to directly address key figures who used the platform to perform a version of themselves (e.g. Jonathan Ross and Grace Dent). It called on them to build buzz virally around the brand by mentioning it, in an accidental example of celebrity fan work. This connects to John Caldwell's (2005: 95) discussion of a "viral marketing scheme" for media where

Each multimedia platform (the Web site and the DVD with extras) serves as a "host body" for the studio/network's mutating content, and various forms of industrial reflexivity (behind-the-scenes, making-ofs, bonus tracks, and interactively negotiated production knowledge) serve as the fuel that drives the endless mutation of this content across proprietary host bodies within the conglomerated world (with) onscreen critical analysis (whether from scholars, publicists, show-biz reports, or industrial marketing departments) (facilitating) the process of repurposing and mutation.

However, this social media push, like the televisual elements of the *Utopia* brand, was not without its issues, despite its useful promotional function. *Utopia* garnered a decidedly mixed social media response, judging by the Tweet-stream of viewers watching live monitored via Zeebox, reacting with bemusement and often vitriol concerning *Utopia*'s themes, narrative and scheduling. The relatively poor ratings due to its late 10.00pm scheduling also bear out problems with Channel 4's multiplatform commissioning and its attempts to coherently blend the paratextual with the textual. It is ironic that spaces designed for social interaction, along with commissions created to engender feedback and user agency, performed highly effectively, yet generated discussion revolving around the problematic demographic targeting and strategic issues that Channel 4 was suffering from. Indeed, Channel 4 used Twitter for its own ends to promote programme brands such as *Utopia*, but also had to cope with the self-same platform being used to voice displeasure (from user audiences) concerning it. This was part of the balance between recognising these platforms as spaces of promotion and recognising them as spaces where fan audiences could create, experience fandom in their own fashion and respond to objects of fandom in a variety of (not always positive) ways.

Although *Utopia* undoubtedly benefited from possessing a strong social media presence, particularly in its innovative usage of Twitter, appreciation of the televisual brand was hampered by its content. *Utopia* did not fit with either the contemporary brand identity or the predominant content of Channel 4, nor would it operate effectively, due to its tone and themes, on the teen-oriented E4, despite that channel brand's predilection for multiplatform drama commissions. Despite following the groundwork laid down by E4's drama commissions (e.g. *Skins*), there was a level of brand incongruity between *Utopia* and Channel 4 that did not exist between E4 and its homegrown commissions. There was a disparity between what Channel 4 wanted to accomplish (seen within its corporate rhetoric) and what it was actually able to accomplish due to its positioning within the televisual marketplace and the ways in which its audiences reacted to its content.

Conclusion

The levels of agency and interactivity outlined above, as well as Channel 4's attempts to innovate within new media spaces and collaborate with start-ups, rather than indicative of Channel 4's desire to truly innovate and empower its youthful users, were evidence of a false dawn. This can subsequently be witnessed within a series of strategic developments and spaces that, despite their links to social networks and practices of new media consumption and production, were not squarely aimed at the demographic that Channel 4 has spent time and money trying to attract – youth. Indeed, the launch of Channel 4's first television channel in seven years (4seven in 2012) was partially in response to the need to belatedly harvest data and "buzz" emanating from users on platforms such as Twitter and Facebook, with its subsequent scheduling being determined to an extent by "social media buzz" (Barnett, 2012). 4seven acted as what current chief executive David Abraham referred to as a "bridge" between traditional modes of television consumption and convergence television consumed by an active audience (Sweney, 2012). In short, it was less a channel that embraced the central tenets (innovation and experimentation in content and form) of what Channel 4 was and rather an example of pragmatic and consolidative strategy to increase multichannel presence, while attempting to appeal to audiences in non-televisual spaces, as part of the shift towards sustaining the Channel 4 brand across a swelling network. This sprawl across a variety of digital spaces could also be seen in Channel 4's "Digital Scrapbook", an initiative pushed by Richard Davidson-Houston (Channel 4 head of online) which tied into Channel 4's pushing of its "4Life" portfolio (4Beauty, 4Food and 4Homes) of digital spaces to its users (Khalsa, 2012).

This strategy was recognition of user practices and fan work within social media spaces outside Channel 4, such as Facebook, while also recognising the possible value of sites such as Tumblr and Pinterest. It was also another way of building and potentially exploiting archives, this time of user-bookmarked materials within Channel 4-branded spaces and of Channel 4-branded materials, as a means to engender brand loyalty within official spaces, rather than have its users escape to platforms such as YouTube (taking their labour with them). The various strategies and texts discussed within this chapter illustrate Channel 4's strategic shifting back and forth concerning modes of audience address in order to cope with their changing consumption practices, as well as the allure of external spaces. This could be seen in projects that encouraged the user experience to be increasingly insular (keeping them within the Channel 4 branded enclosure), collaborations which embraced the messiness of external social media platforms (e.g. Facebook and Twitter) and disparate applications (e.g. the MSN-bot and Zeebox) in order to understand and capture the full range of the user experience.

These various social media platforms (Twitter, YouTube and Facebook) are spaces of struggle between the potential agency of users and their practices, and the desires of media institutions, such as Channel 4, to colonise and exploit these spaces, shaping interactions with texts by controlling paratextual production within these platforms. Although the institutional rhetoric dictates that these spaces allow a variety of different access points, enhancement of the user experience and opportunities for agency and production from fan audiences, if it doesn't benefit the brand identity or commercial interests of media institutions, then the terrain is changed to the point where the use of such platforms and the production of unofficial paratextual material becomes problematic for users. If there is a connection between audiences and Channel 4 in this instance, it is not to facilitate fandom or citizenship, in some kind of egalitarian, public service ideal of universality of access, but a more pragmatically commercial arrangement designed to mine data from audiences in order to shape subsequent endeavours in multiplatform commissioning and social media experimentation. The practices and feedback of audiences is vital to broadcasters (particularly Channel 4) in its quest to evolve commissioning, promotional and production practices to befit a multiplatform network of channel brands and content spaces in the contemporary media environment, performing a version of innovation and experimentation that fulfils a version of its remit. User agency (real or illusory), in Channel 4's ideal world, is something that can be co-opted to help it to evolve into something more effective, rather than something to be embraced for its own sake.

References

"A Nation of Audience Participation." (June 11th, 2012), *Guardian Unlimited.*
Andrejevic, M. (2008), "Watching Television without Pity: The Productivity of Online Fans." *Television & New Media,* 9(1), 24–46.
Barnett, E. (March 8th, 2012), "Why Channel 4's Attempt to Harness Twitter Buzz Is Ambitious." *The Telegraph.* Available from http://www.telegraph.co

.uk/technology/9130898/Why-Channel-4s-attempt-to-harness-Twitter-buzz-is
-ambitious.html

Brooker, W. (2001), "Living on *Dawson's Creek*: Teen Viewers, Cultural Convergence and Television Overflow." *International Journal of Cultural Studies*, 4(4), 456–472.

Burgess, J. and Green, J. (2009), *Youtube: Online Video and Participatory Culture.* Cambridge: Polity Press.

Byerly, A. (2009), "What Not to Save: The Future of Ephemera." Media in Transition (MiT) 6 Conference, MIT, April 2009. Available from http://web.mit.edu/comm-forum/mit6/papers/Byerly.pdf.

Caldwell, J.T. (2005), "Welcome to the Viral Future of Cinema (Television)." *Cinema Journal*, 45(1), 90–97.

Carter, C. (2009a), "Growing up Corporate: News, Citizenship, and Young People Today." *Television and New Media*, 10(1), 34–36.

Carter, M. (November 2nd, 2009b), "Facts in Focus: Interactive Strategies Aim to Grow Audiences: Cross-Platform Documentary Content Has Traditionally Been an Afterthought, but Attitudes Are Changing." *The Guardian* (Newsprint Supplement), 5.

Channel 4 Corporation. (2008), *Channel 4 2008 Annual Report.* Available from http://www.channel4.com/media/documents/corporate/annual-reports/CH4_Report2008_Full.pdf

Davies, J. (November 14th, 2011), "Channel 4 Trials New Zeebox App." Available from https://bramblemedia.wordpress.com/2011/11/14/channel-4-trials-new-zeebox-app/.

Davies, J. (August 17th, 2012), "Channel 4's Utopia Drama Series: Challenges of Multiplatform Storytelling." Available from https://econsultancy.com/nma-archive/58402-channel-4-s-utopia-drama-series-challenges-of-multiplatform-storytelling.

Duncombe, S. (2012), "Imagining No-place." *Transformative Works and Cultures*, 10.

Enli, G.S. (2008), "Redefining Public Service Broadcasting: Multi-Platform Participation." *Convergence: The International Journal of Research into New Media Technologies*, 14(1), 105–120.

Garde-Hansen, J. (2011), *Media and Memory.* Edinburgh: Edinburgh University Press.

Gray, J. (2010), *Show Sold Separately: Promos, Spoilers, and Other Media Paratexts.* New York: New York University Press.

Greenhow, C. and Robelia, B. (2009), Informal Learning and Identity Formation in Online Social Networks. *Learning, Media and Technology*, 34(2), 119–140.

Gwenllian Jones, S. (2003), "Web Wars: Resistance, Online Fandom and Studio Censorship." In M. Jancovich and J. Lyons, eds., *Quality Popular Television: Cult TV, the Industry and Fans.* London: BFI, pp. 163–176.

Jenkins, H. (1998), "The Poachers and the Stormtroopers." Available July 9, 2009 from http://www.asc.upenn.edu/courses/comm334/Docs/poaching.pdf.

Jenkins, H. (2006), *Convergence Culture: Where Old and New Media Collide.* New York: New York University Press.

Jermyn, D. and Holmes, S. (2006), "The Audience Is Dead; Long Live the Audience! Interactivity, 'Telephilia' and the Contemporary Television Audience." *Critical Studies in Television*, 1(1), 49–57.

Johnson, D. (2009), "Fantasy, Labor and the Dunder Mifflin Paper Company: Working for the Office." *In Media Res* ("Overflow", April 27th–May 1st, 2009). Available July 20, 2009 from http://mediacommons.futureofthebook.org/imr/2009/04/27/fantasy-labor-and-dunder-mifflin-paper-company-working-office.

Khalsa, B. (May 2nd, 2012), "More4 Sets Launch Date for Digital Scrapbook." *Broadcast*.

Knight, J. and Weedon, A. (2010), "Editorial: Social Networking vs. Timeshifting." *Convergence: The International Journal of Research into New Media Technologies*, 16(2), 147–149.

Land, K-H. (June 26th, 2012), "Opinion: The End of TV as We Know It." Available from https://econsultancy.com/nma-archive/23656-opinion-the-end-of-tv-as-we-know-it

Lotz, A.D. (2007), *The Television Will Be Revolutionized*. New York: New York University Press.

"Louise Brown, multiplatform, C4." (1 December, 2011), *Broadcast*.

Mair, C. (April 15th, 2009), "Building an Online Community for a TV Show." *Broadcast*.

Marshall, P.D. (2009), "Screens: Television's Dispersed 'broadcast'." In G. Turner and J. Tay, eds., *Television Studies after TV: Understanding Television in the Post-Broadcast Era*. London: Routledge, pp. 41–50.

Matthews, J. (2009), " 'Making It Our Own': BBC *Newsround* Professionals and Their Efforts to Build a News Agenda for the Young." *Television and New Media*, 10(6), 546–563.

Mittell, J. (2005), "Exchanges of Value." *Flow TV*, 3(4). Available 2 August 2009 from http://flowtv.org/?p=264.

Monahan, J. (June 17th, 2008), "Stealth Learning: Creative Approaches: How to Make Education Free-Range." *The Guardian*, 4.

Nelson, R. and Cooke, L. (2010), "Editorial: Television Archives – Accessing TV History." *Critical Studies in Television*, 5(2), xvii–xix.

Newman, M.Z. (2012), "Free TV: File-Sharing and the Value of Television." *Television and New Media*, 13(6), 463–479.

Parker, R. (April 29th, 2008), "C4 Orders Teen Campaign Series." *Broadcast*.

Parks, L. (2004), "Flexible Microcasting: Gender, Generation, and Television-Internet Convergence." In L. Spigel and J. Olsson, eds., *Television after TV: Essays on a Medium in Transition*. Durham: Duke University Press, pp. 133–156.

Prelinger, R. (2009), "The Appearance of Archives." In P. Snickars and P. Vonderau, eds., *The Youtube Reader*. Stockholm: National Library of Sweden, pp. 268–274.

Ross, S.M. (2008), *Beyond the Box: Television and the Internet*. Oxford: Blackwell.

Russell, A., Ito, M., Richmond, T. and Tuters, M. (2008), "Culture: Media Convergence and Networked Participation." In K. Varnelis, ed., *Networked Publics*. Cambridge: MIT Press, pp. 43–76.

Santo, A. (2009), "From *'Heroes'* to 'Zeroes': Producing Fan Vids without Fans." *In Media Res* ("Online Content in an Era of Multiplatform Branding", 16–20 February 2009). Available 20 July 2009 from http://mediacommons.futureofthebook.org/imr/2009/02/20/heroes-zeroes-producing-fan-vids-without-fans.

Simon, R. and Rose, B. (2010), "Mixed-up Confusion: Coming to Terms with the Television Experience in the Twenty-First Century." *Journal of Popular Film and Television*, 38(2), 52–53.

Smith, I.R. (2011), "Bootleg Archives: Notes on Bittorrent Communities and Issues of Access." *Flow TV*, 14(2). Available 10 January 2012 from:http://flowtv .org/2011/06/bootleg-archives/.
Sweney, M. (March 8th, 2012), "Channel 4 to Launch 4seven Catchup Channel in the Summer." *The Guardian Online*. Available from http://www.theguardian .com/media/2012/mar/08/channel-4-launch-4seven-catchup
Willis, L. (April 14th, 2009), "How Battlefront Stood Out in the Digital Jungle." *Broadcast*.
Wilson, P. (2009), "Stalking the Wild Evidence: Capturing Media History through Elusive and Ephemeral Archives." In S. Staiger and S. Hake, eds., *Convergence Media History*. London: Routledge, pp. 182–192.

2
Television Fandom in the Age of Narrowcasting: The Politics of Proximity in Regional Scripted Reality Dramas *The Only Way Is Essex* and *Made in Chelsea*

Cornel Sandvoss, Kelly Youngs and Joanne Hobbs

It takes exactly one hour – and 25 stops – to travel from the edges of London's eastern urban sprawl in Loughton, Essex, to the heart of affluent Chelsea to the south west of the capital's centre on the Central and District lines. What connects these two neighbourhoods in the vast reaches of Greater London, however, is more than a painfully long tube ride: they have both become locations associated with the genre of regional scripted reality drama (RSRD) that has enjoyed growing popularity in the UK since 2010 in the wake of the success and import of MTV's Los Angeles based *The Hills* (2006–2010). Loughton, alongside its neighbouring areas of Buckhurst Hill and Brentwood, serves as the setting for ITV2's *The Only Way Is Essex* (*TOWIE*), which premiered in October 2010. The Royal Borough of Kensington and Chelsea in turn, alongside further central London locations, is home to E4's *Made in Chelsea* (*MiC*), first seen on UK screens in May 2011 on the heels of *TOWIE*'s original success. Both shows, in line with their *spiritus rector*, MTV's *The Real World* and *The Hills* – and in the tradition of much reality television – are part of a hybrid genre category that draws alongside documentary traditions on television drama and in particular serial teen and high-school drama, as well as soap operas and telenovelas. The shows feature a cast that largely compromises twentysomethings with the occasional addition of younger and older members of their families, such as parents, grandparents, siblings or cousins. Thematically, these shows evolve primarily around the representation of interpersonal relationships, principally romance and friendship between cast members.

In addition to personal relationships, both shows focus on mundane, everyday life activities of cast members, primarily on leisure pursuits such as partying and shopping.

Both shows, like those following in their footsteps in the UK – such as MTV's *Geordie Shore*, with a cast of young Geordies and mainly filmed in Newcastle-upon-Tyne, *The Valleys*, set in Cardiff with recruits from the Welsh Valleys, and E4's short-lived Liverpool based *Desperate Scousewives* – drive their narrative frame through spatiality, and their regionality is already reflected in their title. This spatial positioning is less common in reality television in which locations are often changing or devoid of any referentiality to its non-mediated spatial context (such as the *Big Brother* container) and is hence best described as placeless (Relph, 1976). In contrast, these shows draw on the tradition of embedding and constructing a narrative through locality common television drama, such as crime shows (e.g. *Midsummer Murders, Hill Street Blues* and *Crime Scene Investigation*), soap operas (*Coronation Street, Emmerdale Farm* and *EastEnders*) and teen drama (*Beverly Hills 90210, Dawson's Creek* and *The O.C.*).

However, in contrast with the their fictional cousins which, in the case of soaps, are often long running and attract a long-term, committed fan following (see Harrington and Bielby, 1995), and in contrast with prime-time teen drama in the mould of *The O.C.* or *90210*, which rely on high production values, substantive production costs and an associated need for a wide international distribution, the UK's RSRDs reflect a changing logic of cultural production in the era of digital media and the emergence of narrowcasting. These shows are produced with casts of non-professionals and initially non-celebrities, and aired on digital stations away from the major, formerly terrestrial channels of UK broadcasters such as MTV or the digital expansion channels E4 (part of Channel 4 group) and ITV2. As such they are aimed at specific, niche audiences, in particular with regard to age. Their viewing figures remain substantively lower than those of flagship soap operas, which in their prime attracted over 24 million viewers and today reach around 9 million viewers per episode around four times a week (March 2013).[1]

By comparison the most popular part-scripted reality dramas in the UK achieved average ratings of around a tenth of the most popular soap operas (around 880,000) in spring 2013.[2] However, the absolute figures underplay both the relevance of regional reality drama for broadcasters and their wider cultural purchase. RSRDs are cornerstones of digital broadcasters' scheduling. Broadcast on Sunday, Monday or Tuesday at 10.00 pm, again reflecting their young target market, these shows reliably feature among digital stations' most attractive programmes.[3] Beyond their ratings success, regional reality dramas have become a commonplace cultural reference with, for example, the UK's prime minister, David Cameron, referring to *TOWIE* in a quip during Prime Minister's Question Time in April 2012. As such, RSRDs and their cast members increasingly feature heavily across different print and online media.

Like other popular branches of reality television, such as game documentaries (e.g. *Big Brother*) or casting shows (e.g. *Pop Idol* and *The X-Factor*), regional reality dramas are encroaching on the traditional bond between tabloid newspapers and soap operas and their stars by heavily featuring on red top newspapers.[4] The cast of the respective shows also enjoy substantive social media presence, with Charlotte Crosby of *Geordie Shore*, for instance, currently having over 0.75 million "likes" on Facebook, and Spencer Mathews of *MiC* still attracting more than 638,000 followers on Twitter. In turn, cast members have romantic engagements outside the respective shows with celebrities in other fields of popular culture,[5] and they have further cemented a central position of RSRDs in local/national celebrity narratives and popular culture. In this chapter we explore the success of RSRDs, and its consequences, through the study of the practices and motivations of fan engagements with RSRDs, and we examine the role of these programmes within the textual fields of convergence media in the particular context of post-network television.

The cultural niche that RSRDs occupy in the UK, while central in popular culture, particularly among adolescents and young adults, is thus one in which fandom and fan cultures have only been spasmodically explored. Reflecting the longstanding debate about the position of researchers as either insiders or outsiders in the respective cultures of their investigation (see Hills, 2002; Sandvoss, 2005; Duffett, 2013), studies of fan culture have gravitated towards fan objects and cultures that are commonly associated with those of higher educational capital, such as quality television, rock music icons such as Bruce Springsteen, sports or cinema. Less culturally recognised forms of fandom, especially those most popular among younger audiences, have been studied less frequently

Working with a team of three researchers that combined insider and outsider perspectives on both shows, our analysis is primarily concerned with understanding the practices and motivations of RSRD fandom, including the two questions that are essential to understanding the interplay of fandom and narrowcasting in the case of regional reality drama: How were these shows read, including the construction of the "textual boundaries" (Sandvoss, 2007, 2011b) and embedded in everyday life practices and the wider ecology of fans' media use? And, by documenting fans' motivations and affective attachments, how is the bond between these fans and their fan object formed and what does it reveal about the textuality of fan objects in a digital media environment?

Given this concern with individual fans' practices, agency and emotions, we conducted 35 semistructured in-depth interviews with participants (23 female and 12 male) between spring 2012 and spring 2013. Open-ended questions were aimed at establishing the history of interest in the given programme, forms of media use and wider everyday life practices in which the viewing of the show was embedded, as well as a discussion of the programmes and their cast, allowing respondents to comment on storylines, developments and cast members. Interviews also established respondents' wider social and cultural interests and identity positions. All interviews were also conducted by peer interviewers who were familiar with interviewees, following an approach to qualitative audience research that was focused on establishing the personal value of the given cultural text that has previously been applied by Crafts et al. (1993). The sample of interviews was therefore based on snowball sampling in existing informal fan networks of the respective shows. Interview transcripts were coded through thematic analysis, identifying the key themes underscoring the popularity of both programmes. These in turn are reflected in the structure of our subsequent analysis.

Identification and identificatory fantasies in RSRD

A central debate in fan studies remains the question of to what extent fandom is constituted through communal and collective acts of reading and media use, and hence is constituted socially and best understood sociologically, and to what degree it is based upon the bond between fan and fan object, and hence is at its core an individual, subjective act of agency exercising emotions which, at least partially, reflect needs and desires of the self. The same tension between these polarities in fandom, both of which shape fan experiences to varying degrees, are evident in the study of fans of RSRDs.

In the first instance – and across the spectrum of fans with varying degrees of social connectivity and textual productivity – the intrapersonal rather than interpersonal structured fans initial interest in the respective shows. As in other forms of serial television drama, fans of *MiC* and *TOWIE* build a bond with the programme through an affective attachment to particular protagonists with whom they experience a particular affinity. In the following interviews, Matt, Ronan and Violet explained their interest in the show by shifting their discussion to their favourite cast members: Hugo Taylor, Spencer Matthews (both *MiC*) and Mark Wright (*TOWIE*)

> Hugo is a lad. He always looks banging and never fails to impress the ladies. If I were to be one of the characters of *MiC* I'd definitively be him. I wouldn't mind having his life and his "entourage" [laughs]. But, yeah, I think I wouldn't mind being like him for a while.
>
> (Matt, 19)

> Spencer is the best. He's really chilled, gets on with all the girls, he goes out with his boy mates and always looks hot [laughs]. But, really, he's also a sensitive and emotional guy who falls for one girl – oh my God, I sound gay [laughs]. He's basically like me, and I'm sure that if we met we'd be mates.
>
> (Ronan, 21)

> Mark brought a lot of interesting storylines to the programme. I loved his character and his relationship with Arg. I liked their double act but don't think it's quite the same without that. I also loved Amy and I'm quite gutted that they're gone.
>
> (Violet, 21, London, *TOWIE* fan)

The affective bond between fans and text/celebrity highlighted in these accounts is underscored by a series of "identificatory fantasies". In a noteworthy parallel between RSRDs as a textual form distinctly associated with a digital narrowcasting era and Jackie Stacey's (1994) analysis of fans at the height of a mass communication media system – mid-20th-century Hollywood cinema – the fundamental processes of projection and introjection through which a bond is constructed with the fan object and subsequently articulated remain unchanged, despite their radically different textual form and means of distribution. Both the cinematic and the extracinematic identificatory fantasies that Stacey identified in the memories of female fans of Hollywood cinema are echoed in the account of RSRD fans. Stacey summarised four extracinematic fantasies as resembling, copying, imitating and pretending, illustrated in accounts such as this, reflecting aspects of copying, imitating and resembling:

> Now Doris Day... I was told many times around that I looked like her... I bought clothes like hers... dresses, soft wool, no sleeves, but short jackets, boxey type little hats, half hats we used to call them and low heeled shoes to match your outfit.
>
> (Patricia Odgen, quoted in Stacey, 1994: 164)

The same practices of copying and imitating are evident in the account of Mark, a 24-year-old fan of *TOWIE*:

> I watch it 'cos I've noticed myself modelling myself and my lifestyle, my dress sense and stuff on the show. In a way I get fashion tips and stuff like that from it... I would have never have worn a pair of chinos in my life... but chinos are now the in-thing, along with polo shirts buttoned up and I get my hair cut in Loughton now. [I] had a side parting cut in, things like that.

Similarly, Miranda, a 20-year-old student from Surrey, engaged in practices of copying:

> I really love Caggie's style. I try to buy clothes like hers, shoes, dresses, coats, even make-up sometimes. I know I can't get the real thing but I buy the equivalent. She always looks so good and "chic", but at the same time she has that quirky look about her, which I really like.

Juliette, a 22-year-old fellow fan of *MiC*, also echoed the simultaneous processes of resembling in an assumed likeness, and active acts of copying:

> I enjoy *MiC* because some people tell me that I look like Funda, which is really flattering. I know she's only a secondary character in series one but she is really attractive, so I've started to do my hair like hers and try to talk like her, even though it doesn't make me half as hot as she is [laughs]. It's kind of an ego boost to think that I can actually make myself look a little bit like her.

Through these identificatory fantasies, fans thus build a bond between themselves and the fan object based on assumed and practised likeness, and, if we follow Stacey's use of Melanie Klein, the fantasies also serve a fundamental need in positioning one's self in the object world. Stacey argues that work of object relations theorists – rather the narrowly Lacanian framework of analysis prevalent in film studies – is best suited to explain the pleasures, enjoyments and rewards of cinematic fandom in which stars serve as spaces in the processes of positioning oneself in the world while negotiating the inner tension between Thanatos and Eros: projection and introjection, in which the external object as "good object", whose association with the self is maintained through introjection, affirms good elements of self. This loop of self-affirmation through the fan object thus serves as an important identity resource, or what Juliette calls an "ego boost". She does not simply self-describe as attractive but she emphasises the perceived beauty of one of the show's characters while establishing her likeness to her. The shows' cast members thus serve as both affirmation of present forms of appearance to their same-aged friends and potential textual facilitators of aspiration and inspiration. For example, Jessica, a 19-year-old *MiC* fan, illustrated how RSRDs serve textual spaces that in being compared to fans' own practices come to symbolise aspirational desires:

All their couture dresses and high fashion shoes – I love them! The girls are always so nicely dressed and they always go for coffee or drinks in the nicest places in Chelsea. I wish I could do that sort of thing with my mates. All we ever do is get wasted in a dirty club. I wish we were more sophisticated like them and could do the stuff they do, like dinner parties and lunches, or playing polo, fishing and shooting.

Such aspiration in turn informs social and cultural practices, in particular consumption practices for fans who command sufficient financial capital. As 23-year-old *TOWIE* fan Ash from Hertfordshire reported,

I shop more in All Saints now, seeing what they wear...I also liked Joey's Smart Car so I got the same car as him to save me money...I would say the show influenced me, gave me the idea that men could drive smart cars and get away with it.

In a notable contrast with the body of work in fan studies that has emphasised the subversive and emancipatory potential of fans' reading of popular texts and documented forms of social activism associated with particular fan practices and cultures, the reading and appropriations of the show among participants consistently emphasised values of consumerist lifestyles, celebrated a consumerist model of physical beauty and sexual availability, and failed to challenge or even facilitate a wider engagement with contemporary, social, cultural and economic conditions. Ash's empowerment lay in the fact that he now chooses a certain clothes retailer and that the show influenced his choice of car. Such readings in turn reflect the prevalent themes of shopping and consumerism in both programmes.

While we do not argue that either programme could be interpreted as a closed text and readings of the programmes varied widely (especially between fans of the different shows), it is noteworthy that all fans in this study accepted what could be conceived as dominant reading within the wider political and ideological frame of both programmes that leaves private, apolitical consumerism unquestioned and brazenly endorses material wealth through aspiration. In the words of 21-year-old economics student Steve, talking about the wealth on display in *MiC*,

> I know I want to have what they've got. I want to be able to live like them and do everything they do; buy nice cars, expensive clothes, go to really nice places and all that stuff. I like the programme because it makes me realize how cool life is when you've got money [laughs].

Again, such system imminent readings do not warrant an *a priori* textual critique of the text in question. Rather, our argument about RSRD fandom is one about the nexus of text and technology. It is easy to contemplate, and indeed document, readings that do not endorse the frivolous display of inherited wealth enjoyed in *MiC* or the sometimes seemingly militant insularity and anti-intellectualism celebrated in *TOWIE*. In the words of one user's much favoured reaction to MSN UK's article entitled "Joey Essex's Greatest Quotes Ever",[6]

> Idiocy is idolised nowadays... Geordie Shore, TOWIE, these people have NO BRAINS nad [sic] no talent, they are just prats... why is it funny that Joey uses words like CONFRONTATE, why is it funny that he can't tell the time, why is it funny that he doesn't know what the 5 vowels are in the alphabet, why is it funny that he wants to know who the Prime Minister of Essex is? It's not funny, it's annoying... this **** earns more by being a **** in one week, than I do monthly working 9 to 5 Monday to Friday in a Full Time Office Job. And some people will say, it's an act, but even if it is... why is ACTING like a **** something to be praised?

Indeed, fans of *MiC* were often also dismissive of other RSRDs such as *TOWIE*. Drama student Tatiana offered a critique of *TOWIE* that focuses on a comparative appreciation of appearances and aesthetics in both programmes:

I don't really get TOWIE, the characters are all stupid, or they pretend to be – which I sincerely hope so. And they look so ridiculous with all their outrageous make-up, fake boobs and provocative clothing. The storylines are basically the same in both programmes but it's so much more interesting to watch in *Made in Chelsea* because it seems more real.

Converse sentiments existed among *TOWIE* fans about *MiC*. The decisive determining factor in different individual readings and clusters of reading according to fan groups was thus a theme of relateability, or what we will explore further below as proximity. While our study only offers a snapshot of two qualitative, and hence small, samples, this study of fans without exception adopted a reading that affirmed dominant ideological positions of consumerism and a near-exclusive focus on romantic and sexual relations, corresponding with earlier findings of dominant readings in teen drama (McKinley, 1997). While in everyday life conversation fans of either show occasionally articulate an ironic distance from their fan object that Wood's textual analysis (2014) suggests as a dominant reading position, this distance appeared to largely constitute a cultural legitimisation device which reflected the degree to which fans of RSRD remain restrained in their fandom by (internalised) dominant cultural hierarchies. During in-depth interviews, and in the certainty that the interviewer shared participants' fandom, their appreciation and readings of both programmes, however, bore little evidence of such ironic distance or questioning of the perceived ideological frames of the programmes – or even a shared complicity in an ironic narrative tone on behalf of the shows themselves.

In turn, fans' choices of a given RSRD as a fan object is not coincidental. We do not, for example, wish to suggest that Steve's desire for material wealth is a consequence of his *MiC* fandom. Conversely, however, his *MiC* fandom is clearly informed by his pre-existing strong interest in material wealth. In this sense the identificatory fantasies of RSRD fans reflect more than a need to balance the self through a cathexis of parts of the object world. More immediately, they also express fans' values, desires and sense of belonging. It is these aspects we will turn to now.

Desire, shipping and "dating porn"

The aspirational fantasies of RSRD fans are thus not limited to material possessions and lifestyle. They are also, as in many areas of popular culture, motivated by sexual and romantic desires. While Kleinian object relations theory offers a useful starting point in conceptualising forms of identificatory imagination (see also Elliott, 1999) as rooted in the need of the self to build meaningful connections between the self and the object world, popular culture – in particular heavily visual forms of popular culture such as television and cinema – also draw on fans' more narrowly romantic and sexual desires. To fans of both shows, RSRDs offered spaces which facilitated sexual and romantic fantasies – fantasies that often served as a marked contrast with the actualities of their intimate relationships.

MiC fans Oliver and Arthur, for instance, reflect such desires in talking about their favourite cast members Millie Macintosh and Caggie Dunlop. Oliver explained:

> I think Millie is really attractive, really sexy and I would 100% [have sex with her]. I don't really know why she's wasting her time with that Hugo lad because he's not even that good looking! I don't really care about their relationship and I don't really like it anyways, it bores me [laughs]. I think Millie should be with me.

This rhetorically playful but nevertheless sincere attraction illustrates the (in Thompson's (1995) words) mediated quasi-interaction between Oliver and his fan object as an object of romantic and sexual desire, lived out through fantasy. Yet more explicit about the degree that Caggie serves as fantasy object was 21-year-old Arthur:

> I really love Caggie. I think she is absolutely beautiful and would love to meet her. I admit that I have imagined what it would be like to be with her, as, in a relationship with her ... Don't get me wrong, I have a girlfriend and I really like my girlfriend, but I guess meeting Caggie is like one of my fantasies, maybe ... I don't know.

Female respondents equally foregrounded (heterosexual) attraction to cast members as one of the key motivations behind their interest in specific RSRD. Alexandra, a dance student and *MiC* fan, explained her interest in the show in reference to biscuit manufacturer McVitie's heir, Jamie Lang:

I think I like the programme because of Jamie, because he's my type. Like I said before, he makes me want to watch him. So I think I can say I do kind of watch *Made in Chelsea* only because of him. He makes the series, or for me at least ... If I had the opportunity to meet him ... in normal circumstances, I would definitively go up to him, if we were in a bar or a café, and I'd try to chat him up [laughs]. I sometimes dream about that.

There are number of important implications for our understanding of RSRD fandom, with, in turn, wider implications for fandom in the digital age, that follow from these accounts that highlight the significance of sexual attraction and fantasies in the creation and maintenance of interest in RSRDs. First, such accounts stress the importance of the interplay between popular culture, self and sexual desire and fantasy, which in turn is still best understood before the background of a Freudian understanding of desire and its necessary articulation through fantasy for the tripart self between id, ego and super-ego. Here the ahistoricity of Freud's understanding of the self is a rare strength: RSRDs, however much they are an expression of a specific technological and economic context, are in this respect firmly positioned with a strong tradition of popular entertainment facilitating sexual fantasies based on both narrative and visual conventions that emphasise dominant, patriarchal ideas of female youth and beauty, emphasise bodilyness (over other aspects of self) and foster fantasies of sexual availability.[7]

In contrast with, for example, the many studies surrounding science fiction and adult television drama emphasising the creative and subversive erotic engagements with these texts through fan fiction and slash writing, interrogating and challenging existing inequalities and questions of power surrounding gender and sexuality, the sexual fantasies among RSRD fans in our study remained distinctly heteronormative and compliant with consumerists' norms of beauty and romance. Both Oliver and Arthur emphasise physical beauty ("Millie is really attractive, really sexy"; "really love Caggie; I think she is absolutely beautiful"), whereas Alexandra explained her attraction through a number of personality traits concerning interpersonal relationships ("he's so my type. I mean he's sweet and attentive with all the girls and he's got a great sense of humour"). While both *TOWIE* and *MiC*, in contrast with MTV's more overtly laddish and ladettish *Geordie Shore* and *The Valleys*, have featured storylines that have focused on bisexuality and same-sex relationships (which nevertheless remain firmly within narrow conceptions of contemporary monogamous morality), respondents showed little interest in these alternative representations of romance and sexuality, nor did they indicate an interest in the creative appropriation of the shows' narratives in potentially subversive practices such as slash writing. Similarly, there is, at the time of writing, little evidence to be found online of any substantive body of erotic fan fiction surrounding either programme, a commonality with another genre centred on physicality and sexual desire: pornography – a not coincidental parallel to which we will return below.

In the first instance, however, beyond facilitating spaces for the articulation of sexual desires through fantasies surrounding fans' favourite cast members, the reception of RSRDs follow in the tradition of other forms of television drama, with an interest in the characters' romantic relationships being a key motivation in building and sustaining interest in the text. Participants identified a strong interest in the onscreen relations as central to their interest in the shows. *TOWIE* fan Violet recalled:

> I cried when Mark and Lauren broke up because I can relate to those sorts of relationships ... You know, how someone would feel if they saw their boyfriend getting with other girls, because they are the things that would emotionally upset you. I know how I would feel if it happened to me.

Past studies focusing on fans with a particular investment in given romantic relationships as (relation-)shippers, as Williams (2011a) has argued in reference to Bird (2003), have identified shipping, by being associated with melodrama and thus deemed "manipulative" as having "often been perceived as a culturally feminised fan practice due to its associations with romance, love, and emotionality". While female respondents elaborated in greater detail on their interest in particular relationships, some male fans, such as Rupert, a 19-year-old *MiC* fan, were equally heavily invested in particular romantic storylines:

> I really loved the Caggie and Spencer relationship. I think the fact that they never, really officially got together made the show really interesting because you always wanted to know if anything was going to happen between them two. I mean, Caggie is beautiful and Spencer is really hot [laughs]. They would be so perfect together. I love that they are both so distant and don't really tell each other how they feel

at some point, but I think, maybe deep down, I really want them to be in a proper relationship.

Williams' discussion of shipping and gender is embedded in an analysis of the interplay of genre, gender and reception, suggesting that the emphasis on relationships in fans' reading of shows is seen as a feminised frame derived from soap opera viewing that is rejected in traditional constructions of value in quality drama. While Rupert's account evokes traditional, scripted and syndicated television drama such as *Moonlighting*, *X-Files* and *Buffy the Vampire Slayer*, with the two central protagonists being involved in a "will they/won't they" romance that spans across the narrative of various seasons, both *TOWIE* and *MiC* are indeed much closer to the soap operas and teen drama in the narrative prominence and centrality of romance, sex and relationships. In RSRD, as in teen drama in particular, these romances and relationships are also more ephemeral, as indeed are their cast members. The first consequence of this is that RSRD fandom is not among the "many fandoms" in which "any perceived feminisation of a fan object is dismissed by male fans who remain keen to maintain the boundaries of 'appropriate', often masculinised, fan discourses (Jenkins, 1995; Bury, 2005; Williams, 2011b)" (Williams, 2011a). Male fans, such as Rupert, happily employ a shipper frame in their reading of RSRD. The traditional reluctance to foreground romance and relationships by male viewers thus seems to be less a patriarchal response to pleasurable readings of, and investments in, on-screen relationships and more a (gendered) rejection of particular forms of representations of relationships. Here the melodramatic as dominant representational style of soap operas contrasts with the pseudodocumentary, fly-on-the-wall style of RSRD, the exceptional emphasis on quality of visual composition in *MiC* notwithstanding.

As in teen dramas, viewers of RSRD select from a range of narratives tracing romantic and/or sexual relationships between different cast members (rather than the singular romantic narrative in many traditional television dramas, such as those identified above); and as in teen drama, such relationships are distinctly ephemeral, rarely spanning across more than a few (for RSRDs much shorter) seasons. Respondents in our study thus selected both cast members whom they were sexually attracted to and on-screen romances that they could identify with, and hence emotionally invest in, at relative ease from a text that allowed for substantive textual selection, with the guiding principle emerging in respondents' accounts being the degree to which fans' reading of given on-screen romances reflected their own romantic experiences and ambitions. Lucie, a 20-year-old *MiC* fan, recalled:

> Caggie and Spencer are exactly like me and Dan were at the beginning. We liked each other but we'd always been best friends, so it was hard for us to commit to each other in a relationship because we didn't want to ruin our friendship. I love *Made in Chelsea* because I can really relate to what they are going through and I love that now I am happy with Dan and so glad we were able to work it out.

Shipping in RSRD fandom thus functioned primarily as a form of self-reflective reading, in which, as Sandvoss (2005, 2007) has suggested, the bond between fan and fan object is maintained through fans' capacity to so radically appropriate a given text that it reflects their own experiences, values and sense of self, without this fascination with the externalised image of self, as in the myth of Narcissus, being apparent to the self. However, this self-reflective bond between popular text and fan in turn requires closer analysis of the semiotic nature of fan objects that facilitate such a bond (Sandvoss, 2007, 2011b).

This leads us to a second point: Not only do *TOWIE*, *MiC* and other RSRDs offer multilayered narratives containing a number of romantic storylines from which fans in a pick-and-mix approach invest in those mapping closest onto their own desires and experience, but the narrative of RSRDs is composed of little else than these various storylines woven together. Crucially, and in contrast with the narrative traditions of soap operas or even the more closely related teen dramas, they are also presented largely within a contextual vacuum. Romances and sexual encounters in *MiC* and *TOWIE* appear to be unaffected by the social, cultural and economic conditions that are commonly at the heart of soap opera narratives. As RSRDs only feature the interactions between cast members and not their wider everyday life contexts, romances appear to take place in isolation of family and off-screen friends, untouched by working life or economic pressures, by health or illness, let alone explicit references to wider social or political conditions which are absent entirely in RSRD (as indeed they might be in much of contemporary youth culture). The textual worlds of RSRD are fundamentally concerned with the superficial, most prominently with appearance. As Nunn and Biressi (2013: 227) observe, "TOWIE is a social world placing a premium on hyper-groomed appearance". To them, this is a sign that "the characters in *TOWIE* (together with their obsessions, lifestyles, and conduct) ... inhabit, albeit in hyperbolic cartoon fashion, a post-class, postfeminist social, economic, and cultural field". We argue that the seemingly post-classlessness of the show is based on a one-dimensionality of representation, in which romances are thus free to blossom and wilt regardless of material needs or power inequality – although we accept that such one-dimensionality of cast members in a singular focus on appearance and interpersonal relationships in turn may be a hallmark of post-class youth culture.

In this sense, RSRDs offer narratives of dating and textual encounter freed from their wider interpersonal contexts except for fans' knowledge of cast members' past dating history. As in porn, to return to our above comparison, the act of romance/intercourse occurs in isolation, devoid of context and wider meaning. RSRD thus constitutes a form of "dating porn" – romance, love and relationships reduced to the act of dating in the same way as pornography reduced them to the act of sexual intercourse. And it is thus that we can explain the absence of fan fiction in a genre that is so centrally concerned with romance and sex: contextless, the multiple romantic storylines of RSRDs are open to immediate appropriation, or what Iser (1978) describes as "normalisation", by their fans. *MiC* fan Lucie, for instance, finds a readily suitable textual resource in Spencer and Caggie's relationship: in their one-dimensional representation, characters and relationships gain a near-generic quality that emerged as central to the easy "relatability" and hence "normalisability" of the fan text for respondents. Precisely because fans can easily project their own relationships, their ambitions and their self-image on selected cast members and on-screen romances, they can build a self-reflective bond between themselves and the object of fandom as a symbolic extension of the self.

Accommodating these reflections and appropriations seamlessly, generic RSRD representations carry little intersubjective meaning beyond the meaning and significance created in the appropriation through viewers' and fans' identificatory fantasies – albeit that we acknowledge that meaning is always only manifested in the process of reception. No overarching story is being told; there is, in contrast with the other narrative forms such as the novel or other types of television drama, no message, however it is interpreted. It is herein that the particular appeal of RSRDs as fan objects to a particular audience segments lies. The way in which RSRD fans appropriate what in the context of literary theory Wolfgang Iser (1978: 194–195) calls Leerstellen – "the empty space which both provokes and guides the ideational activity" – is thus one which, in Jauss' term, instantly meets horizons of expectation and experience. Aesthetically, this means that RSRDs are what Iser (1971: 8)

labels as trivial: "either the literary world seems fantastic, because it contradicts our experience, or it seems trivial, because it merely echoes our
own". RSRDs are thus lacking the very aspect of the process of reception
in which aesthetic value is created (cf. Sandvoss, 2011b): aesthetic distance in which the reflexive engagement with the previously unknown
and seemingly fantastic leads to a "Horizontenwandel" (Jauss, 1982), a
broadening and indeed alteration of one's previous horizon of experience and expectation. It is through this type of reflexive rather than
reflective engagement that, according to Iser, the literary text "takes its
selected objects out of the paradigmatic context and so shatters their
original frame of reference" with the result of revealing "aspects (e.g.
of social norms) which had remained hidden as long as the frame of
reference remained intact" (Iser, 1978: 109). The appeal and emotional
quality of RSRDs is rooted in the diametrical opposite: not aesthetic
distance but proximity.

Reality television and proximity

To RSRD fans the lack of aesthetic distance constitutes the fan text's
central quality: easily relatable, familiar and closely mapping onto their
own experiences. In other words, the meaning derived from the text
matches fans' horizons of expectation. Notably, while in the interplay
of reading and expectation, the notion of genre commonly plays a central role (see Mittell, 2004). The umbrella term of reality television,
with its numerous hybrid subgenres, did not emerge as a central frame
shaping fans' reading of the show in our study. Respondents – echoing
the ambiguity of the disclaimer in *TOWIE*'s opening sequences which
proclaims that "the tans you see may be fake, but the people are all
real although some of what they do has been set up purely for your
entertainment" – generally did not read the show as aiming to represent something constituting the real or reality and were aware of the
staged and scripted nature of both shows. Some distinguished between
the show as scripted and the cast members as being real, thus being
distinct from authored narratives, such as novels, feature films or television drama, which some participates perceived as less authentic. Work
on reality television has emphasised the significance of authenticity –
or the perception of authenticity on behalf of viewers – as central to the
reception of reality television. While there were echoes of this notion
in respondents' talk about cast members rather than the shows, authenticity constitutes an intersubjective, absolute and ultimately positivist
concept that overstates participants' concerns regarding the actuality

of cast members and plot lines in RSRD. Rather, notions of the real or authentic were used as indicators of the key concern in fans' reflections of the attraction of *MiC* and *TOWIE*: that its characters were perceived as relatable. *TOWIE* fans Sally and Violet explained:

> In a weird way, because they are real people and they remind me of my friends – I suppose what I'm trying to say is I can relate to them... Everything happens so fast and even though it's partially staged it feels like what happens in real life... Also, being from Hertfordshire and being around the same age, they're like neighbours. I think the basics are real.
>
> (Sally)

> It's been built upon people's real lives, whereas soaps are scripted. A lot of it can be unrealistic, whereas this, you can relate to the characters. They seem like everyday people. They're a similar age to me so I can relate to what they're doing. I think that's why I'm a fan of it.
>
> (Violet)

In turn, the capacity to relate to storylines and cast members in these accounts by fans was based on perceived cultural and social proximity. Sally, for example, highlighted a number of perceived proximities: demographic ("being around a similar age"), social ("feels like what happens in real life") and geographical (being from Hertfordshire, which borders Essex to its east). All three themes were present throughout interviewees' accounts that linked proximity to their capacity to relate to the text. *TOWIE* fan Sarah, for example, noted that she has "friends and family from that area, so I can relate to it quite well". Others, such as Jenny, who is from Essex herself, equated geographical proximity to social and cultural proximity:

> I think it's mainly because it's been a success in Essex, so people from the area get involved, because they know all the places they film and the lifestyle they lead. I suppose the people that aren't from Essex look at it and think "wow, look at that amazing place", because they are always glamorous and think I want to be like that.

In these accounts, territoriality, culture and class intersect. *TOWIE* fans frequently reported their connection to Essex and regularly attended venues that were featured in the show, such as the night club Sugar Hut, a converted public house located near London's orbital motorway's route through Essex that hardly shakes stereotypical perceptions of the 1980s Essexman and "Sharon and Tracey" (cf. Thornton, 1995) as late 1980s and early 1990s culturally inept, aspiring working-class figures. *TOWIE* fan Martin recalled such visits to locations featured on *TOWIE*: "We've been to the Sugar Hut, had a walk around there, been to Minnies, and we've been to Bella Sorrella." *MiC* fans conversely emphasised their connection to the phantasmagoric, global urban settings of south west London distinctly associated – alongside the further locations of tourism and global travel such as New York, Dubai or the Swiss resort of Verbier featured in the show – with the presence of members of the transnational capitalist class (Sklair, 2000). Cedric, a 21-year-old marketing management student from Strasbourg, explained, reflecting on the interplay of habitus and place in *MiC*,

> I really like their lifestyle. I love the fact that they are able to travel to Cannes just like that, or go skiing for a week. I personally love to travel and have done a fair few travels with my mates from home. I know Chelsea because I've been there a couple of times and I really like it, because it's posh and sophisticated. I'm not going to say that I am filthy rich like them, but I do relate to what they do, and the fun they have is very similar to my idea of having a good time. I hope I don't sound too much like a snob to you.

Whether such proximity is material, as in Cedric's case, or primarily aspirational, as in Jessica's account cited above ("they always go for coffee or drinks in the nicest places in Chelsea. I wish I could do that sort of thing with my mates"), fans' choice of RSRD's is centrally informed by such proximity. This is Nicola's reflection on her preference for *TOWIE*:

> The only reason I'd say I like *TOWIE* more is because I live there and know the places. So I can relate to it a bit more. It's definitely the original and the others have just followed, but if you lived in areas like *Desperate Scousewives* in Liverpool then you're gonna like that the most.

In turn this geographical and cultural proximity facilitated identificatory fantasies upon which the affective bond and imagined connection between fan and fan objects rested. Tatiana explained her particular interest in *MiC* cast member Hugo Tailor in these terms of proximity:

> I kind of know Chelsea because I've been there a few times and my stepmum has a flat there. So I've been out in the same streets and

same clubs as Hugo. I suppose you could say I also relate to his lifestyle; that's why I think he'd like me if he met me [laughs]. Hugo was supposed to come to our club on campus but apparently he broke his arm so he was replaced by Sophie from ... *Geordie Shore* and that guy Kirk from *The Only Way Is Essex*. I was gutted. I really wanted to see Hugo, not those two randomers from the other shows.

Similarly, Violet emphasised her familiarity with the social and geographical setting of *TOWIE*:

I like to see what they're doing ... it seems weird, I go to the same places as them, and they're just ordinary everyday people who have actually become celebrities out of the programme.

To the fans of both shows it is thus proximity that matters over authenticity or notions of the real, reflecting an implicit awareness of the already inherent nature of performance in contemporary social interaction (see Abercrombie and Longhurst, 1998) by a generation that overwhelmingly engages in forms of mediated performances through social media in their presentation of self already. Expanding on Skeggs and Woods' (2012: 38) observation that "reality television may be less an aesthetic genre than a set of techniques and social experiments in which the audience are not so much engaged through the modes of escapism usually associated with fiction, but ensconced in practices of 'incapism' – a mediated immersion into everyday life (Bratich, 2007)", we suggest that reality television is more accurately described as "proximity television" – television that in its shift from broadcasting to narrowcasting, catering for ever smaller and specific audience groups, presents a mirror of fans' lifeworlds whose affective appeal lies in its near compete lack of aesthetic distance. While thus failing to challenge horizons of experience in any meaningful way, it is important to remember that such proximity is nevertheless mediated and imagined. Despite a number of fans knowing cast members of either show via friends, or friends of friends, their interest remained firmly within the frame of non-reciprocal quasi-interaction (Thompson, 1995). It is through a lack of reciprocity that their identificatory fantasies were maintained. Conversely, reciprocal interaction between fan and fan object can fatally undermine fans' affective investments. Of course, fans often interact with producers, actors or others involved in their favourite shows (see, e.g., Hills and Williams, 2005; Andrejevic, 2008; Chin and Hills, 2008), but it is interactions between fans and their immediate fan object in the form of a given person that are most fraught with the risk of breakdown through reciprocality. Sandvoss (2005), for instance, refers to the case of a young fan of the 1970s and 1980s rock band The Police whose explicit sexual desires and fantasies about the band are detailed in Vermorel and Vermorel (1985). Yet when the fan eventually met the real life Stuart Copeland and Sting, love of the fan object gave way to profound disillusionment: "then I met them. And that crushed it for me...I suppose it just shook me because I'd built up this picture of him and he didn't fit this picture at all. I felt sad, disappointed...All my fantasies about meeting him...they totally collapsed" (quoted in Vermorel and Vermorel, 1985: 166). For all of the interaction with stars and celebrities that the emergence of digital media has facilitated, non-reciprocity through which proximity can be imagined in mediated reception remains of central importance as a premise of RSRD fandom. Janice, a 19-year-old student from Birmingham, echoed the disillusionment of meeting her fan object and favourite cast member, Spencer Mathews:

> I used to seriously think that Spencer was amazing as on the series he seemed like such a cool guy and I always imagined what it would be like to know him in "real life". My mate's sister knows him from back home and she had already warned me that he was a bit of an idiot; but it's only when I saw him in a club...he made an appearance and he was so rude, he didn't even say hello to the crowd and sort of mumbled something on stage and then went back to him VIP area. He was unsociable. And, I know he's sort of famous, but he really seemed to think he was some sort of superstar or something.

There is, of course, a degree of inevitability in fans' disappointment in such encounters as interactions with cast members fall short of the imagined bond and intimacy at a mediated distance. While proximity is central to RSRD fandom, it remains a cultural proximity of lifeworlds rather than socially manifest proximity. RSRD fandom thus relies on a lack of aesthetic distance while maintaining the need for actual social, mediated distance between fans and cast members.

RSRD, textuality and technology

This reading position of proximity at a distance on which fans' identificatory fantasies, and thus by extension affective attachments to the shows, rests is further grounded in the specific textual condition and technological context of RSRDs. Like many other contemporary popular texts (see, e.g., Brooker, 2001), RSRDs lack clearly defined textual boundaries (see Sandvoss, 2011b). On the surface, television shows such as *MiC* and *TOWIE* appear to have textual boundaries determined in the production and scheduling process. The text, we might assume, is what we find between the first and last moment of the broadcast. But to the regular viewer of either show, these boundaries are less clear cut. Viewers of *MiC* are often invited to join cast members in a live online chat after the show; the final episode of each *MiC* series features a talk show format with cast members, which is neither quite part of the show's storylines nor fully outside them, with cast members also partly in and out of character. In another example of broadcaster's efforts to both engage and recruit audiences (and deliver them to advertisers) beyond the medium of television, *TOWIE* makes more explicit use of user-generated content via the continuity announcer's updates on Twitter and Facebook comments about the current episode, culminating in encouraging the audience "to keep tweeting" and promoting the hashtag "TOWIE". Claims that more users followed *TOWIE*'s season in 2011 via Twitter than watched the show (Hill, 2013) may seem hard to verify, not least given the difficulty in defining what following and watching constitutes (and the associated methodologies of measuring total user and viewer figures), but respondents echoed the centrality of social media use as a route into their initial interest in the programme. *TOWIE* fan Debbie explained in the context of reading about the show on Twitter and Facebook: "I hadn't watched it from the beginning so I watched it because everyone else was and I thought, 'I'll see what it's like', and as I caught up...I got more into it I followed it more." Others reported to first encounter the show through YouTube clips shared by friends, further highlighting the interplay between narrowcasting and the distribution of audiovisual content via social media, especially among contemporary youth audiences.

Beyond facilitating user-generated content surrounding both shows, the inherently ambiguous nature of RSRD cast members' media presence created (popular) texts about the show beyond the boundaries of weekly broadcasts. In contrast with performers in television drama or film, RSRD cast members are always in character and media appearances[8] – including their own often extensive social media use, presence in the online and offline versions of tabloid newspapers and celebrity gossip magazines and websites, and appearances in other broadcast formats, such as spin-offs, panel shows and other reality television programmes – are thus an automatic extension of the original show.[9]

Before the disappointment of a face-to-face meeting, *MiC* fan Janice, for example, had been an avid Twitter follower of *MiC*'s Spencer Mathews:

> Well, before meeting him, me and my friends always used to write on each other's walls, or post pictures of Spencer, because we used to think he's was hot... I know I met him and was disappointed, but before we'd always used to try to find out where he was going and if we could meet him. Twitter was useful too because when other characters posted their tweets, I knew what Spencer was up to!

Fans of both shows also reported avidly following news about cast members in celebrity magazines and, less frequently, tabloid newspapers. One of the cast members of the two shows whom we interviewed about the condition of confidentiality emphasised the significance of their Twitter and Facebook followers in the tens of thousands and the relative leverage that it gave them in maintaining a fan base beyond the show. Such direct interactions via Twitter were frequently particularly highly valued by fans. Laura, for example, emphasised the importance of continuing and new storylines beyond the televisual text in cast members' social media use:

> Because you can follow the cast and they can tweet you and you can keep up with them, it's just fun... I want to interact with the show more than just watching it... I go on twitter a lot.
>
> (Laura)

In this mix of the programme, broadcasters' multimedia promotion of the programme, cast's and fans' social media use – as well as fans' everyday life talk and chatter about the shows – the recirculation of the programme via video-sharing portals, and print and online celebrity and tabloid media coverage of cast members, the fan "text" was thus less clearly defined than its initial form as a television programme, with clearly defined temporal parameters, might suggest. Given the dispersed nature of authorship, including, alongside the shows' producers, cast members through their media profiles outside the show alongside the wealth of user-generated texts surrounding both shows, RSRD constitutes less a (singular) transmedia narrative and rather a transmediated "textual field of gravity" which "may or may not have an *urtext* in its epicenter, but which in any case corresponds with the fundamental meaning structure through which all these texts are read". This textual field spans a multiplicity of different textual episodes – from the broadcast programme itself, as the gravitational centre or urtext, to the many textual episodes surrounding the urtext, which Jonathan Gray (2003, 2010) has, in reference to Gérard Genette (1997), helpfully described as paratext and which, alongside promotional material and user- or fan-generated content in the case of RSRDs, also includes the continuation (and introduction of new) storylines by cast members outside the urtext. *MiC* fan Alexandra illustrated how these paratexts become an integral aspect of many fans' engagement with RSRDs:

Twitter is cool because the people in *MiC* always update their tweets about what's going on in the series. Sometimes it's straight after the episode has aired on Channel 4. I got Twitter just because my friends were on it and told me that the *MiC* people were chatting about *MiC* gossip on it.

If in light of the inherent intertextuality of popular culture, and indeed most narrative motifs, distinctions between urtext and paratexts are already blurred, in the case of RSRDs the distinction is yet more problematic given that cast members set parameters through their media performances outside the show which the narrative within the broadcast episodes needs to follow. The widely publicised on/off engagement of *MiC* cast member Milly Mcintosh, for instance, to pop musician Professor Green (who does not feature on the show) led to a reduced role, and eventual exit, as she was no longer able to participate in the romantic entanglements that serve as the show's narrative backbone. In their sum, the textual episodes surrounding cast members in and outside the show thus constituted a wide textual field of gravity, from which fans constructed their individual fan text tailored to their interests. They not only read but also create their specific fan objects through acts of textual selection that maintain identificatory and self-reflective fantasies. In *TOWIE* fan Jessica's words, "I do enjoy a lot of their posts and pictures of them on nights out. It makes them more real the fact that you can connect with them." This decentralised textual nature of RSRD hence facilitates the experiences of proximity on which fandom surrounding the shows rests. It is these paratexts that allow mediated interaction between fans and cast members that are valued by activist fans in particular. Laura, for instance, ran her own Twitter fan page, motivated by a wish to have a greater opportunity to interact with cast members:

Because you can follow the cast and they can tweet you and you can keep up with them. It's just fun ... I want to interact with the show more than just watching it ... I set up this fan page so I could "tweet" the stars, and I "DM" [direct message] Cara and Ricky [cast members] ... I think if I ever tried to get followed on a personal account it wouldn't be as easy to get noticed as it is on a fan page.

Alongside direct interactions with cast members, following and sharing cast member-generated social media content was of particular interest to fans. 20-year-old Danielle from Berkshire recalled: "I actually got Twitter to follow all of the *TOWIE* cast". Similarly, Ash followed "pretty much all" of the cast members: "to be honest, everyone, except Kirk". As in other realms of (digital) fandom, these industry-produced paratexts intersected with fans' own productivity and creation of content. These user-generated paratexts primarily facilitated interaction and proximity among networks of friends and fans by appropriating textual elements and motifs from the show and its surrounding paratexts, thereby facilitating conversations among fans – offline, through forms of communal viewing that many participants reported to enjoy, and online through the use of social media. Cassie, 20-year-old student and *MiC* fan, explained the significance of posting and reading on Facebook about her favourite show:

> I always update my status on Facebook if there's, like, a shocking episode. Because if something dramatic happens, I know loads of people are going to want to talk about it, just like me. It's always interesting to see how many people like or comment;

On the surface, RSRD fandom thus shares the markers of a participatory media culture as outlined in Henry Jenkins' (2006) influential *Convergence Culture*. Yet the purpose of these interpretative communities formed through shared reading practices and the distribution of paratexts on social media networks appears less aimed at endeavours of collective interpretation or textual curatorship. It was firmly anchored in reference to individual fans' selves, both in respect of self-performance and in maintaining a self-reflective reading of the fan object by constructing proximity through acts of textual selection. Cassie continued:

> It also makes me look popular [laughs]. But, really, it's also kind of like gossiping, where everyone has their bit to say about my status and about our common interest of what we've just seen in our favourite programme. And it's always interesting to see how peoples' opinions

diverge, people always have to take sides, and it's all happening on my status!

To Cassie there is then an important duality in being a member of an interpretative community and utilising the show as an identity resource, reflected in her sense of ownership of collective engagements ("and it's all happening on my status"). The show and its paratexts function as important symbolic resources in her presentation of self, echoing Sandvoss' (2005, 2014) analysis of fandom as an identity resource in late and liquid modernity in which community association becomes increasingly voluntary and flexible in shifting away from yet more heavily socially, culturally and economically determined realms. Others equally highlighted the importance of talk about the show as such a means of presentation of self:

> I do say a lot of stuff that goes on during the show and put it on my Facebook... On Facebook I'm always using catchphrases and sayings that they've coined on the show.
>
> (Mark)

Whether such forms of fan-generated online content are more accurately classified as "enunciative" or "textual" productivity, drawing on Fiske's (1992) definition of both terms, has been the subject of recent debate. Matt Hills (2013) has suggested that describing online talk between fans as a form of enunciative productivity misreads Fiske, as the "crucial distinction between enunciative and textual productivity is not 'primarily one of form' (Sandvoss, 2011a: 60), but rather one of mediation". He is correct in noting that, according to Fiske, enunciation presupposes immediate social relationship, although such immediacy is of course no longer limited to face-to-face interactions to the same degree in spaces of digital fandom (and indeed friendships). The more important line of distinction – both, we would argue, in Fiske's work, but especially for our purposes here – is not one of communicative context but of communicative purpose. To us, this critique misses the utility of distinguishing between the aims of user-generated paratexts by employing Fiskes' distinction. The notions of enunciative and textual productivity are at their most useful when employed to differentiate between user-generated texts that are aimed at commenting, appreciating, critiquing and distributing the fan object in a form of metadiscourse, on the one hand, and works and texts aimed at drawing upon, developing and recreating the initial fan object, on the other. Textual productivity thus seeks to both emulate and transform the urtext. In other words, while enunciative textuality is largely paratextual, textual productivity creates alternative urtexts, albeit that these can serve as a form of (paratextual) commentary too.

The key difference in our analysis of RSRD is that while both enunciative and textual productivity can facilitate a critical engagement with the urtext, fans' enunciative productivity here primarily appears to facilitate and maintain proximity through underscoring their textual control and ability to construct boundaries around the fan text, echoing how even seemingly critical enunciative productivity frequently reinforces the economic and cultural parameters of the urtext (see also Andrejevic, 2008). Lacking the *a priori* need to reflect on and thus potentially interrogate the form and structure of the urtext of textual productivity, enunciative productivity in the case of the RSRD fans in our study has two primary aims. First, it serves as a means to articulate and share fandom with others and thereby to both construct a collective sense of identity and community membership, and construct and articulate identity to both the fan and its social environment. Second, through the sharing and circulating of additional information about cast members as well as of industry produced paratexts (including media appearances by cast members), fans contributed to the transmediated textual field of gravity surrounding both shows, which in turn further facilitated fans' ability to construct fan texts and objects in their selection of textual boundaries. Both aims thus sought to maintain the proximity of RSRD fandom through which these shows came to serve as textual home and a symbolic *Heimat* (cf. Sandvoss, 2005) to their fans, reflected in a perceived blurring of territorial, social and textual belonging in the account of some fans. Violet noted reflecting on her use of social media to stay informed about *TOWIE*,

> I like to see what they're doing ... it seems weird. I go to the same places as them, and they're just ordinary everyday people who have actually become celebrities out of the programme.

As a transmediated textual field that is heavily dependent on fans' enunciative productivity, RSRDs with their ephemeral and niche celebrity and simultaneous mediated intimacy in their narrow focus on dating, sex and relationships have successfully translated the tension between mediated distance and proximity that has been at the heart of the affective bond between fans and fan objects to an age of digital narrowcasting and convergence media. Yet, while a prime example of participatory convergence culture and transmediated textuality, RSRDs sit uneasily with an often implicit, and sometimes explicit, assumption in fan studies that participation in digital media landscapes equals a form of empowerment. Jenkins' (2006: 268) assessment below is constitutive of the canon of such work on participatory culture:

> the power of grassroots media is that it diversifies; the power of broadcast media is that it amplifies. That's why we should be concerned with the flow between the two: expanding the potential for participation represents the greatest opportunity for cultural diversity. Through greater powers of broadcasting and one has only cultural fragmentation. The power of participation comes not from destroying commercial culture but from writing over it, modelling it, amending it, expanding it, adding greater diversity of perspective, and then recirculating it, feeding it back into the mainstream media. Read in those terms, participation becomes an important political right ... The emergence of new media technology supports a democratic urge to allow more people to create and circulate media.

As meaningful a connection between broadcast and digital media RSRDs constitute, there was, in this study at least, little evidence that this interaction in a transmediated textual field facilitated greater diversity or perspective, or that it was utilised by fans for anything but (reflecting the eradication of aesthetic distance in the engagement with narrowcast texts embedded in a textual field of indeterminate boundaries) the maintenance of an affective bond with their fan object and a utilisation of the fan object as an identity resource based on perceived proximity.

Conclusion: Participation, proximity and power

The study of RSRDs is thus of wider importance to our understanding of fandom and participation in the age of digital narrowcasting. Popular culture, not least in a digital environment, constitutes a wide and vast field in which large segments of popular entertainment, particularly those that are less attractive to those with high educational capital, remain underexplored. Where these have been studied previously, as in Woods' (2014) textual analysis of both *TOWIE* and *MiC*, the proposed viewing positions at best partly reflected the actual readings of fans that emerge from empirical audience research. To fans, nether class nor gender were central to their enjoyment of the show derived from identificatory fantasies, desire and "shipping".

We have illustrated here that RSRD fandom is rooted in forms of digital participation, and RSRDs exemplify many of the transformations of textuality that are highlighted in the study of digital fandom, from transmedia storytelling to the facilitation of online enunciative communities and the formation of interpretative communities online. RSRDs fans in this study modelled content, found affective cast members and particular relationships that were meaningful to their sense of self, meaningful in how they communicated with friends and maintained social bonds, and ultimately created pleasure and enjoyment through proximity – offering a reflection of self and hence as textual space experienced as home (cf. Sandvoss, 2005). Yet, beyond modelling, there was little evidence of "expanding", the inclusion of industry-produced paratexts aside, or even of the creation of "greater diversity of perspectives". The social and political vector of democratisation, and by extension empowerment, was absent in fans' practices and productivity. As much as the shows themselves, RSRD fandom is distinctly apolitical and unconcerned with the wider social, cultural and economic context structuring the interpersonal relationships that RSRDs are solely dedicated to.

Our analysis here suggests that it is precisely this context-free, neutrosemic quality on which the popularity of these shows among their youthful fan base is based. Reduced to largely decontextualised representations of dating, sex and romance, RSRDs are instantly normalised (cf. Iser, 1978) by their fans, inviting identification, shipping, and imitational fantasies and practices. At the same time, it is this ability of fans to instantly normalise RSRDs that precludes a wider social and cultural critique and engagement through, among other practices, textual productivity.

We thus suggest that the success and impact of RSRDs are more accurately captured in a different model of consumer/user participation in digital media environments than the one that is commonly employed following Jenkins in fan studies: RSRDs are as much a sign of forces of "new forms of capitalism" in the digital age, which are in turn informed by both the narrow application of formal rational principles in consumer capitalism that Geore Ritzer (1996) has described as McDonaldisation and the changes of production, labour and consumption regimes that have been described as the shift from Fordism to post-Fordism by David Harvey (1990).

In their production, distribution and affective reception, RSRDs carry a number of notable characteristics that are associated with both processes. Reminiscent of a global franchise systems with token local adaptations – or what Woods (2014: 211) describes as glocalised reality television – RSRDs constitute, to borrow David Harvey's (1990) terminology, a form of "post-Fordist" popular culture, produced by small, independent operators (Monkey Kingdom producing *MiC* and Lime Pictures both *TOWIE* and *Geordie Shore*) for specific markets, with low overheads; combinable, adoptable and disposable. RSRDs are built on a generic formula while targeting specific markets in terms of regions, interests and lifestyle, mirroring different fashions and representations of class in *MiC*, *TOWIE* and *Geordie Shore*, while all three shows remain firmly committed to a narrow focus on dating and consumption. In comparison with television drama, RSRDs are low cost and flexible, and utilising an amateur cast as storylines are reduced to their most generic and universal essence. Their formulaic nature is easily adaptable to different settings, yet vague enough to evade the legal restrictions of licensed format television. Their efficiency, one of the four principles of McDonaldised production identified by Ritzer (1996), and effectiveness as a sign of prosumer capitalism in an age of digital abundance (Ritzer and Jurgenson, 2010) are further heightened in the symbiotic cross-promotion with celebrity magazines, gossip blogs and tabloid media that happily feature the free content provided by self-promoting cast members. In constructing the textual field in which their fandom is formed, RSRDs thus employ the free labour of cast members, tabloid media and fans.[10] Similarly, what we have described as a lack of aesthetic distance and a high degree of congruity with audiences' expectations also coincides with the second and third principle of McDonaldisation: calculability and predictability. As we have demonstrated here, RSRDs steadily meet their fans' horizons of expectations and echo their experiences, at best rarely challenged through face-to-face encounters, as in Janice's meeting with a cast member of *MiC*.

Predictability thus serves a premise for the bond between RSRD fans and their fan texts. It is through predictability, based on generic neutrosemy of RSRDs, that fans experience a sense of proximity which their identificatory fantasies facilitate. RSRD fandom has thus possibly less in common with television drama fandom and more with forms of actuality-based fandom, such as sports. As in the case of equally transmediated contemporary football teams (see Sandvoss, 2003, 2013) – another fan culture that is both heavily dependent on perceived proximity and subject to the application of McDonaldised production regimes – predictability allows semiotic control, swift normalisation and ultimately the ability to project a sense of self onto the fan text. Like football fandom, RSRD fandom allows for an articulation of self through appropriating aspects of the textual field in the construction of their fan object; and like football fandom, RSRD fan cultures inherently reflect the logic of post-Fordist, digital cultural production. In this tension between structure and agency, the (cultural) products of McDonaldised production regimes are, of course, not beyond appropriation (Parker, 1998; Jary, 1999; Sandvoss, 2003), and yet, the limits of such appropriation appear to be firmly set their macrocontext, as reflected in the readings and reception practices of RSRD fans in this study.

This then leads us to the concluding question of what the politics – and political consequences – of proximity in an age of narrowcasting, participation and digital fandom are. While highly participatory, RSRD fandom does not seem to warrant the optimism of an *a priori* interpretation of digital fandom as a means of democratisation and audience empowerment. A more relevant theme in the analysis of RSRDs is a common concern in the study of participation in digital political communication, where proximity has been expressed as the risk of the solmisation and fragmentation of discourse (Sunstein, 2007; Leccese, 2009). The narrowness of niche politics and the neutrosemic blandness of RSRD's "dating porn" serve as equal reminders that in digital environments, proximity is a source of affect, belonging and associated pleasures that play important roles in the affirmation and articulation of self in late modernity; but that it is only through distance, both communicatively and aesthetically, that engagement remains a meaningful process of communication rather than affirmation. The popularity of RSRD suggests that in the age of narrowcast, transmediated entertainment, such distance may be in short supply.

Notes

1. Source BARB http://www.barb.co.uk/viewing/weekly-top-30?
2. Series eight of the most popular regional reality drama, *TOWIE*, broadcast in 12 episodes from 24 February to 3 April 2013, was watched by an average of 1,168 million viewers on initial transmission (with an additional 160,000–220,000 viewers watching the episodes on ITV+1), peaking at 1,304 million viewers for the first episode and 1,334 million for the season finale (and a low of 949,000 viewers for the ninth episode). E4's 12 episodes spanning season five of *MiC* broadcast following series eight of TOWIE between 8 April and 24 June attracted average audiences of just over 883,000 viewers, peaking at 1,069,000 viewers for the 10th of 12 episodes. *Geordie Shore's* eight episodes spanning season five averaged 810,000 on initial transmission. The latecomer, *The Valleys*, remains the least popular of the four regional reality dramas currently on air in the UK. Following the show's premiere in September 2012, the eight episodes of the second season,

broadcast from 30 April to 18 June 2013, attracted average ratings of just over 430,000 viewers.

3. *TOWIE* was only beaten into second place in weekly ratings by panel shows *Celebrity Juice* on ITV during season eight. E4's *MiC* is commonly its third most popular programmes behind new episodes of US sitcoms *The Big Bang Theory* and *How I Met Your Mother*, only occasionally relegated into fourth place by episodes of *New Girl* or Channel 4's long-running teen soap *Hollyoaks*. *Geordie Shore* and *The Valleys*, while attracting fewer viewers overall, are yet more pivotal to MTV. Both shows lead their weekly ratings throughout their run of season five and season two, respectively, and commonly attract up to eight times as many viewers as the second-placed show in a given week.

4. Between 24 February and 24 June 2013, *MiC* featured in 200 articles in *The Mirror* and a further 140 articles in *The Sun*; and surprisingly no less than 23 times in *The Guardian*. *TOWIE* featured in *The Sun* 279 times, 262 times in *The Mirror* and *Sunday Mirror*, 15 times in *The Times* and 14 times in *The Guardian*.

5. *MiC*'s Louise Thompson, for example, has been linked to members of teen boy band One Direction, and *TOWIE*'s Mark Wright's liaison with *Coronation Street* actress Michelle Keegan have created transgenre narratives, marrying reality television and soap opera entertainment news.

6. User "the world and his uncle", http://celebrity.uk.msn.com/features/joey-essex%E2%80%99s-greatest-quotes-ever.

7. For a succinct summary of relevant approaches to popular culture and such convention, see Sturken and Cartwright (2000).

8. Media appearances have included, in particular, other reality television programmes with a number of cast members from both shows having appeared on UK prime-time reality formats, such *I'm a Celebrity... Get Me Out of Here* or *Celebrity Big Brother*, as well as numerous other celebrity-themed versions of television entertainment formats.

9. Structured reality television programmes are particularly well suited to the development of spin-off formats because of the continuity of cast members' characters beyond the confines of a given format. Such spin-offs have included former *TOWIE* cast members Amy Child's short-lived Channel 5's reality show *It's All About Amy* (2011–2012), and ITV's *Mark Wright's Hollywood Nights* (2012) and *Party Wright Around the World* (2014).

10. Audience participation in creating fan-generated content as part of the textual fields of RSRDs make RSRDs another important site of investigation in the growing number of studies that critically interrogate the role of (free) fan labour in the commercial process of media production (see Baym and Burnett, 2009; Milner, 2009 & 2011; Booth, 2010; Baym, 2011).

References

Abercrombie, N. and Longhurst, B. (1998), *Audiences – A Sociological Theory of Performance and Imagination*. London: Sage.

Andrejevic, M. (2008), "Watching Television without Pity: The Productivity of Online Fans." *Television and New Media*, 9(1), 24–46.

Baym, N.K. (2011), "The Swedish Model: Balancing Markets and Gifts in the Music Industry." *Popular Communication: The International Journal of Media and Culture*, 9(1), 22–38.
Baym, N.K. and Burnett, R. (2009), "Amateur Experts: International Fan Labor in Swedish Independent Music." *International Journal of Cultural Studies*, 12(5), 1–17.
Bird, S.E. (2003), *The Audience of Everyday Life: Living in a Media World*. London: Routledge.
Booth, P. (2010), *Digital Fandom: New Media Studies*. New York: Peter Lang.
Bratich, J.Z. (2007), "Programming Reality: Control Societies, New Subjects, and the Powers of Transformation." In D. Heller, ed. *Makeover Television: Realities Remodelled*. London: I.B. Tauris, pp. 6–22.
Brooker, W. (2001), "Living on Dawson's Creek: Teen Viewers, Cultural Convergence and Television Overflow." *International Journal of Cultural Studies*, 4(4), 456–447.
Bury, R. (2005), *Cyberspaces of Their Own: Female Fandoms Online*. New York: Peter Lang.
Chin, B. and Hills, M. (2008), "Restricted Confessions? Blogging, Subcultural Celebrity and the Management of Producer – Fan Proximity." *Social Semiotics*, 18(2), 253–272.
Crafts, S.D., Cavicchi, D. and Keil, C. (1993), *My Music*. Hanover: Wesleyan University Press.
Duffett, M. (2013), *Understanding Fandom: An Introduction to the Study of Media Fan Culture*. New York and London: Bloomsbury.
Elliott, A. (1999), *The Mourning of John Lennon*. Berkley: University of California Press.
Fiske, J. (1992), "The Cultural Economy of Fandom." In L.A. Lewis, ed., *The Adoring Audience*. London: Routledge, pp. 30–49.
Genette, G. (1997), *Paratexts: The Thresholds of Interpretation*. Cambridge: Cambridge University Press.
Gray, J. (2003), "New Audiences, New Textualities: Anti-Fans and Non-Fans." *International Journal of Cultural Studies*, 6(1), 64–81.
Gray, J. (2010), *Show Sold Separately: Promos Spoilers and Other Media Paratexts*. New York: New York University Press.
Harrington, C.L. and Bielby, D. (1995), *Soap Fans: Pursuing Pleasure and Making Meaning in Everyday Life*. Philadelphia: Temple University Press.
Harvey, D. (1990), *The Condition of Postmodernity: An Inquiry into the Origins of Cultural Change*. Oxford: Basil Blackwell.
Hill, A. (2013), "Book Review: Beverly Skeggs and Helen Wood, Reacting to Reality Television: Performance, Audience and Value." *Media, Culture & Society*, 35(6), 784–785.
Hills, M. (2002), *Fan Cultures*. London: Routledge.
Hills, M. (2013), "Fiske's 'Textual Productivity' and Digital Fandom: Web 2.0 Democratization versus Fan Distinction?" *Participations: International Journal of Audience Research*, 10(1).
Hills, M. and Williams, R. (2005), "It's All My Interpretation: Reading Spike through the 'Subcultural Celebrity' of James Marsters." *European Journal of Cultural Studies*, 8(3), 345–365.

Iser, W. (1971), "Indeterminacy and the Reader's Response in Prose Fiction." In J.H. Miller, ed., *Aspects of Narrative*. New York and London: Columbia University Press, pp. 1–45.

Iser, W. (1978), *The Act of Reading: A Theory of Aesthetic Response*. Baltimore: John Hokins University Press.

Jary, D. (1999), "The McDonaldization of Sport and Leisure." In B. Smart, ed., *Resisting McDonaldization*. London: Sage, pp. 116–134.

Jauss, H.R. (1982), *Toward an Aesthetic of Reception*, trans. T. Bahti. Minneapolis: University of Minnesota Press.

Jenkins, H. (1995), "Do You Enjoy Making the Rest of Us Feel Stupid? Alt.TV.Twinpeaks, the Trickster Author and Viewer Mastery." In D. Lavery, ed., *Full of Secrets: Critical Approaches to Twin Peaks*. Detroit: Wayne State University Press, pp. 51–69.

Jenkins, H. (2006), *Convergence Culture*. New York: New York University Press.

Leccese, M. (2009), "Online Information Sources of Political Blogs." *Journalism & Mass Communication Quarterly*, 86, 578–593.

McKinley, E.G. (1997), *Beverly Hills, 90210: Television, Gender and Identity*. Philadelphia: University of Pennsylvania Press.

Milner, R.M. (2009), "Working for the Text: Fan Labor and the New Organization." *International Journal of Cultural Studies*, 12(5), 491–508.

Milner, R.M. (2011), "Discourses on Text Integrity: Information and Interpretation in the Contested Fallout Knowledge Community." *Convergence: The International Journal of Research into New Media Technologies*, 17(2), 159–172.

Mittell, J. (2004), *Genre and Television: From Cop Shows to Cartoons in American Culture*. New York: Routledge.

Nunn, H. and Biressi, A. (2013), "Class, Gender and the Docusoap: *The Only Way Is Essex*." In C. Carter, L. Steiner, and L. McLaughlin, eds., *The Routledge Companion to Media & Gender*. London: Routledge, pp. 269–279.

Parker, M. (1998), "Nostalgia and Mass Culture: McDonaldization and Cultural Elitism." In M. Alfino, J. Caputo, and R. Wynyard, eds., *McDonaldization Revisited – Critical Essays on Consumer Culture*. Westport: Praeger Publications, pp. 1–18.

Relph, E. (1976), *Place and Placelessness*. London: Pion Limited.

Ritzer, G. (1996), *The McDonaldization of Society*. Newbury Park: Pine Forge Press.

Ritzer, G. and Jurgenson, N. (2010), "Production, Consumption, Prosumption: The Nature of Capitalism in the Age of the Digital 'Prosumer'." *Journal of Consumer Culture*, 10(1), 13–36.

Sandvoss, C. (2003), *A Game of Two Halves: Football, Television and Globalization*. London: Routledge.

Sandvoss, C. (2005), *Fans: The Mirror of Consumption*. Cambridge: Polity Press.

Sandvoss, C. (2007), "The Death of the Reader? Literary Theory and the Study of Texts in Popular Culture." In J. Gray, C. Sandvoss, and C.L. Harrington, eds., *Fandom: Identities and Communities in a Mediated World*. New York: New York University Press, pp. 19–32.

Sandvoss, C. (2011a), "Fans Online: Affective Media Consumption and Production in the Age of Convergence." In M. Christensen, A. Jansson, and C. Christensen, eds., *Online Territories*. New York: Peter Lang, pp. 49–74.

Sandvoss, C. (2011b), "Reception." In V. Nightingale, ed., *Handbook of Media Audiences*. Malden, MA and Oxford: Blackwell, pp. 230–250.

Sandvoss, C. (2012a), "Enthusiasm, Trust, and Its Erosion in Mediated Politics: On Fans of Obama and the Liberal Democrats." *European Journal of Communication*, 27(1), 68–81.

Sandvoss, C. (2012b), "Jeux Sans Frontières: Europeanisation and the Erosion of National Categories in European Club Football Competition." *Politique Européenne*, 36, 76–101.

Sandvoss, C. (2013), "Toward an Understanding of Political Enthusiasm as Media Fandom: Blogging, Fan Productivity and Affect in American Politics." *Participations: International Journal of Audience Research*, 10(1).

Sandvoss, C. (2014), " 'I ♥ Ibiza': Music, Place and Belonging." In Mark Duffett, ed., *Popular Music Fandom: Identities, Roles and Practices*. New York: Routledge, pp. 115–145.

Skeggs, B. and Wood, H. (2012), *Reacting to Reality Television: Performance, Audience and Value*. Abingdon: Routledge.

Sklair, L. (2000), *The Transnational Capitalist Class*. Oxford: Wiley-Blackwell Publishing.

Stacey, J. (1994), *Star Gazing: Hollywood Cinema and Female Spectatorship*. London: Routledge.

Sturken, M. and Cartwright, L. (2000), *Practices of Looking: An Introduction to Visual Culture*. Oxford: Oxford University Press.

Sunstein, C.R. (2007), *Republic.com 2.0*. Princeton: Princeton University Press.

Thompson, J.B. (1995), *The Media and Modernity: A Social Theory of the Media*. Cambridge: Polity Press.

Thornton, S. (1995), *Club Cultures: Music; Media and Subcultural Capital*. Cambridge: Polity Press.

Vermorel, F. and Vermorel, J. (1985), *Starlust: The Secret Fantasies of Fans*. London: Comet.

Williams, R. (2011a), " 'Wandering off into soap land': Fandom, Genre and Shipping *The West Wing*." *Participations: International Journal of Audience Research*, 8(1).

Williams, R. (2011b), "Desiring the Doctor: Identity, Gender and Genre in Online Science-fiction Fandom." In J. Leggott and T. Hochscherf, ed., *British Science Fiction in Film and Television*. Jefferson, NC: McFarland, pp. 167–177.

Woods, F. (2014), "Classed Femininity, Performativity, and Camp in British Structured Reality Programming." *Television & New Media*, 15(3), 197–214.

3
"A Reason to Live": Utopia and Social Change in *Star Trek* Fan Letters

Lincoln Geraghty

Henry Jenkins uses Michel de Certeau's term "textual poaching" to describe how fans rewrite *Star Trek* television shows and movies in order to produce their own narratives, which they then share among each other in the form of novels and music.[1] Constance Penley has also analysed artwork produced by these fans, and Heather Joseph-Witham has looked at their costume-making.[2] These studies have brought critical attention to what might have seemed to be an overdone and outdated subject, and have highlighted how important *Star Trek* fan culture is to the fields of media and reception studies. Yet their work is limited by its exclusive focus on those more marginal fans who are producers of new texts rather than more "ordinary" fans who consume the original text but do not write stories and filk music (a term used to describe science fiction folk singing), dress up or manipulate video material.[3] The *Star* Trek movies and television shows play an important role in the emotional and affective lives of American fans. Therefore in this chapter I want to investigate the ways in which fans actually talk about the show and their engagement with it.[4] Specifically, given the long-running nature of the series, I want to address the differential character and historically shifting contexts of audience reception as found in *Star Trek* correspondence. The letters I have analysed recount *Star Trek*'s impact on fans' daily lives – *Star Trek*'s vision of a future utopia is consistently referred to as the fans' ideal future, a model for how the USA can be changed for the better. Overall, these letters highlight the ways in which fans use and adapt notions of utopia, community and self-improvement to help to express their personal stories and feelings. In the process of the textual analysis of the aforementioned sources,

I want to establish the precise role that *Star Trek* plays in fans' daily lives. As well as eliciting themes from the letters, such as when fans watch it and to what extent particular moods determine the episodes that they choose to watch, I want to understand and conceptualise the affective relationship that *Star Trek* and its utopian vision have with the fans. I conclude that *Star Trek*'s utopia is both something at which the fans can aim and is also an important part of their own lives – it gives them motivation to perhaps try to enact social change (even on a small level) for themselves.

Star Trek's goal is to promote the multicultural future of the USA, however impossible it may seem. Gene Roddenberry's ideological foundation for the series was to show that there was such a thing as "Infinite Diversity in Infinite Combinations" – that through a constant "didactic project to engage the experiences and politics of the 1960s", *Star Trek* could address real problems that the USA was facing when it came to race and the politics of pluralism (Bernardi, 1998: 29–30). Unfortunately, according to Daniel Benardi, this premise was "inconsistent and contradictory", and as a result *Star Trek* only succeeded in participating in the subordination of minorities on the screen and embedding them in a "white-history" narrative which Roddenberry had originally set out to attack (30). However, *Star Trek*'s utopian message of diversity and peace continues to be one to which millions of its fans listen and in which they believe. Their letters indicate just how important *Star Trek*'s conception of utopia is to their daily life and how their vision of life should move on. In effect, the fan letters I look at in this chapter show an enduring faith in the future that Roddenberry created on screen, going against current public and political discourses that emphasise that our future will not be better than our present and that society will continue to decay rather than progress.

In political terms, Russell Jacoby describes an "era of acquiescence, in which we build our lives, families and careers with little expectation the future will diverge from the present". For him, on the eve of the new millennium, the USA's "utopian spirit – a sense that the future could transcend the present – [had] vanished" (Jacoby, 1999: xi). The main reason for this apathetical turn, according to Jacoby, is that the USA has abandoned its utopian ideals that sustained dissent and the inspiration for social change. Furthermore, the critics, writers and intellectuals who once strove to attain these ideals have apparently given up their fight; Americans are losing the will to reclaim their vision of utopia. If this does not seem discouraging enough, Rick Altman believes that the USA is losing its ability to even imagine a utopia, let alone achieve one.

The science fiction genre once offered viewers the chance to imagine their own worlds, and films of the 1950s allowed audiences to talk about the possibilities of science and the images of science fiction. Today, Altman argues that movies such as *Star Wars* and series like *Star Trek* have spoken to the masses and offered them a unified, commercialised vision of the world because producers are interested in creating larger, more homogenous audiences. Whereas science fiction "once served as a monument to real world configurations and concerns", it has "increasingly taken on what we might call a pseudo-memorial function. That is, they count on spectator memory to work their magic ... Their minds filled with prepackaged memories provided by generic memory-masters" (Altman, 1999: 190–191). Therefore, if this is the case, the fans who write letters about *Star Trek*'s future and its impact on their struggle to achieve a utopia are being brainwashed. They are not imagining their own worlds but are replicating a homogenised world that is separated from contemporary society and detached from the contexts of their own lives.

However, I do not believe that this is the case with the fan letters I look at in this chapter. As Anthony Easthope (1990: 50) points out, "someone will only invent a science fiction utopia if they are dissatisfied with the real world they live in". Consequently, *Star Trek* fans not only take inspiration from the utopian framework that Roddenberry created but also want to imagine a better world because they do not believe that this world is good enough. Not only are the fans concerned for their own personal situation but also they are concerned for society as a whole and they want to stress how using *Star Trek* as a guide might help to steer people in the right direction. Social change, as well as utopia, is an important objective for the fans in these letters. Jacoby and Altman's arguments that Americans are losing interest in changing society appears to not apply to these fans, who hold fast to the idea that Roddenberry's beliefs and the *Star Trek* text can be catalysts for social change. In fact, their attempts to imagine and write about a future utopia follows Fredric Jameson's point of view that " 'to imagine utopia' constitutes an important political act because it challenges and criticises the alienation of late capitalist society" (Jameson, 1988: 355). If they are not hardened political activists, *Star Trek* letter writers can at least be described as interested participants in social change.

Richard Dyer states that the two "taken-for-granted descriptions of entertainment, as 'escape' and as 'wish-fulfilment', point to its central thrust, namely, utopianism". Utopia, the manifestation of "something better", is imagined in entertainment through the desire to have something that we cannot get in our own daily life (Dyer, 1981: 177). For Dyer, the particular form of entertainment that he describes is the movie musical – a genre that can provide images of escapism and fulfilment. Like *Star Trek*, the musical provides audiences with a positive representation of reality, where life is significantly different from the more humdrum daily grind that most people endure. However, Dyer sees limitations in entertainment's depiction of utopia. It does not present an accurate model of what a utopia should be like, "as in the classic utopias of Sir Thomas More, William Morris, *et al*. Rather the utopianism is contained in the feelings it embodies" (177). To an extent this is true for the musicals that Dyer has analysed, but for *Star Trek* it cannot apply since the series portrays a future utopian reality that works and acts as a model for its fans. *Star Trek* possesses both the utopian world and the feelings that it embodies; it is the feeling of utopia that fans talk about in their letters in connection with the conception of its reality. Indeed, the coupling of an authentic model for utopia and the relevant sensibilities that go with it persuades fans to believe that *Star Trek* gives them "a reason to live".[5]

As a US utopia, originally imagined by one person and loved my millions more, *Star Trek* shares similar ground with the utopian world imagined by L. Frank Baum in *The Wonderful Wizard of Oz* (1900) and its 13 sequels.[6] Baum created what has been described as a " 'socialist' utopia", which saw Dorothy and Toto transported from a barren Kansas to Oz, a world of plenty and magical characters (Zipes, 1983: 129). In Oz, everyone is equal, there is no poverty or hunger, and (almost) everyone lives in peace and harmony. If there is trouble, such as the Wicked Witch of the West, then by the end of the story, Dorothy and her friends easily triumph. Jack Zipes sees Oz as "a specific American utopia . . . a place and space in the American imagination", and because Dorothy Gale and her family eventually come to live in Oz rather than continue farming in Kansas, "it embodies that which is missing, lacking, absent in America" (Zipes, 1994: 138). The USA, at the time when Baum wrote his first book, was going through a national crisis. Farmers were struggling to make a living, depression and strikes characterised the 1890s, and war with Spain was testing the country's mettle.[7] To his readers, children in particular, Baum's utopia offered something different. Oz's popularity in the early part of the century continues to this day. According to Zipes (1999: 182), it "stems from deep social and personal desires that many Americans feel are not being met in this rich and powerful country".

Like *Star Trek*, then, Oz is a US utopia that many find attractive. Its vision of the simple life allows for escapism and wish-fulfilment. There is also an element of US self-help which characterises Dorothy, Scarecrow, Tin Man and Cowardly Lion's quest. As they search for a way home to Kansas, brains, a heart and courage, it soon becomes apparent that they had the ability to acquire those things all along. Dorothy could have used her magic slippers to go home at anytime, the Scarecrow was always smart but never applied his wisdom, the Tin Man was always compassionate but confused this with his desire to love, and the Cowardly Lion was always brave but he never before had people he cared about to defend. They lacked the faith in themselves to change. As the story progresses, they find their faith to change and as a result all get their wish. Alison Lurie (1990: 28–29) believes this to be particularly true of the 1939 movie adaptation. As a Hollywood allegory of the "rags to riches" story, *The Wizard of Oz* depicts Dorothy and her friends fulfilling their wishes through music, whereas at the same time millions of Americans were still struggling in the Depression.[8] However, as Dyer stipulates about the musical, Oz only gives the feeling of utopia – it is not an accurate model for it. Unlike *Star Trek, The Wonderful Wizard of Oz* and its sequels were "designed solely to entertain the young" and were not didactic moralising stories that offered readers answers to the social problems of the day and possible ways of implementing them (Hearn, 1979: 57). One reason for this could be because the Land of Oz "has no overriding law or principle except variety", Dorothy roams the country and meets extraordinary people and animals, getting into seemingly impossible dangers with them, and then moves quickly on to the next adventure with hardly any explanation or detail (quoted in Hunt and Lenz, 2001: 26–27). *Star Trek's* universe is the exact opposite. It is firmly rooted in the real and regimented – its history is based on actual events that have happened in our history. The enormous amount of scientific technology and technobabble that characterises its future is painstakingly based on the science of today; its accuracy assures a convincing utopia. What is more, because the fans immerse themselves in this history, *Star Trek's* US utopia seems more plausible as the boundaries between reality and fiction keep on merging.

Although Dyer's understanding of entertainment's utopia does not include a suitable model, he does suggest ways in which entertainment can achieve utopia even if it is not sure how it will function. "Dyer categorises the experience offered by entertainment into five 'utopian solutions' ", suggesting that they are related to specific inadequacies, or problems, in society (Geraghty, 1998: 320).[9] These utopian solutions do appear in the letters because fans identify them in the *Star Trek* text, but of course the fans also have an idea of the utopia that they are aiming

Table 3.1   Summary of the five social problems and utopian solutions presented in the US musical

Social problem	Utopian solution
1. Scarcity and the unequal distribution of wealth; poverty in society	Abundance and material equality
2. Exhaustion; work as a grind; pressures of life	Expressions of energy; work and play united
3. Dreariness and monotony	Intensity; excitement and drama
4. Manipulation; the feeling of being controlled: sex roles, advertising, etc.	Transparency: open, spontaneous, honest communications and relationships
5. Fragmentation: job mobility, rehousing, legislation against community	Belonging to a community; communal interests, community activities

Source: Dyer (1981), pp. 183–184; summarised in Geraghty (1998).

for – they see it on the television screen every week. The five problems with their corresponding utopian solutions are shown in Table 3.1.[10]

The first problem is touched upon in a letter by Danielle Ruddy, particularly the ideas of poverty and inequality. She acknowledges the contemporary social problems of today, such as war, hunger and racism, and she hopes "that one day *Star Trek* – a work of fiction – will become a reality". Roddenberry's vision is very important to that reality. She says that he provided the world with "a glimpse of the future", implying that it will happen, and that future utopia will be "one where mankind didn't fight over land and money, where there was no hunger, and it didn't matter what color, race, or gender you were".[11] Gerald Gurian goes one step further and writes about how *Star Trek* made a form of social contract with its audience as it played out its adventures of space travel in the future: "By the 24th century, we were assured that Earth would have solved the devastating problems of mass poverty, hunger, and disease." Not only was Gurian convinced by *Star Trek*'s "promise" but he believed that this "overwhelmingly positive portrait of humanity" was a "major factor in the global appeal" of the franchise.[12]

Expressions of work and play united in fan letters often describe how the *Star Trek* text directly contributes to the person's work day; how their affection for a particular character or series influences their attitude to work and how much enjoyment they get from it. In a letter I examined with regard to *Star Trek*'s pedagogical applications, Mark Emanuel

Mendoza describes his career as being very closely tied to *Star Trek: The Next Generation* (1987–1994). He studied to be "exactly what *Star Trek* indeed is: a teacher". In fact, he describes himself becoming a primary schoolteacher at the same time *Star Trek: The Next Generation* "was born".[13] Mendoza relates how the lessons that he learnt from the show helped him in the classroom as he transferred those lessons to the children. It appears that work for him is a combination of his passion for the show and his passion for teaching kids. Shamira, a bellydancer from New York, writes about her first initiations into the *Star Trek* universe – watching the Orion slave girl dance in the pilot episode "The Cage" (1964). This inspired her to become a bellydancer and now she can live the dream of being part of *Star Trek* by doing her job every day. She describes the series as "a cosmic dance" painting a "romantic and exciting design in the universe, in human thought, in [her] mind", and she says that she was drawn to both *Star Trek* and bellydancing because they "are fascinating, glamorous, and mysterious".[14] Shamira's private life as a fan and her public life as a bellydancer feed off the energy that she sees in the utopian future that the series portrays. The character whom she first admired was the role model for a child wanting to become a professional dancer.

In the same letter by Gerald Gurian previously discussed, issues regarding the "dreariness" of life, as described in Richard Dyer's list of social problems, are addressed alongside his opinions about *Star Trek*'s utopian future. Gurian also believes that the series "played a pivotal role in shaping and influencing" his "character and basic understanding of right and wrong". It was important to him that the original series was fun and provided "exciting action entertainment". This is key to Dyer's analysis of entertainment and utopia; that it was intense and exciting drama which could help to take the viewer away from their ordinary lives and transport them to a place that was exciting and promising. Gurian believes this to be true of the series and that it was an important part of his viewing experience: "*Star Trek* provided a *bona fide* cast of larger-than-life heroes espousing core values such as honesty, integrity, loyalty, bravery, compassion, self-sacrifice, and perseverance despite seemingly insurmountable obstacles."[15] Gurian's statement about what the characters espoused also alludes to the fourth problem and solution proposed by Dyer: manipulation and transparency. Utopia is possible because the main *Star Trek* characters are seen as honest and compassionate, among other things, therefore helping to cure social problems such as racism, sexual discrimination and prejudice: "Mankind would no longer be divided by petty politics or racial prejudice."

For Douglas Mayo, *Star Trek*'s depiction of utopia gives him a place where he feels accepted and wanted. Being disabled has excluded him from some important social relationships in his life, how he relates to his family being the most significant. He sees *Star Trek*'s future as a template for how he can build relationships today and a place where he will be able to have those important relationships tomorrow:

> Because of my CP [cerebral palsy], neither my parents nor my brothers knew to interact with me in any meaningful way, nor did they try... [At school] one month... I spotted a *Star Trek* book... Here was a world through a story in a book that challenged humankind to rise above physical appearances, to work together as a team for a greater good, something I had wanted on a personal level all of my life... Through repeats I watched every episode of *Star Trek*. I understood *Star Trek*'s vision for humankind to take hold, a place where I would be accepted regardless of my disabilities, and I desperately wanted it in my own life. *Star Trek* for me became more than television, it became my hope of a better life... [16]

Problems relating to his disability – acceptance, inclusion, work, daily life – are in Mayo's words addressed by the possibilities that *Star Trek*'s utopian future offers; society will be more open and transparent, therefore utopia is assured.

The fifth pairing in Dyer's definition of utopia in entertainment addresses community and communal interests. It is important to state here that most fan letters that I have studied described the notion of community in a variety of ways: from very simplistic terms, such as watching the series with the family, to meeting fellow enthusiasts at college and remaining friends for life. Underscoring these communal relationships is the idea that *Star Trek* as a television show gave them the opportunity to meet people and have fun that would not ordinarily have been open to them. Dan Harris says in his letter that he is "grateful to *Star Trek*; besides being a great series, it is because of the show that I met my closet friend". Some 35 years later, he and his friend still reminisce about how they met at college, measuring their time as friends by how many *Star Trek* movies have come out since 1968.[17]

Returning to a theme that I touched upon earlier, the notion of *Star Trek*'s promise of utopia is a recurring component of fans' letters. Jason Lighthall, like others, believes that *Star Trek* aims "to teach morals and values" and it does this by having "thousands of different species from different worlds who come together to try to better themselves as a civilisation, while trying to deal with social conflicts in the right way".[18] For Lighthall, the fans have a big part to play in that mandate. For example, he actively sought to join a fan group, thus learning "better communication skills" and "to treat people with the utmost respect", and he believes them to be "intelligent and sophisticated people who love to dream about what our future could be".[19] As we have already seen, Gerald Gurian believes that *Star Trek* "assured" its audience that social problems will be solved by the 24th century, which is a step beyond Lighthall's belief in the possibilities of human achievement. However, both Lighthall and Gurian's opinions differ from those of another fan, whose belief in the future remains firmly based within the fictional text of the series. Marco Di Lalla "embraces" Roddenberry's "ideas and visions", confessing that "not a single day goes by without [him] wondering if, eventually, humanity will conquer all of its problems and difficulties", just like on *Star Trek*.[20] Di Lalla writes that he thinks of *Star Trek* "as actually being the real fate reserved for our species", intimating that not only will society change and utopia be achieved, but what actually has appeared on screen will become reality.[21] A far leap one might think, but with the series' attempts at basing the future on actual events and current technological developments, can some fans conclude anything different?

Throughout the fan letters I have studied, one can identify a narrative progression which talks about *Star Trek*'s utopia in terms of a burgeoning ideal to the conception of a realised reality. Some fans believe in the possibility of achieving utopia but recognise that there is a lot of work to be done if society is to be changed. Other fans see that this change will occur, sooner rather than later, and *Star Trek* has a part to play in initiating that change. Finally, there are some letters that talk of *Star Trek*'s utopia as if that were the ultimate goal, that somehow Roddenberry's vision is an accurate depiction of what the future will be like. This last form of narrative would seem to be heavily based on the idea that *Star Trek*'s future history is taken by some fans as being part of the USA's real future, the merging of the two in the text somehow influencing the audience's take on reality. However, it is important to bear in mind when examining the content of the letters that the overall trend corresponds to a particular narrative of "changing for the better". Fans recognise that work needs to be done to achieve utopia in the USA. Furthermore, I should reiterate here that *Star Trek*'s version of a utopia remains the fans' ultimate goal. It appears that achieving that goal can be made easier by trying to implement one of two things: personal change or social change.

Gregory Newman's letter highlights the delicate position that *Star Trek* occupied in the late 1960s with regard to war in Vietnam and concepts of social change. He describes *Star Trek* as recognising "our world of war, racial prejudice, and poverty", giving "us hope of a future glorious world".[22] Scholars such as H. Bruce Franklin have understood that it also tried to comment on a war that was rarely given coverage on television except for patriotic news reports. For Franklin, *Star Trek* "parabolically displaced the Vietnam War in time and space", showing just how much the USA was being transformed by conflict (Franklin, 2000: 136).[23] These sorts of contemporary message built into the original series are not lost on fans today. Therefore they would not have been lost on those fans who watched the series for the first time or especially those fans who were directly affected by the war, through serving, getting wounded or losing loved ones. DeForest Kelly – Dr McCoy from the original series – when asked about the impact of *Star Trek* in the 1960s, identified the Vietnam veteran as someone who was especially open to the show's ethos: "We struck a note, a chord, with the youth of this country and particularly those who came back from Vietnam."[24]

Franklin has identified a shift in *Star Trek*'s attitude to the war that is similar to a shift seen in Newman's letter. Two episodes – "The City on the Edge of Forever" (1967) and "A Private Little War" (1968)[25] – represent *Star Trek*'s belief that Vietnam "was merely an unpleasant necessity on the way to the future". Two later episodes – "The Omega Glory" (1968) and "Let That Be Your Last Battlefield" (1969)[26] – "openly call for a radical change of historic course, including an end to the Vietnam War and to the war at home", and thus both signify a change due to the "desperation of the period" (Franklin, 2000: 148). Newman's letter also recognises that war might have been needed, yet, instead of being found in a shift illustrated by Franklin's analysis, these two theories exist simultaneously because Newman does not see them as being different from one another but as a result of *Star Trek*'s faith in the future. The letter endorses Franklin in that the series was interested in both showing how the world could be different after war had ended and how important the war was in US society at the time – perhaps war was the only way in which such a utopian future could be secured. When Newman says that he and others "were fighting and dying in Vietnam while prejudice, poverty, and drug wars raged around us, *Star Trek* kept alive a dream of a better world", he implies that *Star Trek*'s future was going to be the result of such extreme sacrifice – something worth fighting for.

However, he also writes how *Star Trek* "gives us hope of a future glorious world, a world of benevolent human beings of all races who work together with beings from other worlds to peacefully explore the vast universe with awe, courage, hope, love, and curiosity", implying that war solves nothing and the only way in which *Star Trek*'s future will become a reality is through a unification of peoples, regardless of race and cultural differences. After, and despite the war, Newman wrote that "*Star Trek* kept Vietnam veterans focused" on the possibility of peace, it helped them find the strength to continue applying its doctrine of universal peace even when they had returned home. This suggests not only that his experience of the war returned home with him – to be identified by the term "veteran" – but also that the war on racism, drugs and poverty had become personal to him and universal to those veterans who shared his love of *Star Trek*.

The author's opening statement that "the year was 1966 and I was a black soldier in the U.S. Army" reveals the highly volatile situation in which he was involved. In 1966 the US Secretary of Defense, Robert McNamara, drew up Project 100,000, which aimed to increase manpower for the war by conscripting large numbers of the poor. This would also serve to help to rebuild "the fabric of black society" by "curing" them of "idleness, ignorance, and apathy". Such a policy caused immeasurable distrust within the African-American community, and they received little comfort from the fact that blacks were disproportionately represented in the officer corps and were more likely to serve and die in combat than their white comrades (Engelhardt, 1998: 248). The war, it seemed, was not about fighting the enemy but rather continuing to fight the kinds of overt racism that had confronted African Americans before they left for South East Asia. According to Tom Engelhardt, it was not only aspects of white racism that made their way to Vietnam but also the ideas that grew out of the Civil Rights and Black Power movements. Furthermore, those ideas which found sympathetic ears in Vietnam returned home with black soldiers who joined militant organisations, such as the Black Panthers, because they felt that they still had fight left in them – that they would be the ones to lead an armed revolution in the streets (Engelhardt, 1998: 249). However, Newman's letter emphasises that he saw a different outcome from his time in Vietnam. Rather than bringing home the "revolution" with the gun, he saw that *Star Trek*'s view of the future could be achieved through adherence to the "dream of a better world" – a sentiment that, according to him, many Vietnam veterans followed and "focused on". It would seem that Newman believes that direct action is not as important as the philosophy of unity and peace in which many fans – especially the veterans – should believe when there is "trouble" and times are hard.

I believe that those fans who communicate through writing letters to fan magazines and edited publications are doing so in an attempt to contact fellow enthusiasts and share their own personal experiences, whether they are positive, emotionally traumatic or descriptive. By doing so, the fans are able to reveal private and delicate information and at the same time realise that others may have had similar experiences. For instance, all of the fans who believe that the world is nowhere near becoming the utopia envisioned by Roddenberry describe *Star Trek* as being integral to the improvement process. This suggests that they see its multiple texts as a form of encouragement. Indeed, some see themselves as part of the process whereby their experiences can contribute to *Star Trek*'s narrative of social change. When talking about this in letters read by other fans, their affection for the series is passed on through a cohesive fibrous network that allows for intimate but positive exchanges. *Star Trek* fan culture is a collective network, multilayered and interwoven with numerous channels of communication, all of which offer communal support on many personal levels.

Notes

1. See Jenkins (1988, 1990, 1992a, 1992b) and de Certeau (1984).
2. See Penley (1991, 1992, 1997) and Joseph-Witham (1996).
3. To clarify what I mean by "ordinary fan", I should point out that the fans I look at distinguish themselves from more extreme fans by invoking various discourses in their form of textual interaction: the fan letter. Letter-writing allows fans to express a particular kind of sociological and emotional discourse through a particular type of "imagined community". The reasons behind this form of fan expression, as opposed to the extreme versions that I have already described, seem to be connected to issues relating to inclusion, belonging and being seen as "normal"/accepted in the public sphere.
   For the purposes of this chapter, I want to focus on those fans who have had their letters published in print rather than online. This is for two reasons. First, the publications at which I have looked are products of the fan community, while the magazines and newsletters are bought by subscription and therefore cater for a specific market. The edited book was a project that specifically asked for fans who wanted to write letters. Second, the Internet is simply too vast to be able to read every single fan response, most of which pertain to the television text rather than the fans' actual emotions. The letters printed on paper are a result of a more focused effort to write their feelings by fans who want to communicate with other fans.
4. Similar work has been done, using models of cultural reception, by Helen Taylor on women's responses to *Gone with the Wind* (1939) and in Ien Ang's analysis of *Dallas* (1978–1991). See Taylor (1989) and Ang (1985).
5. This phrase is taken from a letter received from Elliott Slack printed in Star Trek *Explorer*, 3 (2001), p. 5.

6. See L. Frank Baum. (1900), *The Wonderful Wizard of Oz*. Chicago, IL: Reilly & Lee. The sequels are listed with publication date only: *The Marvelous Land of Oz* (1904), *Ozma of Oz* (1907), *Dorothy and the Wizard in Oz* (1908), *The Road to Oz* (1909), *The Emerald City of Oz* (1910), *The Patchwork Girl of Oz* (1913), *Tik-Tok of Oz* (1914), *The Scarecrow of Oz* (1915), *Rinkitink in Oz* (1916), *The Lost Princess of Oz* (1917), *The Tin Woodman of Oz* (1918), *The Magic of Oz* (1919) and *Glinda of Oz* (1920).

7. See Zipes (1983: 126). See also Erisman (1968) and Littlefield (1964).

8. See also Alison Lurie (2003).

9. In this article, Geraghty uses Dyer's model to analyse women's fiction, enabling us to have an understanding of why "escape" and "fulfilment" also remain persistent characteristics of soap operas. See also Christine Geraghty (1991).

10. This summary is created from the five problems and solutions proposed by Dyer (1981: 183–184) and summarised by Geraghty (1998: 320).

11. Letter received from Danielle Ruddy printed in Stafford, ed. (2002: 83–86).

12. Letter received from Gerald Gurian printed in Stafford, ed. (2002: 126–133).

13. Letter received from Mark Emanuel Mendoza printed in Stafford, ed. (2002: 30–31).

14. Letter received from Shamira printed in Stafford, ed. (2002: 11–14).

15. Gurian, Stafford, ed. (2002: 126).

16. Letter received from Douglas W. Mayo printed in Stafford, ed. (2002: 5–8).

17. Letter received from Dan Harris printed in Stafford, ed. (2002: 167–168).

18. Letter received from Jason Lighthall printed in Stafford, ed. (2002: 2–4).

19. Letter received from Jason Lighthall printed in Stafford, ed. (2002: 4).

20. Letter received from Marco Di Lalla printed in Stafford, ed. (2002: 168–171).

21. Letter received from Marco Di Lalla printed in Stafford, ed. (2002: 169).

22. Letter received from Gregory Newman printed in Stafford, ed. (2002: 9–10). From here on the following extracts are taken from Newman's letter.

23. Cf. H. Bruce Franklin (1994) and Westfahl (2000), particularly his chapter "Opposing War, Exploiting War: The Troubled Pacifism of *Star Trek*", pp. 69–78.

24. An interview with DeForest Kelly on *Trekkies*, dir. Roger Nygard, (Paramount Pictures, 1998).

25. The episode "The City on the Edge of Forever" was awarded the Hugo Award for best Dramatic Presentation in 1968 and its writer also won the Writers' Guild of America Award. After Kirk is sent back in time to 1930s America, the plot centres on the relationship between him and a woman called Edith Keeler who believed that the USA should not join the Second World War. After realising that his presence in the past was changing the timeline, whereby the USA stayed out of the war thanks to Keeler's peace-keeping efforts and Hitler eventually won, Kirk decided to let her die in order to restore the proper timeline. In "A Private Little War", Kirk and his crew uncover the fact that the Klingons are providing weapons to some of the inhabitants of a peaceful planet. Kirk decides to intervene and give weapons to the rest of the primitive aliens so as to even the imbalance and take revenge on the Klingons.

26. The plot of "The Omega Glory" sees Kirk teach a tribe of Yang warriors, who had misinterpreted the preamble to the Constitution as an order to exclude

their Kohm enemies, that the words "must apply to everyone or they mean nothing". "Let That Be Your Last Battlefield" is a famous episode from the last season of the original series. Two aliens arrive on the ship. One alien's face is split down the middle, half black and half white, while the second's is half white and half black. They both hate each other but fail to recognise that the intense racial hatred that fuelled their people's war has resulted in their being the only remaining survivors. In fact, both blame the other for the devastation and beam down to the surface of their wartorn planet to continue their fight.

References

Altman, R. (1999), *Film/Genre*. London: BFI Publishing.
Ang, I. (1985), *Watching Dallas: Soap Opera and the Melodramatic Imagination*, trans. Della Couling. London: Routledge.
Baum, L.F. (1900), *The Wonderful Wizard of Oz*. Chicago, IL: Reilly & Lee.
Bernardi, D.L. (1998), Star Trek *and History: Race-ing Towards a White Future*. New Brunswick, NJ: Rutgers University Press.
de Certeau, M. (1984), *The Practice of Everyday Life*. Berkeley, CA: University of California Press.
Dyer, R. (1981), "Entertainment and Utopia." In R. Altman, ed., *Genre: The Musical*. London: Routledge and Kegan Paul, pp. 175–189.
Easthope, A. (1990), "The Personal and the Political in Utopian Science Fiction." In P.J. Davies, ed., *Science Fiction, Social Conflict and War*. Manchester: Manchester University Press, pp. 50–67.
Engelhardt, T. (1998), *The End of Victory Culture: Cold War America and the Disillusioning of a Generation*. Amherst, MA: University of Massachusetts Press.
Erisman, F. (1968), "L. Frank Baum and the Progressive Dilemma." *American Quarterly*, 20, 617–623.
Franklin, H.B. (1994), "*Star Trek* in the Vietnam Era." *Film & History*, 24(1–2), 36–46.
Franklin, H.B. (2000), *Vietnam and Other American Fantasies*. Amherst, MA: University of Massachusetts Press.
Geraghty, C. (1991), *Women and Soap Opera: A Study of Prime Time Soaps*. Cambridge: Polity Press.
Geraghty, C. (1998), "Soap Opera and Utopia." In J. Storey, ed., *Cultural Theory and Popular Culture: A Reader*. (2nd edition), London: Prentice Hall, pp. 319–327.
Hearn, M.P. (1979), "L. Frank Baum and the 'Modernized Fairy Tale'." *Children's Literature in Education*, 10(2), 57–67.
Hunt, P., and M. Lenz (2001), *Alternative Worlds in Fantasy Fiction*. London: Continuum.
Jacoby, R. (1999), *The End of Utopia: Politics and Culture in an Age of Apathy*. New York: Basic Books.
Jameson, F. (1988), "Cognitive Mapping." In C. Nelson and L. Grossberg, eds., *Marxism and the Interpretation of Culture*. Urbana, IL: University of Illinois Press, pp. 347–357.

Jenkins, H. (1988), *"Star Trek* Rerun, Reread, Rewritten: Fan Writing as Textual Poaching." *Critical Studies in Mass Communication,* 5(2), 85–107.

Jenkins, H. (1990), " 'If I Could Speak with Your Sound': Textual Proximity, Liminal Identification, and the Music of the Science Fiction Fan Community." *Camera Obscura,* 23, 149–175.

Jenkins, H. (1992a), *Textual Poachers: Television Fans and Participatory Culture.* New York: Routledge.

Jenkins, H. (1992b), " 'Strangers No More, We Sing': Filking and the Social Construction of the Science Fiction Fan Community." In L.A. Lewis, ed., *The Adoring Audience: Fan Culture and Popular Media.* New York: Routledge, pp. 208–236.

Joseph-Witham, H. (1996), Star Trek *Fans and Costume Art.* Jackson, MS: University Press of Mississippi.

Kelly, D. (1998), Personal Interview. *Trekkies,* dir. Roger Nygard, Paramount Pictures.

Littlefield, H.M. (1964), "The Wizard of Oz: Parable on Populism." *American Quarterly,* 16, 47–58.

Lurie, A. (1990), *Not in Front of the Grown-Ups: Subversive Children's Literature.* London: Cardinal.

Lurie, A. (2003), *Boys and Girls Forever: Children's Classics from Cinderella to Harry Potter.* New York: Penguin Books.

Penley, C. (1991), "Brownian Motion: Women, Tactics, and Technology." In C. Penley and A. Moss, eds., *Technoculture.* Minneapolis, MN: University of Minnesota Press, pp. 135–161.

Penley, C. (1992), "Feminism, Psychoanalysis, and the Study of Popular Culture." In L. Grossberg, C. Nelson, and P. Treichler, eds., *Cultural Studies.* New York: Routledge, pp. 479–500.

Penley, C. (1997), *NASA/TREK: Popular Science and Sex in America.* New York: Verso.

Stafford, N. ed., (2002), *Trekkers: True Stories by Fans for Fans.* Toronto, ON: ECW Press.

Taylor, H. (1989), *Scarlett's Women:* Gone with the Wind *and Its Female Fans.* London: Virago Press.

Westfahl, G. (2000), *Science Fiction, Children's Literature, and Popular Culture: Coming of Age in Fantasyland.* Westport, CT: Greenwood Press.

Zipes, J. (1983), *Fairy Tales and the Art of Subversion: The Classical Genre for Children and the Process of Civilization.* New York: Routledge.

Zipes, J. (1994), *Fairy Tale as Myth/Myth as Fairy Tale.* Lexington, KY: The University Press of Kentucky.

Zipes, J. (1999), *When Dreams Come True: Classical Fairy Tales and Their Tradition.* New York: Routledge.

Part II
Reading between the Lines

4
Victims and Villains: Psychological Themes, Male Stars and Horror Films in the 1940s

Mark Jancovich

Although Boris Karloff, Bela Lugosi and Lon Chaney Jr are seen as the key horror stars of the 1940s, along with lesser figures such as Lionel Atwill and George Zucco, the period was one in which the horror film was not limited to the low-budget productions of Universal, Columbia and others but, on the contrary, one in which many horror films were "dressed in full Class 'A' paraphernalia, including million dollar budgets and big name casts" (Stanley, 1944: X3). Consequently, a number of romantic male leads became closely associated with the genre – stars such as Ray Milland, Joseph Cotton, Cary Grant and George Sanders. If these stars are hardly remembered in this way today, this is largely because many of their key horror films are no longer associated with the genre, although they were understood as horror films at the time of their original release. For example, the figure of the gangster and the spy were no strangers to the horror film during the 1940s, and many films that would commonly be understood as thrillers today were clearly seen as horror films at the time (Jancovich, 2009b).

One of the reasons for this situation was that all of these figures – the horror villain and/or monster, the gangster and the spy – were linked through their association with psychological themes so that they were supposed not only to be motivated by psychological compulsions but also to primarily threaten their victims' psychological stability. As Kracauer argued in an article of 1946, these films featured "the theme of psychological destruction" so that their villains "no longer shoot, strangle or poison the females that they want to do away with, but systematically try to drive them insane" (Kracauer, 1946: 133).

Furthermore, while one might expect that these romantic male leads therefore functioned as figures of male heroism that save the female victim from their male tormentors, such a scenario was actually relatively rare. There are clearly some examples of male heroism in horror films of the period, but these romantic male stars were more often cast as terrorised victims or villainous victimisers, as was intended for Cary Grant in *Suspicion* (1941), although the studio eventually shied away from making him the killer and absolved him of the crimes of which his wife suspected him. Alternatively, Ray Milland came to specialise as terrorised victims, men whose charm and good humour crack under the terrors to which they are subjected. Even when Joseph Cotton appears as a detective in *Gaslight* (1944), he remains a peripheral figure to the main action and one who performs very little effective action. Indeed, he is largely reduced to an emotional support for Ingrid Bergman's character, who is the film's terrorised victim/hero.

In other words, these films were preoccupied with issues of dominance and submission, in which the villains both "systematically [tried] to drive" women "insane" and attempted to control and dominate the world in general. On the one hand, this meant that some male stars played victims/heroes who were subjected to terrifying forces that drove them to psychological breakdown, while other male stars were cast as the cruel and dominating villains who sought to psychologically dominate others. However, these two figures – the male victim and the male victimiser – were not simply two sides of the same coin; they also shared many crucial features. Most particularly, while the victims/heroes were subjected to domination, the victimisers were also psychologically motivated figures: their desire to control others was usually presented as the product of psychological compulsions over which they had no control. In this way, both the victim and the victimiser were figures who experienced a profound crisis of subjectivity and no longer seemed to be the authors of their actions. Instead their actions seemed to be the effect of forces beyond their control, forces that challenged any sense of clear division between the internal and the external, the self and the other. As a result, these figures were unable to trust themselves or their perception of the world.

This chapter will therefore examine the ways in which Milland, Cotton, Grant and Sanders were discussed in commentary at the time in order to explore how they and the films in which they appeared were understood. The intention is not to suggest that these "original" meanings are the only legitimate meanings but only to clarify how they were understood within a specific historical context and, in so doing, to demonstrate that understandings of them today are neither necessary nor inevitable but a product of our own historical context. I shall start with Milland and Cotton who predominantly figured as victims/heroes before moving on to Grant and Sanders who often specialised in darker and more villainous roles.

"Suavity and Shock": Frivolous façades, psychological crises and the films of Ray Milland

Milland is rarely seen as a horror figure today although some note his association with Corman in the 1960s (Brosnan, 1976: 278–279) when he replaced Vincent Price in *The Premature Burial* (1962) and starred as Doctor Xavier in *X – The Man with the X-Ray Eyes* (1963). He would also go on to both direct and star in horror films, such as *Panic in Year Zero* (1962). However, these films and numerous other films and television horror roles are usually seen as late entries within his career that have little or no precedent, despite the high regard for one of his key horror films of the 1940s, *The Uninvited* (1944). As Newman puts it, "he ended his career as a dependable character actor in TV movies and exploitation films" (Newman, 1996: 217). However, *The Uninvited* was hardly an isolated case and many of Milland's key roles in the mid-1940s were directly identified as horror films at the time: *Ministry of Fear* (1944), *The Lost Weekend* (for which he won an Oscar, 1945), *So Evil My Love* (1948) and *The Big Clock* (1948). Milland even played the devil in *Alias Nick Beal* (1949). Indeed, these roles were crucial to establishing his relationship to the genre, a relationship that accounts for his later roles with Corman and beyond.

However, Milland is probably best remembered as a smooth, light-comic actor and certainly, in the late 1930s and early 1940s, he made a series of films with Claudette Colbert that led reviewers to describe the duo as "two charming exponents of frivolity" (Crowther, 1940a: 33). Nor was this the only time when he and his films were referred to in this way: he was claimed to be "diligently lighthearted" in *Everything Happens at Night* (Crowther, 1939: 12); a figure of "frivolity" in *The Doctor Takes a Wife* (Crowther, 1940b: 12); and a perfect choice for those with a taste "for frivolous fun" in *Skylark* (Crowther, 1941a: 39). He was also cast along side Dorothy Lamour in a series of exotic tales, such as *Jungle Princess* (1936) and *Jungle Love* (1938), which were generally dismissed as preposterous affairs. In these films, his persona was not only "light hearted" but often "chivalrous" (Crowther, 1939: 22), a word also used to describe him in *Three Smart Girls* (1936). Similarly, *Beau*

Geste (1939) was said to feature "the screen's most gallant gestures" and "absurd nobility" (B.R.C., 1939: 15), even if certain aspects of the film were still eerie enough to "give one the creeps". He was therefore often seen as playing a "trademark aristocrat" in *Skylark* (Crowther, 1941a: 39) and was described as a "Prince Charming" in *Irene* (Crowther, 1940c: 23). Similarly, he was supposed to be "handsome and personable" in *The Gilded Lily* (Sennwald, 1935a: 11) and "more likeable than ever" in *The Next Time We Love* (Nugent, 1937: 16).

Despite this light-comic persona, his early roles were not free from dark shadows. For example, in *Payment Deferred* (1932) he played a murder victim in a film that focused on the "terror"-induced mental breakdown of his murderer, Charles Laughton, following the crime (Hall, 1932: 26). Milland also appeared in *Charlie Chan in London* (1934) and *Menace* (1934), in which "three doomed persons find themselves under the lash of terror" (F.S.N., 1934: 27). He would play another murder victim in the 1935 version of Dashiell Hammett's *The Glass Key*, and he also briefly took the role of gentlemen crime-fighter Bulldog Drummond in *Bulldog Drummond Escapes* (1937). He even got mixed up with Nazi agents in *The Lady has Plans* (1942), even if this was largely seen as "a flyweight comedy edged with melodrama" (Crowther, 1942a: 27).

The pivotal moment in his career, however, seems to have been another comedy, *The Major and the Minor* (1942), which was written by Billy Wilder and Charles Brackett but also represented Wilder's first job as a director in Hollywood. The film flirted with taboo material but was anything but a dark thriller. Nonetheless, when Wilder went off to make *Double Indemnity* (1944), a film clearly identified as horror at the time, Brackett wanted no part of this film and decided to make his own horror film, *The Uninvited*, in which Milland was cast as the male lead. It was clearly seen as one that "sets out to give you the shivers – and will do so, if you are readily disposed" (Crowther, 1944a: 19) and that features all "the old standbys". It may contain some comic elements but is "as solemnly intent on raising goose flesh as any ghost story weirdly told to a group of shivering youngsters around a campfire on a dark and windy night". Nor is Milland's comic persona seen as out of place within the film, but rather as contributing to its effect. He and Ruth Hussey (who plays his sister) are "sufficiently humorous in spots to seem plausibly real" while the way in which the film's horrors crack his "diligently light hearted" façade only emphasises the magnitude of the threat.

Ministry of Fear was also seen as an "eerie" horror film that not only featured a "spectral tone" but in which director Fritz Lang gave

"something of the chilling quality of some of his early German shock-
ers" (Crowther, 1945a: 15). The film is so chilling that audiences were
advised to "keep your overcoats on when you go to see this thriller,
for it dumps you and douses you fast". Again Milland plays "the old
harassed hero", whose performance is balanced between "suavity and
shock" as he battles to retain his composure when he becomes "weirdly
involved in a complex of London experiences". The film also highlights
the psychological dimensions of his situation. Not only has he just
been released from an asylum for the mentally disturbed but the experiences in which he finds himself are "baffling" and create a "shocking
disturbance" that threatens to shatter his fragile mental state.

These psychological themes were more pronounced in Milland's next
film, which reunited him with Brackett and Wilder and won him
an Oscar. *The Lost Weekend* was described as a "realist horror film"
(Cameron, 1945: 90) that "puts all recent horror films to shame"
(Crowther, 1945b: 17), and it presented the "stark and terrifying study
of a dipsomaniac" in terms that were both "gruesome" and "blood
chillingly real". In the role of the dipsomaniac, Milland was claimed
to give a "splendid performance" which "catches all the ugly nature
of a 'drunk,' yet reveals the torment and degradation of a respectable
man who knows his weakness and his shame". Again, it was claimed
to establish Milland's "diligently light hearted" exterior before detailing
his progressive mental breakdown in which his persona gradually cracks
and eventually shatters.

So Evil My Love further probes beneath Milland's charming and personable exterior and presents a tale of "blackmail and poisoning", in which
an "exquisitely proper" Victorian lady is seduced by Milland's "suavely
deceptive ... cad who lures her" into becoming the "smooth perpetrator
of subtle crime" (Crowther, 1948a: 27). In this film, Milland's charm is
revealed as manipulation, and his lack of seriousness is seen as callous-
ness and as stemming from weakness. Nonetheless, while changes from
the original novel were regarded as softening the climax, the film was
still seen as a story of "monstrous malevolence".

Finally, *The Big Clock* is another exercise in bewilderment and paranoia along the lines of *Ministry of Fear*, in which Milland is once again
required to play "a well tailored smoothie" who gradually transforms
into "a desperate haunted man" (Crowther, 1948b: 34). In this film,
Charles Laughton is a tyrannical publisher who "runs his business on
the split tick of a huge electric clock" and who kills his girlfriend
in a "mad, jealous moment". He then seeks to divert suspicion onto
the unknown cause of his jealously and sets the "editor of his crime

magazine", Milland, to identify the killer, unaware that Milland is also the other man. Once again, Milland finds himself caught in a dizzyingly complex situation, in which he is both hunter and hunted, and while the film is "fast moving, humorous, atmospheric, and cumulative of suspense", it is still a dark tale in which Milland becomes ever more desperate, and on the edge of mental breakdown, while his antagonist is also the victim of psychological disturbance, being a "sadistic" figure who is both tyrannical and controlling.

"Frightened protagonist": Joseph Cotton's weak heroes and confused victims

Joseph Cotton also appeared in a range of horror films throughout the 1940s, which might explain his later appearances in horror films such as *Hush, Hush, Sweet Charlotte* (1964), *The Abominable Doctor Phibes* (1971) and numerous television shows from *Alfred Hitchcock Presents* (1955–1962) to *Tales of the Unexpected* (1979–1988). As Thompson notes, he had a "detached and dreamy" quality (Thomson, 2003: 182) and he often played the dreamer who couldn't quite cope with reality, a persona that perfectly suited him to the role of weak male leads and victims in horror films.

Of course, his first roles were with Welles who, as has been demonstrated elsewhere, was clearly identified with horror during the period (Jancovich, 2009a). Even *Citizen Kane* was seen as a film whose protagonist was a "titanic egomaniac" or a figure of "terrifying selfishness", against which Cotton's character offers little effective resistance (Crowther, 1941b: 25). If Cotton is overshadowed in reviews of *Citizen Kane* (1941) and receives little attention compared with Welles, whose presence is as dominating as that of Kane himself, he does receive more acknowledgement in reviews of *The Magnificent Ambersons* (1942), where he played the "fun-loving" Eugene Morgan (T.M.P., 1942: 13), who is again pitted against another dominating figure, Tim Holt's "devilishly spoiled brat", a "vain, arrogant youth [who] cruelly wrecks the bitter sweet romance" between his mother and Cotton's Eugene Morgan.

However, if these Welles films were often associated with horror in reviews of the time, *Journey into Fear* (1943) was explicitly described as "a tale of terror", in which Cotton played "its frightened protagonist", an "American ordnance expert caught in a web of international intrigue" (T.S., 1943: 15). Although a spy story in many senses, it bares similarities with other horror thrillers of the period, such as *Ministry of Fear* and

The Big Clock, in which the heroes are driven to the edge of mental breakdown as they are menaced by vague and shadowy conspiracies so that they cannot make sense of the world around them and don't know who to trust. Furthermore, this story of "Nazi spies" is also one "that sets the audience's pulses pounding" and underscores the protagonist's "fright" through "an uncanny use of light and distorted shadows". The use of the word "uncanny" is particularly telling here and emphasises the uncertain, monstrous and even irrational threats in this "tense invitation to heart failure by fright".

If these earlier characters are sane men in a seemingly insane world, Hitchcock's *Shadow of a Doubt* (1943) inverts Cotton's distance from his world so that this "bumper crop of blue ribbon shivers and chills" (Crowther, 1943a: 18) starred Cotton as "a murderer of rich, fat widows", a serial killer who detests the world. In this film, Hitchcock is claimed to "raise more goosepimples to the square inch of a customer's flesh than any other director of thrillers in Hollywood", and Cotton is claimed to have "obviously kept an eye on Orson Welles" and to therefore play his serial killer "with smooth, insinuating ease while injecting a harsh and bitter quality which nicely becomes villainy".

After *Shadow of a Doubt*, Cotton took a brief sabbatical from horror to play a pilot in the Deanna Durbin vehicle, *Hers to Hold* (1943), but he returned to horror with his next film, *Gaslight*, a "dark and shivering study of Victorian villainy" that had audiences "giggling with anxiety", even if it lacked "the horror and frustration" of the play on which it was based (Crowther, 1944b: 17). In this film, Cotton is not the killer but "a stubborn detective" who lends some support to Ingrid Bergman's "fear driven wife", whose husband is trying to "drive...slowly mad". In this case, then, it is Bergman's character, rather than Cotton's detective, who "goes to pieces in a most distressing way", but Cotton does not offer much in the way of narrative heroics either. He offers Bergman's character a sympathetic ear and some sense of validation but the action is very much restricted to the relationship between the villainous husband and his abused wife.

Since You Went Away (1944) is the story "of one mid-West family's experiences under the abnormal strains of war", and here Cotton "is droll as the Navy playboy" who is a "charming old pal of the family" and "bobs up quite often at the fireside to offer the flattering attentions of a male" to lady of the house, Claudette Colbert (Crowther, 1944c: 16). As such, Cotton's presence is very dual edged one, both male support in the absence of the man of the house and potential threat to the family: he clearly has a more than platonic interest in Colbert and vice versa.

The wartime theme continued with Cotton's next film, *I'll Be Seeing You* (1944), which was not identified as a horror film either but was a psychological film, at a time when the horror film and the psychological film were closely related and almost interchangeable terms (Jancovich, 2009b). Here he played a "psychoneurotic" war veteran with an "apathetic air" (Crowther, 1945c: 20), and the film therefore made use of Cotton's persona as a dreamer who can't cope with reality, while also introducing a young woman who succeeds in bringing him out of his malaise. In contrast, *Love Letters* (1945) reversed the dynamic and featured Cotton as a "soulful and poetic fellow" who helps Jennifer Jones out of her mental problems – she is a young woman who suffers from amnesia – a process which is complicated by a thriller plot involving "a murder...and a good bit of wounded veteran gloom" (Crowther, 1945d: 22).

In *Duel in the Sun* (1946), Cotton is yet another unworldly figure, and in *Portrait of Jennie* (1948), he literally seems to retreat from the world into fantasy, when he plays a "morbidly solemn" painter who "falls in love with a ghost" (Crowther, 1949a: 31). He worked with Hitchcock for a second time in *Under Capricorn* (1949), a dark tale of love and frustration in which he once again starred with Bergman. But this time, Michael Wilding was her support and Cotton played the "gruff and sullen" husband (Crowther, 1949b: 28). Furthermore, although this husband "was not trying to drive his wife mad", the film was another Gothic (or paranoid) woman's film, like *Gaslight*, but one that did not earn the same levels of critical praise. On the contrary, critics dismissed it as a fairly tawdry affair "of penny dreadful substance", which was therefore seen as drawing on very old-fashioned horror conventions without providing any fresh approach to them.

The same year, Cotton once again played a dreamer who is unable to deal with reality in *The Third Man* (1949), and one who is again chasing a wraith. The film was described as a "ghostly" and "macabre" story that is supported by "the brilliant and triumphant device" of using "eerie and mesmerizing music" as "its sole musical background" (Crowther, 1950: 29). If Welles appears as another "dark and treacherous shadow" against whom Cotton has little resistance, Cotton plays "a young American [who] attempts to get to the bottom of the mystery of a friend's dubious 'death' in Vienna's streets" but "who blunders upon mystery and romance" rather more by accident than design, and never really seems to grasp the world in which he finds himself. As in many of his other films, Cotton plays a man whose mind cannot cope with the shocking realities of life and is either driven to the edge of mental breakdown or retreats into a cocoon of fantasy in order to deny these realities.

"Oddly mysterious": The dark side of Cary Grant

Like Milland, Cary Grant was best known for his light comic roles until the 1940s, and also like Milland, although he played a variety of non-horror roles during the 1940s, his horror roles are his most celebrated ones from this period, at least until the later 1940s when the cycle went into decline. However, unlike Milland and Cotton, his horror roles did not cast him as likeable figures who register the strains of victimhood but as darker and more disturbing characters who are more victimiser than victim. Even in the case of *Arsenic and Old Lace* (1944), in which he is a likeable and sympathetic victim/hero, the film raises questions about his sanity – he seems to come from a family of homicidal maniacs and he comes to suspect that he is as deranged as the rest of his family.

For Thompson, these roles brought out the "dark side" that was always present, even in his comic roles, and the sense that a mania lay beneath the poised and polished surface (Thomson, 2003: 351). Similarly, McCann argues that many of his 1940s roles emphasised his potential to be mysterious and that, in both of his Hitchcock roles, he played a "professional dissembler" (McCann, 1996: 160). Indeed, the poise and composure that is often seen as central to Grant's charm always suggested a sense of veneer or performance, a façade that made him seem to be both mysterious and suspect.

In other words, while Milland and Cotton tended to play victim/heroes in their horror roles, but could play darker roles, Grant's horror roles tended to emphasise the darker depths that lay beneath the charming exterior of his comic non-conformists, and even hinted at the mercilessness and cruelty that are a feature of many of his screwball comedies (*The Awful Truth* (1937) and *His Girl Friday* (1940)).

Of course, the key role in this context was Hitchcock's *Suspicion*, a film that was clearly intended as a contribution to what is now referred to as the Gothic (or paranoid) woman's film but was simply referred to as horror in the period. It even starred Joan Fontaine, who had played the nameless heroine in the most celebrated of these films, *Rebecca* (1940). The story is one in which Fontaine's "shy deeply sensitive English girl married a charming rakehell", Grant, and then "through accumulated evidence begins to suspect him of murdering two dear people and finally of having designs upon herself" (Crowther, 1941c: 23). The film therefore follows a "straight psychological progression" until "a mountainous tower of suspicion looms forbiddingly" and, although Hitchcock is seen as the key figure behind the film's success, Grant is also praised. If his character is "provokingly irresponsible" and "boyishly gay" in familiar ways, he also manages to be "oddly mysterious" at the same time, even if the studio ultimately insisted that his character was cleared of every wrongdoing and entirely vindicated by the conclusion.

He also made *Arsenic and Old Lace* in 1941, although Capra's war duties postponed its release until 1944. The film was one of many comedy-horror films of the period, and featured Raymond Massey as a serial killer who looks "like Boris Karloff" (Crowther, 1944d: 17) and was originally played by Karloff on the stage. The comic elements did not work to undermine the horrific elements, however, and the film was said to offer "some genuine melodramatic thrills" despite its "large number of laughs". Some reviewers even found it too grisly, although others complained about Capra's adaptation: "That Mr. Capra wasn't satisfied the stage product and insisted on adding a few camera capers of his own doesn't do the picture any good." Grant's comic routines also met with criticism so that, although he "turns in a creditable performance", his "energy is likely to wear down, eventually, even the stoutest spectator. As a hyper-vitaminized drama critic, he bounds, bellows, howls and mugs through practically two hours and that, combined with Jack Carson, makes those two long hours ones indeed." Nonetheless, the role also explored the mania of Grant's screwball roles, and even has Grant's character questioning whether he is a demented killer like his relatives. (In addition to Massey's serial killer, whom Grant believes to be his brother, the film features another relative, who thinks he is Teddy Roosevelt, and "two gentle" maiden aunts, who turn out to be mass murders who poison sad old men out of misplaced pity and charity.)

These roles did not establish a trend and Grant's following films were not horror projects. However, they did make a break from his lighter comic fare, being darker and more ambiguous roles. *Talk of the Town* (1942) was not a horror contribution but his character is still described as "slightly disturbing" (Crowther, 1942b: 22), while *Once Upon a Honeymoon* (1942) tried "mixing romantic comedy" with Nazi persecution, even "casting [its leads], momentarily, into a mournful concentration camp", a moment that made the film "downright offensive" to one reviewer (Crowther, 1942c: 28). *Destination Tokyo* (1942) was a "purely melodramatic" war film (Crowther, 1944e: 9), and both *Mr. Lucky* (1943) and *Once Upon a Time* (1944) were films that presented his charm as a form of manipulation. In these films he played "slick and slippery" conmen, although these characters are eventually redeemed during the course of the narrative (T.M.P., 1943: 21).

However, it was *None But the Lonely Heart* (1944) that really impressed reviewers as "an uncommon picture" of "haunting moods" and "profound meaning" (Crowther, 1944f: 16). Not only was Grant described as "exceptional" in a darker and more complex vehicle but it was also claimed that the film might actually be ahead of its time: "It may possibly be that this picture will not be widely accepted just now, but we are sure that it will be remembered – and revived – long after many current favorites are forgotten."

Then, after "an idealistic smattering of biography" (T.M.P., 1946: 16) in *Night and Day* (1946), which starred Grant as songwriter Cole Porter, he returned to the horror thriller in *Notorious* (1946). Grant plays an American intelligence agent who recruits Ingrid Bergman to spy on "a South American Nazi-exile gang". The movie features many of the characteristics of the Gothic (or paranoid) woman's film "when the nature of her assignment is discovered by one of the Nazi's who she has wed" (Crowther, 1946: 19). However, while Claude Rains plays her menacing husband, the film's twist is that he is far more able to acknowledge, and demonstrate, his love for Bergman than Grant's agent, whose job is to persuade her to seduce and then marry another man, and then to place her in danger in the hope of getting information.

When Grant first meets Bergman's character, she is "a lady of notably loose morals" and he finds it hard to trust her feelings for him, particularly given her willingness to marry another man. Furthermore, it is also difficult to read his emotional feelings for her or to tell how genuine they are – he is, after all, a spy who uses his charm as a tool and is trained to lie and deceive. As a result, he seems at least as callous and cruel as her potentially murderous husband, and "the unpleasant suspicions and concealed feelings of the two [Grant and Bergman] form the emotional drama of the film".

"Much flesh creepy business": Cynicism, contempt and cruelty in the films of George Sanders

If Grant had a few key roles in horror during the 1940s, George Sanders was heavily identified with the horror film despite Newman's suggestion that his only significant role was as Sir Henry Wotton in the highly expensive and commercially successful film version of Oscar Wilde's *The Picture of Dorian Gray* (Newman, 1996: 283). *Rebecca, The House of the Seven Gables* (1940), *The Lodger* (1944), *Hangover Square* (1945), *The*

Picture of Dorian Gray (1945) and *Uncle Harry* (1945) were all explicitly identified as horror at the time, and many of his other roles were strongly associated with horror too. His association with the genre was such that he was even commissioned to write a novel for Simon and Schuster's *Inner Sanctum Mysteries*, a series that was not only clearly associated with horror but was even turned into a series of horror films by Universal Studios between 1943 and 1945, all of which starred their key horror star of the period, Lon Chaney Jr.

Often a leading man, Sanders was also frequently cast as villains, particularly Nazi villains, the line between his heroic and his villainous roles being very thin. As Thompson claims, he "cultivated" an air of "offensiveness", "disdain" and "malice" in most of his roles and, even in his roles as the Saint and the Falcon, where he played playboy adventurers who fought crime around the globe, he gave the impression that he did not really believe in the virtues for which he was officially fighting (Thomson, 2003: 774–775). Sanders was therefore claimed to play a "stock cad" in *Her Cardboard Lover* (Crowther, 1942d: 19), a persona that he actively cultivated as a star (Vanderbeets, 1990). He even actively promoted the persona of a misogynist, although his biographer sees this as a protective mask that he used to hide his insecurities (Vanderbeets, 1990). Certainly it transpired that he had been keeping his marriage a secret to maintain the notion of his supposed disdain for women.

Consequently, while *Photoplay* identified him as one of "the top ten dream boys" in Hollywood, he was described as an "homme fatal" who a woman dates "at her own risk – but who wouldn't risk it?" (Kilgallen, 1945: 77). He is therefore described as a man who treats women badly: he is not only likely to "turn up anywhere from two hours to three months" late for a date, but a woman shouldn't "expect him to compliment" her hat but simply "consider [herself] lucky if he doesn't knock it off [her] head". This "cynic" will therefore give a date "a good inferiority complex" and has the "impression – real or faked – of being able to see through woman the way you can see potato chips through a cellophane bag". However, these qualities are not his problems but his attractions, and he is "a nice change" for the "spoiled belle, jaded with flowers and candy and swains who are putty in [their] lily-white hands".

This calculated misogyny, contempt and cruelty were not simply directed against women but were part of an air of misanthropy that was directed at the world more generally. They were also strongly associated with a quality of aristocratic arrogance that could be turned to heroic chivalry and, just as easily, to play tyrants, particularly Nazis. It is therefore hardly surprising that he played doubles on a number of occasions, one of the first being in *Lancer Spy* (1937), a spy story set during the First World War. In this film, Sanders plays "a young British naval officer who is called upon by His Majesty's Intelligence Service to impersonate a young German nobleman prisoner in order to take over his life back in Germany" (B.R.C., 1937: 29). The film therefore presented Sanders in a dual role as both hero and villain, and it also featured a number of players who were strongly associated with horror at the time, particularly Lionel Atwill and Peter Lorre, who was very much understood as a horror star at the time. The role was even claimed to provide Lorre with "a very adequate scope for his gifts" at a time when he was claimed to be "a one man chamber of horrors" and "as malignant a flower of evil as the screen has produced" (Sennwald, 1935b: X3).

Similarly, in *Confessions of a Nazi Spy* (1939), Sanders played the head of a Nazi spy ring. The film that was accused of portraying Nazi's strictly in terms of "melodrama" so that all Nazi's are "restricted to the rat-faced, the brute-browed, the sinister" and are played so that their "mouths twitch endlessly whenever they mention our constitution or Bill of Rights" (Nugent, 1939: 13). It was even suggested that "this school of villainy had gone out" of fashion before the First World War, having "sacrificed much of its dignity by making its villains twist their long moustaches".

If the associations with horror are implied here, they are more pronounced in one of Sander's later roles as a Nazi in Fritz Lang's *Manhunt* (1941). This "grim and suspenseful film" is told with "stark and terrifying ruthlessness" and tells "the sinister tale" of an English hunter who "conceives the fantastic notion of simply staking Hitler for sport" but is then "hounded" by "cold and merciless pursuers", who are led by Sanders's Nazi villain (Crowther, 1941d: 20). Similarly, in Hitchcock's *Foreign Correspondent* (1940), Sander's plays another Nazi agent who orchestrates a "monstrous spy plot" that results in "much flesh creepy business" (Crowther, 1940d: 15).

The Saint and the Falcon were also closely associated with horror in various ways. Most notably, when Sanders surrendered the role of the Falcon to his brother, Tom Conway, Conway spent the next few years alternating between playing the Falcon and appearing in Val Lewton horror films, such as *Cat People* (1942), *I Walked with a Zombie* (1943) and *The Seventh Victim* (1943). Also, *The Saint in London* (1939) was said to induce "cozy gooseflesh", even if it does not feature "as much bloodshed and screaming in the dark as one generally fancies" in these types of "detective thriller" (B.C., 1939: 23), although this "deficiency is made up (for those with a more cultivated taste) by some racy character acting" and by Sanders's Simon Templar: "The handsomest and most urbane of all the current practicing Gentlemen detectives." Indeed, his casting in the role had been seen as an excellent device in the previous film, where "Mr. Sanders and his very British accent, which is admirably suited to the soft, humorous answer and the well-turned phrase, have created a debonair and polished 'Saint' " (T.M.P., 1939: 18).

The Saint's Double Trouble (1940) even had Sanders playing another dual role as both the Saint and a "murderous rogue who is a ringer for the Saint" (Nugent, 1940a: 27). Not only is this dual role claimed to have "uncanny" aspects but the film was described as a "penny shocker" that even featured the presence of Bela Lugosi. By the time of *The Saint in Palm Springs* (1941), however, reviewers did not find it a pleasure to "watch the sluggish plot unfold", although "George Sanders is still the hero [and] it is a pleasure just to watch him have fun" (Crowther, 1941e: 15).

The shift from the Saint to the Falcon was seen as hardly even cosmetic: "now, without giving [Sanders] so much as a pair of dark glasses and a false beard, [RKO] have set him to play 'The Falcon' another fellow with a taste for solving crimes. 'Saint' or 'Falcon', what's the difference?" (Crowther, 1941f: 33). If the series still featured "uncanny" elements such as "fortune tellers' haunts and lonely houses", there was a strong sense developing that, given "Mr. Sanders' cool talents", these films were a "distinct waste of time" (T.S., 1942: 9).

When he gave up the series in late 1942, or rather passed it over to his brother, he continued to be associated with the sinister. *Quiet Please: Murder* (1942), for example, was an "inducement to shivers" that also raised the psychological themes that were central to many of Sanders' films, and particularly his horror films. He not only plays the villain of the piece but "has to pretend some business about being a masochist" (Crowther, 1942e: 31). Similarly, in *Confessions of a Nazi Spy*, Edward G. Robinson's FBI agent clearly states that the Nazi plotters lead by Sanders "must be mad" (Nugent, 1939: 13), a comment that is not idiomatic but a serious diagnosis. Meanwhile, in *Rage in Heaven* (1941), Sanders is the best friend of a "paranoiac" who "suspects his wife and his best friend of being in love and against him" and then "takes his own life in a manner which involves his friend" (Crowther, 1941g: 19).

These psychological themes are most pronounced, however, in his horror films, the most celebrated of which is *Rebecca*, where he plays a "blackguard", Rebecca's favourite cousin, Jack Flavell (Nugent, 1940b: 25). If this film focuses on the psychological terrors of the heroine, *The House of the Seven Gables* featured Sanders as the "brutal Jaffery", whose "false accusations and deceits" have driven his brother, Clifford, to the edge of madness (B.C., 1940: 21). Although an adaptation of a Hawthorne novel, "there have been some changes made" to this "nineteenth century shocker" and to its tale of a "strangely haunted house" and "family curses". Consequently, the film played at the Rialto, New York's premier horror revue, where owner Arthur Mayer "generally feeds [his customers] on raw meat", even if the film was predicted to be a disappointment for its audience, being too "dull" and "watered down" for their tastes.

Other films, such as *Manhunt*, were also claimed to feature "psychological overtones" (Crowther, 1941d: 20), although *The Lodger* was an overtly psychological horror film that featured Laird Cregar as Jack the Ripper and George Sanders as the "capable Scotland Yard inspector" who stops him (T.M.P., 1944: 15). This film was clearly "designed to chill the spine" and featured Cregar as "the mysterious, psychopathic pathologist of the title", who not only goes "around trying to scare the daylights out of everyone" but is even associated with Frankenstein's monster when, at the end of the film, Sanders' inspector "pours more bullets into the murderer than even Frankenstein's monster was ever asked to absorb".

This association is also present in reviews of the next confrontation between Cregar and Sanders, *Hangover Square*, in which Sanders plays "a doctor from Scotland Yard" who uses his knowledge of psychology to combat Cregar's "homicidal maniac" (T.M.P., 1945: 15). This "period horror piece" may not have "a first class shiver in the whole picture" but it does feature Cregar as a dual personality, whose "transformation from man to beast is accomplished with wild grimaces, the while he clutches his neck in a manner reminiscent of Frankenstein's monster".

The Picture of Dorian Gray was also seen as a horror film about "diabolic enchantment" (Crowther, 1945e: 15), in which Lord Henry (played by Sanders) is a "cynic who [has] corrupted Dorian's mind". He is not only the perpetrator of psychological harm but is also described in psychological terms as a "misogynist of the mind" (Char., 1945: 20). Similarly, in *Lured* (1947), his attitudes towards women lead Scotland Yard to suspect him of being a demented serial killer, "a character who specializes in killing pretty girls [that he targets through] the personal columns of the newspapers" (E.J.B., 1947: 14).

Alternatively, in *Uncle Harry*, he is cast in the rare role of the psychological victim, a man whose "neurotic sisters, consumed by jealousy, throw a wrench in the machinery" when he falls in love with "smart young" Ella Raines (Crowther, 1945f: 14). This "spinetingling study" was not only directed by Robert Siodmak at the height of his Hollywood career, when he was promoted as the "master of goosepimples" (Greco, 1999), but also starred Ella Raines, who had played the female detective in his earlier horror thriller, *Phantom Lady* (1944), and would also appear in another of Siodmak's horror thrillers, *The Suspect* (1945). If the film caused a controversy, it was not due to its carefully disguised incest plot but to its trick ending in which "another seeming killer wakes up to find his crime a dream again", as had also happened earlier in the year with Fritz Lang's horror thriller, *Woman in the Window*. Sanders was also seen as being "badly cast as the murderous milquetoast, giving neither an illusion of timidity nor the menace of ugly temperament". Today, Sanders looks far more interesting in the role of a man driven to the edge of psychological breakdown, his part suggesting the vulnerabilities that his screen persona usually worked to conceal. But even at the time it seems to draw on the same weakness and corruption that underpinned so many of Sanders' roles, particularly his Nazis, Jack Flavell, Lord Henry Wotton and the range of cynical tyrants that he would later play in historical epics such as *Samson and Delilah* (1949) and *Ivanhoe* (1953). Indeed, in *This Land is Mine* (1943) he played a "cowardly collaborationist" (Crowther, 1943b: 19), who finally resorts to suicide, while in *Summer Storm* (1944) he plays a man "who, cognizant of and tortured by his failings, is still too weak to overcome them" (A.W., 1944: 14).

Indeed, his next role would be as "Eugene Francois Vidcoq, the archcriminal who became police chief of Paris during the Napoleonic era" (A.W., 1946: 9). This character is another "charming poseur" who is too knowing to commit himself to anything – neither law nor crime – until he finally makes "the sudden realization of his great love" for a young woman, "which causes Police Chief Vidcoq to forego what would have been his most daring escapade – the robbery of the bank of Paris". He also followed this film the next year with a role in a romantic ghost story, *The Ghost and Mrs. Muir* (1947), in which he plays "a perfumed parlor snake", a weak and cynical author who leads the heroine into an "ill-fated romance" (T.M.P., 1947: 17). However, this author, Miles Fairly, is more complex than Sanders' usual cad and exposes the weaknesses and pathos that underpin this philanderer.

In this way, while Sanders specialised in cynical, contemptuous and cruel figures, whether heroes or villains, he was particularly adept at conveying the psychological weaknesses that motivated their personas, psychological weaknesses that made them at least as fragile as the weak victims played by Milland and Cotton.

References

A.W. (1944), "At the Gotham." *New York Times*, 23 October, 14.
A.W. (1946), "A Scandal in Paris." *New York Times*, 16 September, 9.
B.C. (1939), "At the Rialto." *New York Times*, 19 July, 23.
B.C. (1940), "The House of the Seven Gables." *New York Times*, 15 April, 21.
B.R.C. (1937), "At the Rivoli." *New York Times*, 4 November, 29.
B.R.C. (1939), "Beau Geste." *New York Times*, 3 August, 15.
Brosnan, J. (1976), *The Horror People*. London: Macdonald and Jane's.
Cameron, K. (1945), " 'Lost Weekend' Daring Film of Drunk's Orgy." *New York Daily News*, 2 December 1945; reprinted in *New York Motion Picture Critics' Reviews 1945*, New York: Critics' Theatre Reviews, Inc., p. 90.
Char. (1945), "Film Reviews." *Variety*, 7 March, 20.
Crowther, B. (1939), "Everything Happens at Night." *New York Times*, 16 December, 12.
Crowther, B. (1940a), "Arise My Love." *New York Times*, 17 October, 33.
Crowther, B. (1940b), "The Doctor Takes a Wife." *New York Times*, 15 June, 12.
Crowther, B. (1940c), "Irene." *New York Times*, 24 May, 23.
Crowther, B. (1940d), "Foreign Correspondent." *New York Times*, 28 August, 15.
Crowther, B. (1941a), " 'Skylark,' Lively Comedy Which Takes of from Triangle, at the Paramount." *New York Times*, 20 November, 39.
Crowther, B. (1941b), "Citizen Kane." *New York Times*, 2 May, 25.
Crowther, B. (1941c), "Suspicion." *New York Times*, 21 November, 23.
Crowther, B. (1941d), "Man Hunt." *New York Times*, 14 July, 20.
Crowther, B. (1941e), " 'The Saint,' Relaxes." *New York Times*, 31 January, 15.
Crowther, B. (1941f), "A Date with the Falcon." *New York Times*, 25 November, 33.
Crowther, B. (1941g), "Rage in Heaven." *New York Times*, 21 March, 19.
Crowther, B. (1942a), " 'The Lady Has Plans,' Opens at the Paramount." *New York Times*, 5 May, 27.
Crowther, B. (1942b), " 'The Talk of the Town,' a Smart Comedy, Starring Cary Grant, Ronald Colman, Jean Arthur, Arrives at the Music Hall." *New York Times*, 28 August, 22.
Crowther, B. (1942c), " 'Once Upon a Honeymoon,' with Ginger Rogers, Cary Grant, Opens at Music Hall." *New York Times*, 13 November, 28.
Crowther, B. (1942d), " 'Her Cardboard Lover,' Remade by Metro Studio, with Norma Shearer and Robert Taylor, Presented at the Capitol." *New York Times*, 17 July, 19.
Crowther, B. (1942e), "Murder by the Books." *New York Times*, 22 December, 31.
Crowther, B. (1943a), " 'Shadow of a Doubt,' a Thriller, with Teresa Wright, Joseph Cotton, at Rivoli." *New York Times*, 13 January, 18.
Crowther, B. (1943b), " 'This Land of Is Mine,' A Moving Drama about Freedom, with Maureen O'Hara and Charles Laughton, Opens at the Rivoli." *New York Times*, 28 May, 19.
Crowther, B. (1944a), "Whooooooo!" *New York Times*, 21 February, 19.
Crowther, B. (1944b), " 'Gaslight,' Adapted from Play 'Angel Street,' at Capitol." *New York Times*, 5 May, 17.

Crowther, B. (1944c), " 'Since You Went Away,' a Film of Wartime Domestic Life with Claudette Colbert and Others, Opens at the Capitol." *New York Times*, 21 July, 16.

Crowther, B. (1944d), " 'Arsenic and Old Lace,' with Cary Grant, in Premier at the Strand." *New York Times*, 2 September, 17.

Crowther, B. (1944e), " 'Destination Tokyo,' a Highly Eventful Submarine Drama, with Cary Grant and John Garfield, Opens at the Strand." *New York Times*, 1 January, 9.

Crowther, B. (1944f), " 'None but the Lonely Heart,' in Which Cary Grant and Ethel Barrymore Star, at Palace." *New York Times*, 18 November, 16.

Crowther, B. (1945a), " 'Ministry of Fear,' a Mystery Thriller, with Ray Milland, at the Paramount." *New York Times*, 8 February, 15.

Crowther, B. (1945b), "The Lost Weekend." *New York Times*, 3 December, 17.

Crowther, B. (1945c), " 'I'll Be Seeing You,' Drama of a Shell-Shocked Solider, with Joseph Cotton, Ginger Rodgers, Opens at Capitol." *New York Times*, 6 April, 20.

Crowther, B. (1945d), " 'Love Letters,' Drama in Which Jennifer Jones Stars, Comes to Rivoli." *New York Times*, 27 August, 22.

Crowther, B. (1945e), " 'The Picture of Dorian Gray,' Film Version of Wilde Novel, with Hatfield and Sanders, Opens at Capitol Theatre." *New York Times*, 2 March, 15.

Crowther, B. (1945f), "Uncle Harry." *New York Times*, 24 August, 14.

Crowther, B. (1946), " 'Notorious,' Hitchcock Thriller Starring Ingrid Bergman and Cary Grant, Opens at Radio City – Claude Rains Featured." *New York Times*, 15 August, 19.

Crowther, B. (1948a), "So Evil My Love." *New York Times*, 22 July, 27.

Crowther, B. (1948b), "The Big Clock." *New York Times*, 22 April, 34.

Crowther, B. (1949a), "Selznick's 'Portrait of Jennie,' with Cotton and Jennifer Jones, Opens at Rivoli." *New York Times*, 30 March, 31.

Crowther, B. (1949b), "Under Capricorn." *New York Times*, 9 September, 28.

Crowther, B. (1950), "The Third Man." *New York Times*, 3 February, 29.

E.J.B. (1947), "Lured." *New York Times*, 29 August, 14.

F.S.N. (1934), "Death in the Evening." *New York Times*, 22 November, 27.

Greco, J. (1999), *The File on Robert Siodmak in Hollywood: 1941–1951*. Parkland: Dissertation.com.

Hall, M. (1932), "Charles Laughton in a Pictorial Version of Jeffrey Dell's Play, 'Payment Deferred'." *New York Times*, 8 November, 26.

Jancovich, M. (2009a), "Shadows and Bogeymen: Horror, Stylization and the Critical Reception of Orson Welles during the 1940s." *Participations: A Journal of Audience and Reception Studies*, 6(1).

Jancovich, M. (2009b), " 'Thrills and Chills': Horror, the Woman's Film and the Origins of Film Noir." *New Review of Film and Television*, 7(2), 157–171.

Kilgallen, D. (1945), "Ten Knights in My Hollywood Date Book." *Photoplay*, 20–21 June, 77.

Kracauer, S. (1946), "Hollywood's Terror Films: Do They Reflect and American State of Mind?" *Commentary*, 2, 132–136.

McCann, G. (1996), *Cary Grant: A Class Apart*. London: Fourth Estate.

Newman, K. (1996), *The BFI Companion to Horror*. London: Cassell.

Nugent, F.S. (1936), "Talkative Is the World for 'Next Time We Love,' Current at the Radio City Music Hall." *New York Times*, 31 January, 16.

Nugent, F.S. (1937), "Deanna Durbin's Debut in 'Three Smart Girls,' at the Roxy." *New York Times*, 25 January, 22.

Nugent, F.S. (1939), "Confessions of a Nazi Spy." *New York Times*, 29 August, 13.

Nugent, F.S. (1940a), "The Saint's Double Trouble." *New York Times*, 13 February, 27.

Nugent, F.S. (1940b), "Rebecca." *New York Times*, 29 March, 25.

Sennwald, A. (1935a), "Claudette Colbert as the 'No Girl' of 'The Gilded Lily,' at the Paramount." *New York Times*, 9 February, 11.

Sennwald, A. (1935b), "Peter Lorre, Poet of the Damned: The Chilling Baby Killer of 'M' Contributes Another Evil Portrait in 'The Man Who Knew Too Much'." *New York Times*, 31 March, X3.

Stanley, F. (1944), "Hollywood Shivers." *New York Times*, 28 May, X3.

Thomson, D. (2003), *The New Biographical Dictionary of Film, Fourth Edition*. London: Little, Brown.

T.M.P. (1939), "At the Rialto." *New York Times*, 9 March, 18.

T.M.P. (1942), "'Magnificent Ambersons,' Welles's Film From Novel by Tarkington, Opens at Capitol." *New York Times*, 14 August, 13.

T.M.P. (1943), "Cary Grant and Laraine Day Are Bewildering Yet Fun in RKO Film 'Mr. Lucky' Presented at the Radio City Music Hall." *New York Times*, 23 July, 21.

T.M.P. (1944), "At the Roxy." *New York Times*, 20 January, 15.

T.M.P. (1945), "At the Roxy." *New York Times*, 18 February, 15.

T.M.P. (1946), "'Night and Day,' Warner Version of Cole Porter's Life, Opens at Hollywood – Cary Grant and Monty Woolley in Leads." *New York Times*, 26 July, 16.

T.M.P. (1947), "The Ghost and Mrs. Muir." *New York Times*, 27 June, 17.

T.S. (1942), "At the Rialto." *New York Times*, 30 May, 9.

T.S. (1943), "At the Palace." *New York Times*, 19 March, 15.

Vanderbeets, R. (1990), *George Sanders: An Exhausted Life*. New York: Madison.

5
"I Want to Do Bad Things with You": The Television Horror Title Sequence

Stacey Abbott

An extreme close-up of a mosquito perched on a human arm followed by a jump cut to a close-up of the arm as a hand comes down and swats the mosquito; red splatters of blood twist and swirl in fluid patterns against a pristine white background; an underwater close-up of a catfish as the camera cranes up above the water to reveal a swamp, accompanied by the opening guitar riffs to Jace Everitt's now iconic "I Want to Do Bad Things". These are the distinct and gripping opening images in the title sequences for *Dexter* (2006–2013), *Hannibal* (2013–present) and *True Blood* (2008–2014). Completely different in tone and style, each of these shots, along with their distinct musical accompaniments, is designed to hook the audience and draw them into the television series, whether through the shock of Dexter's mosquito swat, the hypnotic quality of the blood red swirls or the seductiveness of Everitt's unsettling musical rhythms. These three sequences also introduce the audience to three completely different approaches to television horror. The opening title sequence, an area that has only recently come under scholarly scrutiny, serves as an entryway into the narrative. For such examples of television horror, however, it also serves to establish a series of expectations about the programme's approach to the genre. The aim of this chapter is therefore to consider the role of the title sequence within contemporary television production contexts, but more importantly to examine how it serves to establish generic expectations for each series' new aesthetic approach to the construction of horror.

The title sequence is a curious part of television production and consumption. For many viewers it is a necessary but sometimes tiresome part of a television show that performs a series of perfunctory industrial/

contractual functions. It provides the name of the show, a list of production credits and the names of cast members – usually organised by star value and meeting certain contractual requirements about the order of the names. The order of the production credits often varies from show to show but usually ends with the "created by or executive producer credits" – clearly attributing authorship credentials to the series, which is particularly important for series aspiring to quality or cult television status. The title sequence also provides a clear marker distinguishing an individual programme from the broadcast flow of what came before. It is one of a series of such markers, including the "end credit squeeze", in which upcoming programmes are announced, the channel identification that often introduces the next show to be aired, and the "previously on" for many examples of serial television (see Johnson, 2013). Janet K. Halfyard notes that the "title tune" in particular serves as "a call to attention, a sonic signal for the start of the programme" (Halfyard, 2013). The title sequence is often repetitive, in most cases presenting the same set of images with the same theme music on a weekly basis. This provides the show with a necessary brand identity, reminding audiences of the commercial nature of much television, but also encouraging some viewers to turn away, or fast forward if watching on DVD, video or catch-up television, as the sequence provides a set of overly familiar images that don't seem to require attention.

Of course, broadcast flow is but one way of viewing contemporary television, and has possibly been surpassed in popularity by other time-shift options, such as streaming services, digital download and DVD. These new platforms for viewing television raise the question as to the role of titles. If you are "binging" on a favoured television series via DVD, do you want to rewatch the credits each time or do you prefer to fast forward? As Lisa Coulthard argues, "whether viewing streaming on-air, on video or downloaded online, the attention paid to the opening sequence is a non-compulsory and discretionary activity" (Coulthard, 2010). This is supported by Annette Davison's audience research, which demonstrates that, whether watching at the point of broadcast or via various time-shift platforms, audience's engagement with the title sequences varied, and decisions to watch or not to watch were "often inflected by the demands of the sequence, a viewers' engagement with a particular serial, its theme music and titles imagery, and a viewer's relationship to televisual paratexts more generally" (Davison, 2013).

I would therefore argue that for certain cult audiences, and I include myself in this group, the title sequence, whether watched on broadcast television, DVD or through streaming services, is part of the ritualised viewing of a show, marking the start of appointment viewing, building anticipation for the episode and establishing the appropriate mood. This is demonstrated by the occasional fan practice of singing along to the *Game of Thrones* (2011–present) instrumental theme music during the show's epic title sequence.[1] Annette Davison's research demonstrates that the title sequence sing-along also happens during shows such as *The Wire* (2002–2008) and *The West Wing* (1999–2006), both of which feature distinctive and memorable music. According to her, "singing along to a show's signature music thus enables viewers to share their knowledge of the music, but also to ritualise the (social) viewing experience" (Davison, 2013).

David Kociemba points out that the "saturated primary colors of the images of the Pacific Northwest, the languorous rhythms of its montage, and Angelo Badalamenti's theme music create, [for *Twin Peaks*] a tone teetering on the edge of intensity and dreamy, banality and fascination. It evokes the oneiric experience of watching this strange series to *prepare* the viewer for another episode" (Kociemba, 2006; my emphasis). The repetition of a familiar sequence is part of the repeated ritual of television viewing because, as the creators of the *Six Feet Under* (2001–2005) title sequence explain, titles provide "the sole, consistent, and iconic moment that carries through a show's lifespan and beyond. The title sequence is what you remember most" (Digital Kitchen, 2013).

I would argue, therefore, that in addition to its industrial/broadcast role, the title sequence serves a multitude of textual functions for the show, most significantly serving as a threshold between the diegetic and non-diegetic world. This is particularly important for television horror because this is a genre that is often preoccupied with thresholds, reinforced by the manner in which audiences invite vampires, werewolves and serial killers into their homes on a weekly basis while simultaneously being invited to cross over into the monster's world. As a result, the credit sequence stands as an exemplary illustration for television of Gerard Genette's notion of the paratext. According to Genette, no text appears in its "naked state" on its own but rather is surrounded by a range of accompanying materials that facilitate our entry into and reception of this text. As he explains, this material offers "anyone and everyone the possibility either of entering or of turning back" (Genette, 1991: 261), and while his discussion of texts is focused on the book, this particular choice of phrase does seem to evoke the title sequence whether for film or television. In particular, titles offer an invitation into the morally ambiguous world of television horror and place the onus on the audience to choose to enter. As Steven E. Jones, drawing upon Genette's work, argues, the paratext is a space of "formal mediation between the inside and outside of the text, between the text per se and the rest of the world" (Jones, 2007: 73). Genette argues that this paratextual material is not simply a buffer between the text and the real world, offering a zone for transition, but rather a space of transaction – suggesting a two-way engagement between text and reader or audience (Genette, 1991: 261).

The title sequence of a television series exists in this liminal space between inside and outside the text. First, it brings together elements that evoke the content. More traditional titles draw clips from the show to display key narrative moments from previous seasons, or to preview upcoming moments of the current season. They also often highlight familiar character actions and behaviour – Buffy fighting vampires (*Buffy the Vampire Slayer*, 1997–2003) or Brennan examining skeletons (*Bones*, 2005–present). A more recent development, popular with cable or pay-per-view channels such as HBO, Showtime, FX and AMC, is to commission design companies to construct standalone sequences that do not contain actual footage from the show but rather specially conceived images and graphic designs that are constructed to evoke the narrative and thematic landscape of the series. For instance, the *Six Feet Under* sequence, produced by Digital Kitchen, connotes notions of death and spirituality alongside the quotidian reality of the funeral home. *Carnivàle*'s (2003–2005) fusion of Tarot card imagery with depression-era documentary footage, created by A52, embodies the series' location of the uncanny within social realism.

Second, these sequences remind audiences of the context of a show's production by overlaying these images with production details. These details often call attention to themselves such as when recurring characters are elevated to the position of regular cast by being included in the opening credits. In the season six episode of *Buffy the Vampire Slayer*, Amber Benson was credited in the title sequence for the one episode in which her character was killed ("Seeing Red" (2002)) while Andy Hallet joined the *Angel* credits in season four at a point when his character was coming under threat, causing fans to worry that his appearance there would be a repeat of the Amber Benson tease ("Players" (2003)). The special guest star credits in *Dexter* identify seasonal villains, such as John Lithgow in season four, and Edward James Olmos and Colin Hanks in season six. The names of favoured writers or directors set up a series of expectations for each episode. For instance, fans take note of when the show's creators – Joss Whedon for *Buffy* Alan Ball for *True Blood*,

Eric Kripke for *Supernatural* (2005–present) and Steven Moffat for *Doctor Who* – are writing or directing specific episodes. These credit sequences therefore invite us to straddle the diegetic and non-diegetic world of the paratext and to negotiate these two sets of readings.

Certain examples of telefantasy, particularly shows with a devoted cult following, often demonstrate a self-conscious recognition of this duality, a playful blurring of lines between diegetic and non-diegetic worlds, such as the presidential debate on *The West Wing* which was broadcast live ("The Debate" (2005)), or the 3D episode of the psychic investigation series *Medium* (2005–2011) ("Still Life" (2005)). Both of these episodes called attention to the nature of the show's production but within limits that serve the narrative. The live debate fits in with the season's arc narrative surrounding the presidential election, and the 3D in *Medium* is explained as an element of Alison Dubois' weekly psychic dreams that fuel the investigative narrative. As I've argued elsewhere, however, within cult television "the point of many 'event episodes' is to undermine, albeit briefly, the conventions of the series and to rupture its narrative diegesis, laying bare the construction of meaning within the text" (Abbott, 2010: 94). Manipulating the credit sequence is one way of "playfully" disrupting the diegesis as a form of an interaction between cult fan and producers, in which fans' knowledge of the credits or traditions of television credit sequences are being called upon to engage in the joke. These sequences invite inclusivity within the cult audience. For instance, the episode "Superstar" (2000) from *Buffy the Vampire Slayer* includes a plot in which a previously peripheral character, Jonathan, casts a magic spell that transforms him from a geek at the bottom of the social ladder to a James Bond-style super spy, who both starred in *The Matrix* (1999) and invented the Internet. The teaser begins with Buffy and the Scooby Gang fighting a group of vampires in a graveyard but then uncharacteristically backing off from a fight, stating that there "are too many for *just* us. You know who we need?" They then travel to a mansion, where Jonathan is dramatically revealed behind a mahogany desk, offering his help to the seemingly needy Scooby Gang. Fans of the show recognise Jonathan and the incongruity of this sequence.

Before the full extent of Jonathan's tampering with "reality" is revealed, the show's creators use what Janet K. Halfyard describes as "deviant titles" to confirm that something is wrong in Sunnydale, for the sequence not only includes Jonathan within the montage (although the actor Danny Strong is not credited there) but the sequence is re-edited to present Jonathan as the star character instead of Buffy

(Halfyard, 2013). The episode even concludes with Jonathan walking towards the camera in slow motion, with his long leather coat billowing behind him, in a reverse of the concluding shot of the credits for *Angel* (1999–2004), *Buffy*'s spin-off series. The reworked sequence depends upon audience familiarity with both the traditional *Buffy* credits, and to a lesser degree *Angel*'s titles, in order to understand that we are being presented with some form of alternate universe.

This is a trope that *Fringe* (2008–2013) has repeatedly utilised both to present flashback and flashforward episodes and to indicate their parallel and alternative universe narratives.[2] A 20-second graphic sequence with repetitive, investigative and slightly science-fiction-like theme music, these titles are structured as a single-take digital shot simulating a backward crane movement through atoms, molecules, fibres and a human handprint before pausing on the image of a series of fragments that gradually reform into the show's title. As the camera seemingly pulls back through this abstract space, words appear on screen that connote the fringe sciences explored within the show, such as psychokinesis, teleportation, suspended animation and dark matter. The colours, fonts and scientific terminology of this simple graphic sequence were, however, repeatedly altered throughout the series run to inform the audience that the episode takes place in the past, present, future, parallel universe or alternative universe. For instance, in seasons two and three, when the narrative is focused on the discovery of a parallel universe, the credits shift from the original green for the first universe to red for the parallel universe to indicate the location of the episode. In the episode "Entrada" (2010), which cuts back and forth between both universes, the title sequence fluctuates between red and green. The scientific terminology presented in each title sequence also changes to highlight the key preoccupations of each season (e.g. psychokinesis, telephathy, artificial intelligence in season one; neuroscience, parallel universes, astral projection and mutation in season two). In particular, a flashback episode to the 1980s altered the sequence in terms of style and content to represent this alternative time period ("Peter" (2010)). The terminology used reflected the fringe science of the day, such as personal computing, cold fusion, cloning, DNA profiling and stealth technology. The digital pull-back was reworked as a series of dissolves with the visual designed based upon the aesthetic lines of a 1980s computer game, evoking the imagery that was used to represent the inside of a computer in the film *Tron* (1982), while the show's musical theme was rerecorded to capture an 1980s synthesiser techno-style. These credits involve a transaction between the audience and the creators, as the audience is tasked with reading the imagery to know where they are within the various timelines.

The television series *Supernatural* takes this metatextual approach to new levels by repeatedly integrating this show's construction within its diegetic narrative, and this includes a self-awareness about its credit sequence. *Supernatural* is part of a group of contemporary television series that forego the usual title sequence in favour of a simple title card in which the word "Supernatural" bursts onto the screen out of fire, black crows, angels wings or black oil, depending upon the show's seasonal villains.[3]. On occasion these idents are changed in order to reflect certain generic shifts within the show. When Sam and Dean Winchester travelled back in time to the Wild West in "Frontierland" (2011), the credits were altered to reflect the memorable titles for the television series *Bonanza* (1959–1973), in which a map of the Ponderosa in Nevada burns outwards from the centre to reveal the image of the four main characters riding their horses toward the camera. In "Frontierland" a map of Wyoming is pictured burning as the word "Supernatural" emerges from the centre. Similarly, an episode in which Sam and Dean investigate possible alien abductions features a complete title sequence done in *X-Files* style ("Clap Your Hands if You Believe" (2010)). Most significantly, in the episode "Changing Channels" (2009), the Winchesters find themselves trapped by a trickster in "TV Land", in which they are forced to perform various television formats, including hospital drama, police procedural, Japanese game show, sitcom and even a commercial for STD medication.

Not only does this episode offer comic metatextual commentary on the ephemeral nature of television – Sam and Dean jump from show to show with the ease of a remote control – but the choices of programme into which they are thrust positions *Supernatural* in opposition to certain types of television. Sam and Dean might be at home in *Buffy*, *Angel*, *The X-Files* (1993–2002) or even *True Blood*, but they aren't sent into these programmes. They are, however, out of their depth in *Dr Sexy* (a parody of *Grey's Anatomy* (2005–present)), *CSI Miami* (2002–2012), *Nut Cracker* (a Japanese game show in which they don't even speak the language and therefore have no hope of answering the questions) and a *Supernatural* sitcom which features a 53-second title sequence, replete with a catchy theme song. These credits, comprising specially shot footage of demon-hunters Sam and Dean cavorting on a tandem bicycle and minimotorbikes, playing football, toasting each other with a beer and comically scaring each other before bursting out laughing, evoke the credits for such notable and light-hearted series as *Laverne and Shirley* (1976–1983), *Scooby-Doo, Where are You?* (1969–1972) and *Friends* (1994–2004). They deliberately parody the frivolity of the sitcom in comparison with the dark edginess of Sam and Dean's weekly battles against the apocalypse. This is captured by the titles' largely daylight lighting scheme and colourful imagery, in contrast with the show's usual muted colour palette and dark and expressionist visual landscape. Furthermore, the lyrics of the theme tune accurately reference key aspects of the series' structure and narrative – "town to town", "two-lane roads", "family biz", "two hunting rogues" – but the melody and rhythm of the music lend the theme an upbeat and positive feeling. The hopefulness of this catchy tune, seemingly modelled on Norman Gimbel and Charles Fox's theme song for *Laverne and Shirley* "We're Gonna Make it", stands in stark contrast with the show's apocalyptic narrative and melodramatic themes. In this manner, this sequence, along with the rest of the episode, offers an implicit value judgement exchanged here between the creators and the fans about the quality of *Supernatural* in contrast with other examples of more mainstream television.

The title sequence as paratext does not, however, only operate as a transactional space – a dialogue between show and audience. Jonathan Gray argues that industrial practices around hype and synergy, designed to market and promote new media texts, are further examples of paratexts. For instance, as a means of generating interest and expectations around a new television series or film, hype, he argues, "aims to be the first word on any text, so that it creates excitement, working to create frames through which we can make sense of the text before even consuming it" (Gray, 2008: 34). While he is speaking about "promotional previews for new television series", his argument highlights a key role that the title sequence as paratext plays, which is to "guide our entry to texts, setting up all sorts of meanings and strategies of interpretation, and proposing ways to make sense of what we will find 'inside' the text" (2008: 34). In fact, the promotional use of the title sequence for the first season of *American Horror Story* (2011–present) blurred the line between titles and preview, as this sequence was launched online in advance of the first broadcast of the show as a means of developing audience interest. I would argue that it was designed and previewed as it was to overtly signal this series as horror – a generic signifier highlighted by the show's name but perhaps undermined by the association with the "makers of *Glee*", Ryan Murphy and Brad Falchuk. Those who knew of Murphy from *Nip/Tuck* (2003–2010) might be less surprised about him doing a horror series, but horror fans could easily see a disjunction between the upbeat rhythms and colourful imagery of *Glee* (2009–present) and the dark, disturbing and unsettling tones expected of horror. The advance preview of the credit sequence went a long way towards alleviating those concerns and generated much online discussion about the meaning of the credits and their implications for the show. It was an invitation to the horror fan.

The title sequence therefore provides audiences with the lens through which much interpretation of the series is made, and this is particularly important for examples of television horror because it serves to establish generic signifiers. Lorna Jowett and I argue that while many still view the contemporary horror genre as being defined by graphic gore, it is better defined by the presence of visual and aural excess utilised to generate emotional responses such as fear, disquiet, terror and/or disgust (2013: 131–154). Much of this excess is initiated in the title sequence, which establishes the stylistic and generic approach to the series as well as links to other examples of the genre. This is particularly the case with regard to the specially designed title sequences produced by companies such as Digital Kitchen, Prologue and Momoco, many of which, as argued by Lisa Coulthard, have "garnered awards, attention and a wide popularity verging on cult fandom with sequences characterized by atmospheric, tonal and audiovisual sophistication and ambiguity" (forthcoming). I would like to turn my attention to a selection of such credit sequences that raise very interesting points for the construction of horror on television.

The Seattle-based Digital Kitchen has come to be one of the best known of such companies, partly as a result of its landmark work with HBO on such series as *True Blood* and *Six Feet Under* (for which it won the Primetime Emmy for Outstanding Main Title Design in 2002). For HBO, Digital Kitchen produces not only title sequences but often commercials, music videos and *True Blood*-themed faux-ad campaigns targeted at the vampire communities among us and designed to create a buzz about the show. In so doing, this material, much like title sequences, extended the series' diegetic universe into the real world, once again blurring the lines between diegetic and non-diegetic.[4] The titles for *True Blood* have come to be one of the most popular of television credit sequences, repeatedly appearing in online lists of favourite television titles, discussed and analysed by aficionados (Art of the Title) as well as by professional journals like *American Cinematographer* (see Stasukevich, 2008).

For television horror they marked a significant turning point at which the title sequence could be used to signal disjuncture, discomfort and unease rather than a soothing, occasionally inquisitive or sometimes near-hypnotic entry into the narrative world (see title sequences for *Twilight Zone* (1959–1964) and *The Night Gallery* (1969–1973)). Shot with a combination of 16 mm, 35 mm and high definition, and made up of found footage, documentary and pseudohome movies, alongside diegetic fiction material, the sequence is edited together with an abrasive and disjunctive style that both startles and embroils the audience in this dark and disturbing world. Described by Digital Kitchen as a "love letter to the Gothic South" (2013), this sequence embodies, as Lorna Jowett and I have argued, the "gothic excess of style and juxtaposition that dominates the series" (2013: 118). This is a schizophrenic show, featuring "a frenzy of imagery, including sultry eroticism, graphic depictions of sex and violence, hallucinatory visions, comic interludes and action set pieces", and the show has schizophrenic, discomforting titles to match (118). The horror genre aspires to generate these emotions and while it was once felt by some that television was too cosy a space to facilitate the generation of horror, this sequence openly signals in its aesthetic approach that this show "wants to do bad things" like never before.

In contrast, Digital Kitchen's credit sequence for the television horror series *Dexter* (winner of an Emmy in 2007) does soothe and seduce the audience into the world of a serial killer, but the sequence's emphasis upon close-ups, both visually and sonically, of mundane morning routines (getting dressed, flossing teeth, preparing breakfast) highlights in their grotesque exaggeration the violence that underscores *Dexter's* world. (For a full discussion of this aspect of the credits, see Jowett and Abbott, 2013: 137–138 and also Brown and Abbott, 2010.) This sequence emphasises the moral questionability of being seduced into the world of the USA's favourite serial killer. In fact, *Dexter* and *Hannibal* make two very interesting and interconnected companion programmes, both inviting the audience to follow the exploits of a serial killer and his parallel life as he works alongside the police in the pursuit of other serial killers – Dexter as a blood spatter analyst and Hannibal as a psychiatrist consultant for the FBI. *Dexter* chooses to focus upon the serial killer over the investigators, prioritising the killer's perspective, offering an insight into his mind, making him a sympathetic, if morally ambiguous, protagonist and implicating the audience along the way, all of which is conveyed by the titles. The series invites the audience to be complicit in Dexter's actions and even if, as Douglas L. Howard argues, "we do not like the character of Dexter and instead ... 'get the creeps from him,' the very act of viewing itself puts us in an uncomfortable position, as if any enjoyment that we get from the show at all amounts to complicity on our part" (Howard, 2010: xvii).

Hannibal, on the other hand, spreads its attention across three main characters – FBI investigator Will Graham, head of the FBI's Behavioral Science Unit Jack Crawford, and psychiatrist/serial killer Dr Hannibal Lecter – often fluctuating between their individual perspectives. The *mise-en-scène* of the series is, however, dominated by two points of view: Graham, as he mentally deconstructs each crime scene in order to put himself into the position and thought process of the killer to produce a profile, and Lecter, as he orchestrates and oversees many of the murders, often constructing elaborate and ornate crime scenes in the same manner that he meticulously prepares and artistically presents his elaborate dinners. The *mise-en-scène* of this series is in many ways enacting a meeting of Graham's and Lecter's minds. As the first season progresses, however, the degree to which Lecter is manipulating Graham's mental state becomes apparent, reasserting Lecter as the creative auteur of this series' *mise-en-scène*, a fact that is made obvious by the show's increasingly ornate and artistic murders in which the body is treated as a Gothic canvas upon which the killers construct their art. The exquisite and disturbing beauty of the fungal corpses of "Amuse-Bouche" (2013) leads naturally to the exquisiteness of the human cello in "Fromage" (2013), and then onto the magnificence of the totem pole of the dead in "Trou Normand" (2013). These murders are mirrored each week by the superbly ornate meals that are prepared by Lecter, presumably from human flesh, for his frequent dinner guests.

So if the titles for *Dexter* are designed to embody the series' preoccupation with violence within the mundane, complicity within seduction, the titles for *Hannibal* capture the show's hallucinatory quality and artfully grotesque imagery. Produced by London-based company Momoco, designers of such notable television titles as *Misfits* (2009–2013), *Ripper Street* (2012–present), *Luther* (2010–2013) and *The Fades* (2010), the titles for the new series *Hannibal*, completing its first season as *Dexter* enters its final one, make a break from the earthy, textured, collage-style effects of the company's other sequences in order to establish a lineage with *Dexter* while also suggesting something distinctively new. Beginning as a series of shots of splashes and swirls of a red liquid, potentially wine/possibly blood, against a bright white background, the swirls gradually take the form of faces. The red on white is a colour palette that has become intrinsically associated with *Dexter*. The title sequence in particular features key images of red blood dripping on the white porcelain sink, as well as blood being absorbed into a white cotton swab. The emphasis upon the contrast between red and white is further established by the framed images of blood spatter on the walls of Dexter's lab; in his blood spatter room where Dexter creates blood patterns for analysis; and in early scenes of Dexter "stringing" a crime scene in which he tracks the reverse trajectory of the blood spatter through an intricate web of thin red strings, often set against a stark white background ("Pilot" (2006)). This colour palette is so prevalent in the early seasons that they have become a signature brand for the series, featuring on the show's website and merchandise, and also evoking the cable channel Showtime's own branded use of this colour scheme, reinforcing Dexter's position as one of the channel's signature series.

The use of this red/white colour palette in the *Hannibal* titles – for a new serial killer series emerging on the screens as *Dexter* comes to a conclusion – seems to be putting *Hannibal* in dialogue with *Dexter*. Yet it also conveys that this new show will not be a copy of *Dexter* as the titles also highlight key differences. While *Dexter* emphasises a singular point of view, there are three faces that appear out of the blood/wine in *Hannibal*, namely Graham, Crawford and Hannibal. This signals that the series is structured around three points of view, and yet the manner in which one face morphs into the other also suggests the interconnectedness of their identities and perspectives. Having said that, the sequence ends on Hannibal's face, eyes open and facing the camera, an image of control and violence, particularly as the streams of blood roll down his face, calling to mind the vampiric mask worn by Anthony Hopkins as Lecter in *Silence of the Lambs* (1991). Furthermore, while Dexter's credits call attention to the violence within the mundane, there is nothing mundane about the *Hannibal* credits, which instead emphasise, like Hannibal's approach to both food and murder, an artistic sensibility and a beauty within the grotesque. These credits establish *Hannibal* within a tradition of horror, both televisual and cinematic, but also highlight its own distinct approach to the genre for television.

While *Dexter*, *Hannibal*, and *True Blood* offer televisual explorations of the serial killer and gothic genres, *The Walking Dead* (2010–present) and *American Horror Story* are even more overtly associated with horror through their explorations of the classic subgenres: the haunted house and the zombie. While *Dexter*, *Hannibal* and *True Blood* appeal to both horror and non-horror fans, *The Walking Dead* and *American Horror Story* seem to be deliberately targeting fans of this genre. As a result, their titles need to clearly acknowledge their place within a broader generic landscape. I therefore do not think that it is a coincidence that the title sequences for both series were produced by the company Prologue, run by one of the best known of title sequence creators – after Saul Bass – Kyle Cooper.

Cooper, described by Sarah Boxer (2000) of the *New York Times* as "the king of grunge" aesthetics, earned his reputation for the title sequence for David Fincher's *Se7en* (1995). A self-confessed fan of the horror genre, he introduced in this film a style of title sequence that would be icon- ically associated with horror throughout the rest of the 1990s and into the 21st century: stylistically it is abrasive, jittery, replete with jump cuts and, as described by Boxer, a "twitching, hand-hewn type" of aes- thetic. The sequence also features the song "Closer" by *Nine Inch Nails*, offering a jarring and discordant accompanying soundtrack. In terms of the content of the images, the sequence builds on a title tradition that was established by Stephen Frankfurt for *To Kill a Mockingbird* (1962) in which the titles are shot on a tabletop filled with significant props and objects relating to the film's narrative. In the case of *To Kill a Mockingbird*, the sequence shows a child's hands sifting through a box of prized treasures – dolls, a pocket watch, marbles and drawings – that feature within the film and capture the child's eye view of what matters in their innocent life. *Se7en*, according to Cooper, uses this approach to offer, in contrast, "a fetishistic survey ... of a serial killer assembling a diary 'documenting the murders he will execute during the film'" (cited in Boxer, 2000). As such, this sequence offers a series of clues for what will follow.

The title sequence for *American Horror Story* has clearly been made in this tradition because it evokes *Se7en* in its dark visuals, jittery, hand-held camera style, jarring jump cut editing, accompanied by an equally abrasive title theme by Cesar Davila-Irizary and musician Charlie Clouser, from *Nine Inch Nails*, reminiscent of "Closer". If the *True Blood* titles mix a disjunctive visual style with a seductive blues soundtrack to create a sultry Southern Gothic aesthetic, then *American Horror Story* marries an unsettling montage of disturbing and violent images with a harsh discordant title theme that proclaims this series as horror. It offers an experiential engagement with horror as the image and sound physi- cally unsettle its audience, while also telling us that the house in which this show takes place is what Carol Clover describes as the "terrible place", a "venerable element of horror" presented in such notable horror films as *Psycho*, *The Texas Chainsaw Massacre* and *The Amityville Hor- ror*. These locations are defined as "terrible" as much because of their "Victorian decrepitude" as by the "terrible families – murderous, inces- tuous, cannibalistic – that occupy them", themes with which *American Horror Story* is intrinsically engaged (Clover, 1996: 78).

While engaging with horror on a sensorial level, the sequence also draws attention to the narrative by continuing in the *Se7en* tradition of presenting the audience with a series of seemingly unconnected images which are clues to the mysteries that unfold during the first season. This approach is all the more effective and inviting in a television series than in a film, for in a film we see the sequence once before all is revealed. However, on television we see the sequence every week as the narrative unfolds, providing fans with the task and opportunity to decipher the credits. In this manner, title sequences serve both as what Jonathan Gray describes as "entryway" *and* "in-media res" paratexts (Gray, 2010: 40–41). Audiences encounter title sequences upon first entry into a series, serving to help to establish initial expectations and interpretive frameworks with which to approach the show, but then re-encounter them repeatedly with every viewing of the next episode (unless you choose to ignore or fast forward). In this manner, as Gray argues, they "are free to invade the meaning-making process" (2010: 42), offering material for the audience to analyse as they attempt to unravel the series' narrative and themes. Ryan Murphy made it very clear that this was their intention in an interview for *Entertainment Weekly*, after the *American Horror Story* credits were initially released and before the series went on the air:

> The title sequence is almost like a mystery, says Murphy. "By the time you see the ninth episode of this season, every image in the title sequence will be explained."
>
> (Cited in Carp, 2011)

The violent visual style, macabre household imagery and abrasive soundtrack all clearly signal this show as horror, and they not only provide clues to the narrative but situate the series within the well-established tradition of "family horror" in which the institution of "the all American family" is deconstructed through narratives of dangerous household spaces, monstrous children and bloody household tools. *American Horror Story: Asylum* equally used the credit sequence as a means of establishing the new premise for the show's second season. Unlike most serial television, each season of the show is a self-contained narrative, representing – "attacking" – particular cultural institutions. The first was about the horror of family, and the second used horror to deconstruct issues surrounding the institutions of the church and science. In both cases the title sequences provide clues to the mysteries of the series, but more importantly they prepare the audience for the jarring and unsettling style of the show, which is disjunctive, surreal and nightmarish.

Like *American Horror Story*, *The Walking Dead* is interested in deconstructing – or perhaps, more strongly, stripping away – all of the traditional institutions of modern US life through its depiction of a post-zombie apocalypse. As such I think these two series make interesting companions. In the world of *The Walking Dead*, institutions such as government, religion, marriage and family come under assault before eventually being abandoned as the heroes come to terms with the reality of their new existence. The title sequences produced by Prologue effectively evoke these themes. They share the sepia colour tones of the *American Horror Story* titles, but where this fills each frame with meaningful images, *The Walking Dead* empties the frame of imagery by photographing abandoned spaces or objects. The pacing of the cutting is slower, although the music captures the relentlessness of the living dead and the driving spirit of the main characters as they fight for survival. This pacing, along with images of empty streets, abandoned houses, Dale's forsaken caravan, a forgotten teddybear and our three main characters – Rick, Shane and Lori – presented as photographs in a discarded newspaper and two broken picture frames, evokes the feeling of hopelessness that is an indelible part of the zombie genre and lends the series a visual and aural style that is distinct from the graphic novel upon which it is based.[5] The walking dead of the series title of course refers not to the zombies but the living who are doomed to die. These empty frames are the future to which our heroes seem to be running, in which humanity becomes extinct. By season three the images of the people are gone and all that remain are empty landscapes and icons that stand in for key characters (e.g. Rick's badge and Daryl's arrows). Like *American Horror Story*, *The Walking Dead* embeds key narrative signifiers within its titles and the audience must wait to watch the show develop to understand their significance. Does the emptiness of the frame imply the eventual demise of our team of survivors, or that they must always remain one step ahead of those who pursue them?

The titles designed by Digital Kitchen, Momoco and Prologue, among others, join a long tradition of title sequences that serves to construct a brand image for these shows and to establish the interpretative frames through which we understand them as horror. For television horror they serve a vital role in establishing and maintaining the aesthetic of excess which generates feelings of horror, and they invite fans to engage with each show's particular approach to the genre, be it controlled violence, gothic eroticism, disjointed domestic or institutional nightmares, or apocalyptic despair. The titles therefore serve as a useful paratext to understand how the show's creators perceive the generic signifiers and legacy of their programme and how they wish to engage their audience. They each tell their audiences that they "want to do bad things", but more importantly they tease and prepare the audience with a glimpse of just how "bad" they will be, and it is left to the audience to choose to enter at their own peril.

Notes

1. An example of this can be found in the following YouTube recording during a group viewing of a season finale (http://www.youtube.com/watch?v= wEZpB7AyTyQ). Thank you to Lauren Randell for sharing this particular fan practice with me at the Bad Things: A Gothic Study Day at Lancaster University, June 2013.
2. In fact, this trope is used so consistently throughout the series that Janet K. Halfyard distinguishes it from what she describes as "deviant titles", which involve "a one-off deviation from the usual titles", and describes these as "variant titles: sequences that combine fixed material with the regular inclusion of elements that are different or unpredictable each time and which make specific reference to the episode in some way" (2013).
3. Other such shows include *Lost, Vampire Diaries* and *Revolution*.
4. For a full discussion of the various transmedia marketing techniques used for *True Blood*, see Anyiwo (2012).
5. Contrast this with the unofficial title sequence produced by *The Walking Dead* fan/professional graphic designer Daniel M. Kanemoto, which privileges the visual style of the graphic novel as its key stylistic reference (available at http:// exmortisfilms.com/category/title-sequences/).

References

Abbott, S. (2010), "Innovative TV." In S. Abbott, ed., *The Cult TV Book*. London: I.B Tauris, pp. 91–99.

Anyiwo, U.M. (2012), "It's Not Television, It's Transmedia Storytelling: Marketing the 'Real' World of *True Blood*." In B. Cherry, ed., *True Blood: Investigating Vampires and Southern Gothic*. London: I.B. Tauris, pp. 157–171.

Boxer, S. (2000), "Making a Fuss Over the Opening Credits." *New York Times*, 22 April. Available from http://www.nytimes.com/2000/04/22/movies/ making-fuss-over-opening-credits-film-titles-offer-peek-future-more-ways -than.html.

Brown, S and Abbott, S. (2010), "The Art of Sp(l)atter." In D.L. Howard, ed., *Dexter: Investigating Cutting Edge Television*. London: I.B. Tauris, pp. 205–220.

Carp, J. (2011), "American Horror Story's Creepy, Clue-Filled Opening Credits." *Television Blend*. Available from http://www.cinemablend.com/television/ American-Horror-Story-Creepy-Clue-Filled-Opening-Credits-35519.html.

Clover, C. (1996), "Her Body, Himself: Gender in the Slasher Film." In B.K. Grant, ed., *The Dread of Difference: Gender and the Horror Film*. Austin: University of Texas Press, pp. 66–113.

Coulthard, L. (2010), "That's Not Blood, That's Music: *Dexter*'s Musial Seriality." *FlowTV*, 12(5). Available from http://flowtv.org?2010/07/dexters-musical-seriality/.

Davison, A. (2013), "The Show Starts Here: Viewers' Interactions with Recent Television Serials' Main Title Sequences." *Sound Effects: An Interdisciplinary Journal of Sound and Sound Experience*, 3(1–2).

Digital Kitchen. (2013), Website. Available from http://thisisdk.com/work/hbo.

Genette, G. (1991), "Introduction to the Paratext." *New Literary History*, 22(3), 261–272.

Gray, J. (2008), "Television Previews and the Meaning of Hype." *International of Cultural Studies*, 11(1), 33–49.

Gray, J. (2010), *Show Sold Separately: Promos, Spoilers, and Other Media Paratexts*. New York: New York University Press.

Halfyard, J.K. (2013), "Unstable Edges: The Changing Title Sequence of *Fringe*." Unpublished Conference Paper Presented at the Titles, Teaser and Trailers Conference, University of Edinburgh, 22–23 April.

Howard, D.L. (2010), "Introduction: Killing Time with Showtime's *Dexter*." In D.L. Howard, ed., *Dexter: Investigating Cutting Edge Television*. London: I.B. Tauris, pp. xiii–xxiv.

Johnson, C. (2013), "The Experience of Watching Television in the Digital Age." *CST: Online*, 23 May. Available from http://cstonline.tv/experience-of-watching-tv.

Jones, S.E. (2007), "Dickens on *Lost*: Text, Paratext, and Fan-Based Media." *The Wordsworth Circle*, 38(2), 71–77.

Jowett, L. and Abbott, S. (2013), *TV Horror*. London: I.B. Tauris.

Kociemba, D. (2006), "'Actually,' it Explains a Lot': Reading the Opening Title Sequences of *Buffy the Vampire Slayer*." *Slayage: The Online International Journal of the Whedon Studies Association*, 6(2). Available from http://slayageonline.com/essays/slayage22/Kociemba.htm.

Stasukevich, I. (2008), "Short Takes: *True Blood* Titles Set Southern Gothic Tone." *American Cinematographer*, 89(2), 10, 12, 14.

6
Cannibal Holocaust: The Paratextual (Re)construction of History

Simon Hobbs

Cannibal Holocaust (1980), as a filmic text, is inseparable from the numerous discourses and dialogues that construct its cinematic history. Inherently controversial, the film's extreme content instigated various scandals which have irrevocably impacted its understanding within the wider film discourse. Thus the text harbours numerous meanings, personas and characteristics while maintaining a series of externally acting reference points entrenched within differing social memoires. It is therefore impossible to fully understand *Cannibal Holocaust* without navigating and assessing these externally circulating agendas because they perform an important role in defining the film's cultural image.

A key way in which one can more thoroughly comprehend how these meanings shape our understanding of a film is to explore how it performs as a commercially available artefact. Through the adoption of a paratextual framework, this chapter will examine how *Cannibal Holocaust*'s most recent DVD remediation embodies its various historical discourses, and therein creates a tangible object which projects a communal and widely accessible impression of the film. In order to correctly undertake this investigation, I will seek to combine Jonathon Gray's work on the paratext (Gray, 2010) and John Ellis's notion of the narrative image (Ellis, 1992). Through this grouping, this study will provide a framework in which the DVD can be addressed as an independently functioning bearer of meaning. Herein the chapter will partly address the film's history, its ongoing connection to paratextual forms and its use of established taste structures, while finally looking to conclude regarding how its public face is being presented, shaped and manipulated within the contemporary filmic climate. Within this approach I wish to assert the importance of paratextual remediation in reshaping the histories of seminal exploitation narratives, and in a more general sense the worthiness of exploring media texts through their differing proliferations.

The artefact used to instigate this exploration will be the Shameless Screen Entertainment (Shameless hereafter) two-disc DVD special edition, which was released on 26 September 2011. This particular issue of *Cannibal Holocaust* was distributed on both DVD and Blu-ray, and significantly it represents the least censored version ever released within the UK market.

Cannibal Holocaust: Cultural performance and critical readings

Before finalising the chapter's methodology, it is vital to first explore the text and its cultural history so as to appropriately examine the ways in which these are positioned upon and projected through the paratextual form. Ruggero Deodato's *Cannibal Holocaust* is considered to be one of the most extreme exploitation narratives ever released, and through its depiction of rape, violence and cannibalism it can be read as a synecdoche for the broader industry. The film details Prof. Harold Monroe's search for a lost group of documentary filmmakers who, Monroe later discovers, have been killed and eaten by an indigenous jungle tribe. The professor is able to recover the footage that they filmed during their expedition, where the narrative subsequently consists of viewing the fictional (although presented as real) documentary *Green Inferno*. The film exposes the indiscretions of the crew, wherein they exploited the native tribes in order to gain more sensationalist footage. During the unedited version of the fictional documentary we witness the crew encouraging brutal abortions, burning the indigenous huts and raping female tribeswomen.

Within this structural composition, the film rejected the giallo style that dominated Italian horror of the period. Instead it deployed a realist mode which imitated the visual register of documentary filmmaking, and therein can be seen as a forerunner in the now common "found" footage subgenre. Julian Petley neatly summarises the key traits of this aesthetic:

> The "found" footage itself is an absolute compendium of visual devices which one associates with the documentary mode...shaky, hand-held camerawork, accidental compositions, crash zooms, blurred images, lens flare, inaudible or intermittent sound, direct address to camera, scratches and lab marks on the print.
>
> (Petley, 2005: 178)

This notion of reality was enhanced by the presence of genuine ani-mal slaughter, whose indexical bodies were used to break through layers of fictional meaning (van Ooijen, 2011: 10). While these aesthetic and thematic choices hint at the artistic lineage of the Italian neorealist tradition, they also made *Cannibal Holocaust* a target for censorship in various geographic locations. In the UK the film became embroiled within the "video nasty" scandal, which reached its apex in the 1980s and early 1990s (Walker, 2011: 116). During this period of heightened censorial practice and moral panic, which Johnny Walker claims has become interwoven into the make-up of UK cinema and cultural mem-ory (Walker, 2011: 118–119), *Cannibal Holocaust*'s reliance on gore and sensationalism made it a central artefact, and therein a buzzword for exploitation extremity.

Significantly, due to its prominence within this specific era, *Canni-bal Holocaust*'s history is intrinsically associated with the "video nasty" scandal. However, this particular period of UK censorship has received extended coverage in other academic locations (Egan, 2007; Petley, 2011) and therefore will not be addressed in detail here. Instead, this chapter will look to briefly illustrate the fundamental role that the paratext performed within the instigation of the original contro-versy. In doing this, Petley's assertion that the first concerns regarding media violence were not raised about the films themselves, but the advertising that promoted their content (Petley, 2011: 17) becomes central to my argument. Vitally, Kate Egan supports Petley's claim, stating:

> Distributors...gave these films a public face in the British video mar-ket, a face that, potentially, would not only determine how these films were perceived by potential video renters, but would also have a key influence on the ways in which they would subsequently be perceived by the press and moral campaigners.
>
> (Egan, 2007: 48)

As this public face was so often based around transgressive imagery, sug-gestions have been made that the industry itself was partly to blame for the moral panic (Petley, 1984: 68), as the video sleeves and poster art-work deliberately encouraged conflict with moralists (Egan, 2007: 47). This centralisation of the paratextual form suggests that during *Canni-bal Holocaust*'s original mediation, the externally functioning presence of the narrative was fundamental in characterising it as violent, extreme and taboo – a tradition which, as will be assessed later in this chapter, still defines its distribution.

Predictably, *Cannibal Holocaust*, due to its eminence within the media outcry instigated by these paratextual images, was banned as part of the newly legislated 1984 Video Recordings Act. While this distinct history moulds the paratextual composition of the feature, it has also influenced how the film has been read within the academic discourse. Essentially, due to the combination of brutality and formal experimentation, and its role within a crucial era of UK film history, *Cannibal Holocaust* has become a widely discussed text. Importantly, within these critical dialogues, the film has come to preserve a hybridity, wherein it slips between academic validation and cultural condemnation. For example, Winston Wheeler Dixon claims that the film is "inherently inhumane and senselessly cruel" (Dixon, 2010: 138) due to its depiction of violence, while Carolina Jauregui argues that for many the narrative remains a colonial text (Jauregui, 2004), which Neil Jackson claims actively exploits the environment that it is filmed in (Jackson, 2002). In contrast, Ed Morgan argues that the film makes profound statements about sensationalist journalistic violence (Morgan, 2006: 557), while Petley claimed during an interview that I conducted with him in January 2013 that "in a way *Cannibal Holocaust* is a kind of art movie, [as] it does so many things art movies do; it's very self reflective. If it wasn't for the nature of the subject ... I think people would have taken it rather more seriously" (Petley, 2013).

While the aim of this chapter is not to redeem or condemn the narrative, or explicitly side with these prevailing scholarly dialogues, their presence is vital within the forthcoming exploration of the film's paratextual presentation. The unstable critical landscape, coupled with the vast censorial history, has an adverse impact on the manner in which *Cannibal Holocaust* is presented as a tangible object of commerce. Clearly, due to the balance of legitimisation and denunciation, one can position *Cannibal Holocaust* as a narrative that has the potential to drift between the cultural spaces of "high" and "low", simultaneously harbouring the traditional capital of critical validation and the subcultural kudos of excess and extremity. Therefore, during the analysis of the film's latest DVD incarnation, the chapter will explore whether this artistic validity is promoted, or if the paratextual features trade off the film's reputation as a text of considerable social scandal and illegitimacy.

The paratext and the direction of consumption

Before examining the product itself, it is essential to first outline and survey the methodological framework which will be employed throughout the study of the DVD artefact. In essence, paratextual theory locates itself as an investigation into how, in reference to the work of Christian Metz, the outer machine and the inner machine actively perpetuate a spontaneous desire to consume (Metz, 1977: 7–8). Essentially, the work of Gray, which suggests that viewing decisions are based around the understanding of paratextual entities (Gray, 2010: 3), begins to consider the ways in which the cinematic sphere directs audience consumption habits. Significantly, Gray locates his discussion of the paratext within the current climate of technological advancement that is outlined by the likes of Paul McDonald (2007) and Barbara Klinger (2006), stating that

> Media growth and saturation can only be measured in small part by the number of films or television shows … as each and every media text is accompanied by textual proliferation at the level of hype, synergy, promos, and peripherals.
>
> (Gray, 2010: 1)

Crucially, the DVD is positioned by Gray as a principal artefact within the broader paratextual sphere as it combines differing sites of interaction, such as special features, jacket sleeves, collectable items and commentaries (Gray, 2010: 91).

Importantly for the assessment proposed within this chapter, Gray states that these commercial entities act as "book covers" – small segments of information which help the audiences to create their first impressions of a particular film (Gray, 2010: 4). Herein, the paratext performs a central function in coding the film and positioning it within the established filmic culture. Gray extends this concept:

> Given their extended presence, any filmic or televisual text and its cultural impact, value, and meaning cannot be adequately analyzed without taking into account the film or program's many proliferations. Each proliferation, after all, holds the potential to change the meaning of the text, even if only slightly.
>
> (Gray, 2010: 2)

Thus paratexts, in their numerous incarnations, can affect the market and academic domains of particular films, transforming the space in which the film is located and its understanding within the consumer demographic. This idea of transfiguration will become vital later in this chapter, as the manner in which certain images and symbols actively encourage particular readings is fundamental in mapping the way in which *Cannibal Holocaust*'s cultural history is re-formed within the cinematic sphere.

When considering the DVD as a paratext which retains the ability to alter the meaning of a film text, John Ellis' concept of narrative image proves vital. Although the term, originating in *Visible Fictions: Cinema, Television, Video* (Ellis, 1992), pre-dates the era of technological advancement and media saturation outlined by Klinger, McDonald and Gray, the concept neatly correlates with their work. Ellis states that a film's narrative image is its circulation outside its performance (1992: 31), a definition that neatly reflects Gray's conceptualisation of paratextual artefacts. In essence, the narrative image offers a freely circulating definition of a particular film (Ellis, 1992: 30), created through a series of cinematic ingredients, such as taglines, images, titles, star histories, generic templates and cultural memories. Importantly, these components have to provide a balance between the familiar and the innovative, so as to simultaneously generate a reference point within the audience's understanding of cinema and the curiosity which will make them want to consume (Ellis, 1992: 30). Within this combination it is useful to refer to the recent work of Lincoln Geraghty, who claims that while DVDs represent archival objects, the originally created features and artwork locate them within a new history (Geraghty, 2014: 57). This mixture, which he states allows older narratives to become appealing to younger audiences (Geraghty, 2014: 58), is central to the forthcoming exploration of the *Cannibal Holocaust* artefact because it has a large bearing on the reconstruction of the film's history.

Yet, to more thoroughly comprehend this idea of newly renovated histories being presented through remediated paratextual artefacts, it is vital to refer to Jacques Derrida's notion of trace. His writings on trace theory are located within *Of Grammatology* (1976). However, here it is sufficient to refer to Gayatri Chakravorty Spivak's summation: "Derrida's trace is the mark of the absence of a presence" (Spivak, 1976: xvii). Herein, the trace of an object becomes a sign through a comprehension of its precirculating understandings (Spivak, 1976: xvii). In their simultaneous absence and presence, trace becomes a signifier grounded within a communal memory, and, read through a framework of paratextual study, it is central to the creation of a text's cultural and commercial identity. Therefore certain images and objects used throughout the paratextual world carry a historical significance which informs and directs their reproduction and comprehension within the present. As an example of this, the semiotic signifiers of the horror genre used on posters, which Gray states are limited to an icon of the murder or an image of disturbed innocence (Gray, 2010: 53), work to produce meaning through their previous encounters with the category. Thus the icon of murder – for example, Freddy Kruger's bladed glove in *A Nightmare on Elm Street* (1984) – utilises the trace memory of Norman Bates' kitchen knife in order to locate the film within an understood concept of horror cinema, which has its own structures of value, expectations and templates of knowledge.

Importantly, within the chapter's ambition to consider a text which retains the ability to transgress cultural boundaries, and in order to further assess how the text's history is being reformed through continued remediation, the exploration will look to examine whether this particular paratextual incarnation of *Cannibal Holocaust* seeks to express its transgressive nature or ensconce it within a new history. Herein, I wish to place the chapter within an adjacent critical framework to that of paratextual studies, one populated by the likes of Mark Betz (2013) and Joan Hawkins (2000), and which deals with notions of taste slippage and the porous nature of "high" and "low" cultural spaces. Thus, within the broader discourse of cult distinction, and in reference to the film's fluctuating critical image, I will seek to evaluate how certain semiotic signifiers present on the DVD artefact, such as auteur branding, evidence of critical legitimisation, images of nudity, representations of violence and an employment of generic templates, actively manipulate the public history of Deodato's text and place it within differing cultural environs through the activation of specific memories.

Cannibal Holocaust: DVD aesthetic, marketing and paratextual identity

Essentially, in order to understand the manner in which *Cannibal Holocaust*'s cultural image is constructed through this particular DVD release, one must assess the distributor because it retains an inherent cultural trace that influences the film's narrative image. As stated, this edition was released by Shameless, a UK company started in 2007, which specialises in the distribution of European exploitation films of the 1970s and 1980s and retains a sizable distribution catalogue within the UK. Some of its most important releases include Deodato's *House on the Edge of the Park* (1980), Lucio Fulci's *Manhattan Baby* (1982) and *The House of the Laughing Windows* (1976).

Due to the generic implications of the films released by Shameless, the company is not legitimised within the confines of the "high" cultural space, which in the UK is populated by companies such as Artificial

Eye, Eureka Masters of Cinema and BFI distribution. Instead, through its continued presence within the fan domain, the company has achieved a substantial level of subcultural capital which is grafted onto any film that is released under its branding. Herein, *Cannibal Holocaust* is immediately placed within a marginal discourse and bestowed an additional level of subcultural credence.

A large part of achieving this standing comes from the company's active engagement with its consumer base. The main platform for this interaction is its official forum, which has several main threads, including "Current and Upcoming Shameless Titles", "The Shameless Collection", "Why Don't Shameless Release...?" and "Shamelessly Creative". This forum is crucial in recognising the demographic of Shameless as a fan community because "since its inception, fans, who are often geographically and socially isolated and yet crave association with others of a like mind, have congregated on the Internet" (Cherry, 2010: 69). Furthermore, within these threads, especially "Why Don't Shameless Release...?" and "Shamelessly Creative", the consumer base is encouraged to actively engage with the company, which is an important aspect of modern fandom:

> This ability to transform personal reaction into social interaction, spectatorial culture into participatory culture, is one of the central characteristics of fandom. One becomes a "fan" not by being a regular viewer of a particular program but by translating that viewing into some kind of cultural activity.
>
> (Jenkins, 2006: 41)

Therefore, while failing to achieve a culturally authenticated level of capital, Shameless preserves a valuable subcultural capital based around the distribution of key horror narratives and a fan-orientated company directive.

In order to control and propagate this capital, Shameless maintains a strong market presence through the replication of a uniform DVD aesthetic. The foremost aspect of this commercial composition is the yellow covers that adorn its releases. These carry important (sub)cultural connotations, as the colour references the Italian giallo genre. Herein, the DVD sleeves and cases instantly connote a set of generic conventions, and therefore serve a central purpose in the placement of the filmic narrative. Essentially, the comprehension of this colour scheme can only be decoded if a communal cultural capital exists (Thornton, 1995: 11), in which both distributor and consumer understand the importance of the reference and receive pleasure in understanding its meaning. Crucially, within this centralisation of a communal reading, the giallo, as evidenced within Brigit Cherry's detailed exploration of horror fan cultures, is well respected within the genres hierarchy (Cherry, 2012: 26). Therefore Shameless's use of the distinctive yellow enables it to appropriate part of this subcultural value and graft it to its own commercial image, and each film within its library.

However, it is essential to understand the generic significance of this colour palette. Essentially the colour scheme homogenises the films under a giallo semiotic coding, a notion that affects the understanding of *Cannibal Holocaust*. While violent and sexual, *Cannibal Holocaust* does not follow the giallo narrative template and therefore this particular visual trace effectively contradicts the film's generic composition. Even though this is not an instance of "high" to "low" cultural slippage, it can be recognised as a case of intercanon fluidity, wherein the paratextual packaging misrepresents the narrative content of *Cannibal Holocaust* and thus promotes an inaccurate yet marketable narrative image. In relation to Cherry's earlier comments concerning the subcultural status of the giallo, marketing *Cannibal Holocaust* through the memory of giallo allows Shameless to exploit the popularity of the subgenre, while actively rerouting the film's historical origins.

Nonetheless, the comprehension of these generic connotations is still dependant on a level of subcultural competence, which is not available to those outside the fan community and is deeply entrenched within a learnt set of sophisticated decoding skills. Furthermore, the nature of the narratives, which feature extreme violence and explicit sexual activity, further entrenches the company within a marginal and exclusive discourse. Importantly, this grafts a cult-like status onto the company, wherein the anti-mainstream product can only be properly understood by a small market sector. Significantly, Shameless encourages this reading of its product through the taglines and images used across its catalogue. For example, Joe D'Amato's *Love Goddess of the Cannibals* (1978) features the taglines "You'll die of pleasure!" and "Hold on to your manhood, the Love Goddess is hungry!", in addition to multiple images of female nudity. Moreover, *Killer Nun* (1979) has the tagline "At last the slut is uncut", while prominently featuring the text "Father I've been a murderous whore!" Herein, the exclusive and therefore cultish status of the Shameless brand is confirmed, allowing the company to operate outside the mainstream, and to protect and propagate the inherent marginality of its product.

Within this self-consciously exploitative marketing aesthetic, Shameless employs a promotional approach ensconced within the traditions of ballyhoo. Ballyhoo marketing, pioneered by the touring freak shows and circuses that were popular in the USA in the 1930s, lends itself easily to the marketing of exploitation films (Kattelman, 2011: 63) due to its reliance on hype and curiosity. Beth Kattelman provides a neat summary:

> Throughout the ages, pitchmen have known that some good, effective ballyhoo could help them sell almost anything. Phrases such as those listed above [we dare you to see this!, you won't believe your eyes!, you've never seen anything like this!] have long been a part of sales campaigns promising to deliver an original, unique, bizarre and/or terrifying product to expectant audiences.
>
> (Kattelman, 2011: 61)

This type of hyperbolic advertisement involved the talking up of a film's content in order to make it visible among its peers and desirable to the audience, and become an artform within itself (Kattelman, 2011: 63). In the most part, the term "ballyhoo", when used in relation to the marketing traditions of exploitation cinema, has been employed to describe historical customs. However, as the comments present across the Shameless library prove, a modernisation of the concept can facilitate an understanding of existing exploitation marketing practices, and thus will be a continued site of reference within this chapter's assessment of *Cannibal Holocaust*.

Thus the brand identity of Shameless is split between a promotion of sexuality, violence and disgust; a traditionalist ballyhoo marketing tactic entrenched within "low"-brow cultural practices; and a complicated understanding of genre codes, fan desires and historical contexts. This shifting discourse and instability between sophistication and hyperbolic representation remains prevalent throughout the *Cannibal Holocaust* release. Importantly, the very presence of *Cannibal Holocaust* on a digitalised viewing platform desired due to its quality is central to rewriting the film's history as it removes what Peter Hutchings terms the anti-commercial, anti-official culture and anti-state "badge of honour" retained by "video nasties" during their time as illicit VHS objects (Hutchings, 2008: 225). Herein, the renewal of the product instantly elevates it from its past as an illegitimate filmic text and begins to recast its history within the established discourse of cultural validity. Additionally, this edition contains two different cuts of the film: the aforementioned nearly uncut version, which has only 14 seconds of excessive animal cruelty removed, and an exclusive director's cut, which aims to address the film's previous condemnations. Both of these versions are vital to assessing how this paratextual artefact recodes the films public persona through the adoption of various cultural traces and traditions. First, as Klinger argues,

> Special-edition marketing in particular provides an opportunity to elevate film to the status of high art,...In addition, through the often extensive background materials that accompany it, a special edition appears to furnish the authenticity and history so important to establishing the value of an archival object.
>
> (Klinger, 2006: 66)

Herein, the Shameless release instantly grafts a pre-existing level of cultural worth onto *Cannibal Holocaust* by awarding it special edition status, and further removes the film from the paratextual discourse that characterised its previous distribution and cultural identity.

Furthermore, while the near uncut version shares an inescapable relationship to ballyhoo, as it promises the most violent version of the narrative, it also presents the most authentic and thus authorial account of the film, allowing the artefact to perform as a historically valid release which restores the film to its original condition. This is vital because the previous cuts of this and many other European horror titles of the 1970s and 1980s were addressed as objects of low quality due to the presence of severe censorship (Guins, 2005: 21). Additionally, the original Deodato cut suggests a strong authorial presence, which, as Stephen Thrower claims, is rare within the exploitation industry due its unique production conditions (Thrower, 2007: 18) and the aforementioned censorial regulations. Importantly, these interlinking channels of commercialisation dress the product in the familiar furnishings of cultural significance, and thus allow the film to transcend the liminal space of "low-brow" exploitation.

Aiding the film's transcendence into an artefact of worth, the DVD is equipped with a "collector's reversible sleeve", which further enables fan interaction by allowing the consumer the choice of how they display the item. Within the following section, both covers will be assessed as they begin to expose the artefact as a hybrid and fluid article that is capable of presenting Deodato's film within a dualistic history. The first cover features newly commissioned artwork and thus creates an original narrative image of the film. The image is an artistically stylised version of the film's iconic impaled women scene, and it contains the key ingredients of extreme horror marketing. The silhouette of the woman's breasts and pubic region is visible, giving the cover sexual overtones, while the cascading red blood works to combine this sexuality with violence. Within its presentation of sexualised violence, the jacket art acts as an indicator to the transgressions present within the film while recalling the ballyhoo marketing techniques surveyed earlier through an isolation of extremity.

Extending the hyperbolic nature of this sparse cover, which only includes the main image, the film's title, Deodato's name and Shameless branding, is the tagline which reads "the most controversial film ever made". A classic example of the ballyhoo tradition, the tagline dares the consumer to watch the film as a test of their threshold. This challenge is restated within the blurb on the back of the box: "a film so violent and depraved that the director was charged with killing his own cast!" and "still **THE most controversial film ever**". The repetition of the statement further centralises the film's transgressive standing, confirming its exclusive nature and suggesting a self-aware promotion of the film's "low" cultural status. Importantly, the construction of this cover and the combination of image and text illustrates how the film's original identity as an artefact of notoriety still informs its current meditation, while contradicting the validity obtained through the collector's edition remediation and dual disc presentation.

This recollection of the film's specific historical image, and the idea that this current paratext is trading off the film's initial controversy, is also fundamental to the reversible cover. An exact replica of the illustration that adorned the original 1982 Go Video release, the reproduced image shows a drawn savage eating flesh surrounded by tall grass, with the dual taglines "Eaten Alive" and "The Ultimate Terror Movie...". The image is a marked example of its type as it represents a conventional "video nasty" aesthetic by showing the forbidden spectacle of violence (Egan, 2007: 52), and therein recalls a tradition steeped in national nostalgia. Crucially, this artwork is identical to the image which became ensconced within the censorial scandal instigated on the film's initial release, and therefore carries an important and influential cultural weighting within several key frameworks.

Significantly, the replication of the original cover self-consciously attracts an existing fan base. Mapped in detail in Egan's *Trash or Treasure* (2007), the fandom exists

> As a marked example of how *past* nationally-specific commercial and political circumstance can inform... present day video collections,

and the hierarchies of selection, value and categorisation through which such collections are constructed.

(Egan, 2007: 157–158)

Subsequently, the importance of the past and notions of authenticity motivate the collectors, further underscoring the significance of this cover within the context of the film's commercial desirability. As Geraghty claims, the appropriation and duplication of nostalgia is imperative to consumption cultures of fan communities (Geraghty, 2014: 61–64), and therefore this replica artwork partakes in a long-standing commercial dialogue between the industry and the fan. This becomes even more prevalent when the dedicated Go Video website is considered. Set up for "fellow collectors", it acts as a way in which enthusiasts can view the artwork of Go Video releases, collate their desirability and authenticate their value. On the *Cannibal Holocaust* page, the film's rarity as a precertificated VHS sporting the original Go Video cover replicated here is rated at two stars (represented by asterisks), while its desirability gets five stars. This website and its grading system stress the importance of authenticity to the fan discourse, consequently suggesting that the duplication of the image entrenches the film within its existing subculture. Petley furthers this discussion by stating:

You couldn't really not have that cover could you? In our country that became so iconic of the movie, you know it's in fairly bad taste and is fairly shocking, but I think ... not having it, one would have wondered why it was not there. It seems to me at least in the UK, not perhaps in other countries, it has become ... part of the movie text.

(Petley, 2013)

Essentially, Petley and the work of Egan suggest that an exclusion of this artwork would affect the product's credibility, and therefore its ability to appropriately trade off a legitimised subcultural capital. While this is a commercial decision in the most part, it does have repercussions for the cultural coding of *Cannibal Holocaust*. The image aims to accurately replicate the original artefact, and therefore adopts the role of a modernised archival artefact. Within this it is clear that the modern remediation of the film is still reliant on its past cultural performance and historical significance. Consequently, the product retains a level of historical, cultural and national importance within the UK market, as a signifier not only for the film but also for its inseparable relationship with nationally based controversy.

However, it would be wrong to ignore the hyperbolic nature of the cover and the pre-established and widely recognised cultural stigma that it retains. When asked about this during the aforementioned interview, Petley noted that the use of the cover can be seen as existing within inverted commas, a joke entrenched within a communal knowledge of the film's censorial history (Petley, 2013). Egan supports these claims, stating that rereleased versions of the "video nasties" trade off the visual humour of the replicated covers rather than trying to rekindle the controversy (Egan, 2007: 205–211). However, due to the purposeful application of exploitation marketing techniques that is apparent throughout the rest of the cover, wherein eight of the nine small images on the back cover suggest either violent or sexual themes, the images' commitment to originality invokes the infamy that circulated on the film's initial release. Therefore the two covers trade off a similar employment of ballyhoo marketing, through a reincarnation of the film's historical notoriety and an isolation of the violent spectacle. However, this understanding is reliant on a sophisticated recognition of the film's past, and it works to create a level of authenticity central to notions of "high" cultural reappraisal. As such, the edition harbours an internal contradiction through its refined replication of history and re-creation of a sensationalist aesthetic.

Importantly, this balance and slippage between notions of validation and exploitation are prominent within the various paratextual features that are stored within the edition's two discs. This section will investigate Disc One before considering Disc Two, in order to maintain a chronological parity. Ahead of the main title page on Disc One are three trailers which are vital in understanding the manner in which the contemporary cultural image of *Cannibal Holocaust* is constructed through paratextual artefacts. The first trailer, promoting *House on the Edge of the Park*, portrays scenes of nudity and violence while alluding to the auteur brand of Deodato. The second trailer strays from this authorial notion and promotes *Don't Torture a Duckling* (1972) through a similar framework of nudity and brutality. The third trailer, again Italian and therefore confirming notions of a national trace, advertises *New York Ripper* (1982). Another Fulci film famed for its incredibly violent content, the trailer centralises a particular line of dialogue – "a very sharp knife, rammed in her vagina" – in order to confirm its transgressive kudos. While sharing a geographic parity, the collective violence of these films suggests that Shameless is positioning *Cannibal Holocaust* as the centrepiece of a transgressive distribution catalogue, while trading off the pre-existing status of the film to promote equally extreme narratives.

A short introduction by Ruggero Deodato appears after theses trailers. Within this, the importance of the auteur, which was downplayed on the cover with the minimisation of his name, is re-established. Herein, the disc appropriates a traditional art film marketing strategy and uses the academic theory of autuerism to validate the feature. This centralisation of the director also begins to rewrite the history of the film, which in previous incarnations would have acted independently from the artistic discourse of authorial legitimacy. This notion is furthered during the consumption of the Deodato cut, which is preceded by an explanation from the director. While the justification of the new cut sees a validation of the auteur and the feature itself, the appearance of a colloquial intertitle dilutes this legitimacy and again exposes the instability of *Cannibal Holocaust*'s historic linage. The intertitle portrays a mock road safety logo, in which a red outer circle has a diagonal line crossing through a cartoon turtle and axe. The superficial nature of the image undermines Deodato's strong sense of remorse regarding the film's use of genuine animal slaughter. This contradictory discourse is continued throughout Deodato's monologue, as the *leitmotif* that characterises the film's most extreme sequences is used alongside images of animal slaughter. As such, notions of Deodato's guilt and artistic integrity are suppressed by decontextualised images of extremity and transgression. Therefore, while the new cut looks to actively address the history of the film by removing the animal slaughter that proved to be so damaging to the narrative's cultural image, the paratextual composition of the feature looks to promote that same historical infamy.

Disc Two contains two special features which will be assessed in the order in which they appear. The first, entitled *Film & Be Damned* (2011), is an interview with Carl G. Yorke (who starred as the director of *Green Inferno* by Alan Yates) and Deodato. The paratextual extra balances notions of legitimisation and ballyhoo, advancing the film's commercial fluidity and supplementing the claim that the paratextual form can recode and manipulate the film's cultural comprehension. Deodato, the first subject on screen, instantly discusses how one can place the film within the tradition of satire, stating that the narrative was born out of his dissatisfaction with the violent journalism of the period. This gives the film's transgressions an allegorical context, subsequently justifying its use of extreme violence and recalling parts of the academic scholarship addressed earlier. Moreover, the construction of this context is similar to the rationalisation that is often afforded many art films, where notions of intellectual thought and metaphor validate the violence within the "high" cultural discourse. Therefore a sense of historic reconsideration comes to the fore, which activity contradicts the hyperbolic images projected on the release's cover.

However, as stated earlier, ballyhoo tactics can still be located. On several occasions the film's censorial history is mentioned, as Deodato details *Cannibal Holocaust*'s seizure and the suspended prison sentence that he received. While notions of trace legitimacy can be found within this section, as Deodato compares the controversy with that of *Last Tango in Paris* (1972), the details of the court trial and the subsequent outcome only verify the film's most transgressive aspects. Through this anecdote, the interview adopts the principles of ballyhoo, daring the viewer to see a film that resulted in the director's near imprisonment. Importantly, this recalls the findings of Egan, where she states that within the market discourse of previously banned materials, the longevity and severity of the censorship is a crucial aspect in making the film more desirable (Egan, 2007: 194). Clearly, in this first interview, while parts endeavour to break away from the existing consensus of the narrative, the centralisation of censorial histories increases the film's desirability within the exploitation consumption site.

The second feature on this disc is entitled *The Long Road Back from Hell with Kim Newman, Prof. Julian Petley, Prof. Mary Wood. Featuring Carl G. Yorke, Ruggero Deodato & Francesca Ciardi* (2011) and was directed by Dr Xavier Mendik. The subtitle is fundamental to understanding how this paratextual feature moulds the cultural understanding of *Cannibal Holocaust* as a whole as it foregrounds academic intervention into the prevailing discourses of the film. Through the use of "Prof", a level of "high" cultural capital grounded within academic longevity can be located. This validates the interviewees' statements within the feature, suggests that *Cannibal Holocaust* is a film worthy of academic consideration and elevates the text to the realm of scholastic (re)consideration.

Again, similar to the *Film & Be Damned* interview, the documentary balances notions of legitimisation and ballyhoo. With regard to the foregrounding of the film's more transgressive moments, the talking heads segments are intercut with sequences from the film. These include the finding of the impaled women (which opens the documentary), the abortion sequence and the final slaughter of the crew. While not shown in their entirety, these isolated moments represent the most controversial parts of the narrative, and their decontextualisation projects a narrative image grounded in violence. This is supported by the comments of both a returning Yorke and Francesca Ciardi, who focus heavily on the animal slaughter and the distinct feelings of distrust which followed those incidents. These proclamations construct an image of the film based around depravity, mistrust and a filmic roguishness that is culturally associated with the exploitation film circuit.

However, through the continued presence of academic personas and conceptual frameworks, the documentary ultimately acts as a spoken reappraisal of the narrative. Mendik's voiceover narration continually foregrounds *Cannibal Holocaust*'s influence on modern horror, making it an important part of the wider horror film discourse. These statements are then supported by both Mary Wood and Petley. Additionally, Wood frames the film as a response to the Italian sociopolitical climate of the era, claiming that the narrative is an allegory for the Italian man's loss of power. In doing so she moves the discussion of *Cannibal Holocaust* away from notions of violence and censorship into a consideration of the film's symbolic meaning. Petley's comments operate in the same manner as he locates the text within the Italian tradition of realism by claiming that it should be approached as a piece of metacinema. Here the scholarly practice of reappraisal mapped briefly at the start of this chapter is definitively grafted onto the tangible paratextual object. Therefore the special features present on the second disc seek to reposition the film and furnish it within the conventions of academic study. Here the paratext, operating externally from the main body of the film, has the capacity to alter the cultural perceptions of a narrative and reappraise it within a previously unavailable and impenetrable cinematic environs.

However, essential within the assessment of this release and recognising it as a cultural artefact that breaches the barriers of "high" and "low", while actively reshaping the history of *Cannibal Holocaust*, is the role that Petley held outside the features on the disc. He served as a consultant for Shameless regarding an advice screening with the British Board of Film Classification (BBFC) (Petley, 2013). Within this role as advisor, Petley completed the form which had to be submitted to the BBFC as part of a re-evaluation of the film in the hope that it could be passed with fewer cuts than previously seen in the UK. Petley, talking about the advice screening form, claimed: "the main point I made [was] that this was to be not kind of exploitative or sensationalised..., it was an attempt to present what I think is generally regarded by many people now as an important film in a way that did it justice" (Petley, 2013). Through this role, Petley acted as a signifier of legitimisation and a cultural anchor with an inherent capital, within which a broader sense of acceptance could be comprehended. Due to his involvement, his legitimacy became attached to this edition of *Cannibal Holocaust*, equipping it with an academic validity that was not present during its original release.

Importantly, Petley noted that it is not just his position as an academic liaison that resulted in the BBFC's leniency. He stated:

> I think a long long period of time had passed since *Cannibal Holocaust* was so badly demonised and trashed and I think the writing of people like me, but obviously there are others, . . . have helped to give the film a kind of . . . "respectability" that it hadn't had before.
>
> (Petley, 2013)

What Petley alluded to here is the importance of an extended series of academic interactions. As such, the respected scholarship that has come to take *Cannibal Holocaust* as its focus has resulted in its removal from a critical quarantine of controversy, and encouraged the BBFC to be more sympathetic and thus pass it with fewer cuts (Petley, 2013). This notion has been suggested elsewhere within studies of Italian exploitation cinema and its various paratextual identities. Raiford Guins usefully notes that "the voice articulating the Italian horror film now has a historical tone, on that is educational and premised in informative criticism and genre knowledge" (Guins, 2005: 27–28). Herein, the Shameless release created what Egan has termed a historical portrait of the film (Egan, 2007: 186), in which its exploitative past is contextualised within an academic present.

It is within this conclusion that we can return to the paratextual object as a whole, and reflect not only on the way it creates and recreates *Cannibal Holocaust*'s cultural meaning but how paratexts influence the cinematic environs in general. With regard to this chapter's case study, it is evident that the Shameless release represents an inherent contradiction, and shifts between differing forms of legitimisation, both "high brow" and "low brow". Ultimately, through the study of the various features and images present throughout the object, it becomes clear that the distributor has succeeded in employing "high" cultural validation practices within the distribution of an archetypal exploitation narrative. Herein the artefact effectively collapses the barriers between taste economies, subsequently becoming a transitional object for the film. Through the use of critical and academic anchoring, familiar within the art film discourse but rare within the exploitation realm, the paratext positions *Cannibal Holocaust*, a text which was previously demonised within the home entertainment consumption space, as an important piece of legitimate cinema. Therefore, to use Guins' work on the remediation of Italian horror cinema, the film is repaired and refashioned on entrance to the DVD market (Guins, 2005: 25). While the images of transgress recall a ballyhoo tradition and deliberately incite the film's historical stigma, they also rely upon a complex and sophisticated exchange of subcultural capital and competency, which, in line with the work of Jeffery Sconce, can be as intricate and exclusive as "high" cultural taste structures (Sconce, 1995). Subsequently, while the paratext is able to fit comfortably within the horror genre consumption site, its remediation here suggests that it has been reappraised within the wider cinematic sphere.

In essence, this chapter exposes the importance of the paratext in examining the manner in which filmic paraphernalia manipulates the cultural histories of certain narratives. By understanding this particular artefact, this chapter maps how its identity is reshaped and remoulded, becoming a hybrid form which slips between art and exploitation in a manner that was previously ignored. Therefore the DVD, and the paratext in a wider sense, is a central vessel of meaning in the modern film climate, and must be properly assessed in order for one to comprehend the vast histories of remediated texts.

References

Betz, M. (2013), "High and Low and in between." *Screen*, 54(4), 495–513.

Cherry, B. (2010), "Stalking the Web: Celebration, Chat and Horror Film Marketing on the Internet." In I. Conrich, ed., *Horror Zone: The Cultural Experience of Contemporary Horror Cinema*. London: I.B. Tauris & Co Ltd, pp. 67–85.

Cherry, B. (2012), "Beyond Suspiria: The Place of European Horror in the Fan Canon." In P. Allmer, E. Brick, and D. Huxley, eds., *European Nightmares: Horror Cinema in Europe Since 1945*. London: Wallflower Press, pp. 25–35.

Derrida, J. (1976), *Of Grammatology*. Baltimore: The John Hopkins University Press.

Dixon, W.W. (2010), *A History of Horror*. New Jersey: Rutgers University Press.

Egan, K. (2007), *Trash or Treasure? Censorship and the Changing Meanings of the Video Nasties*. Manchester: Manchester University Press.

Ellis, J. (1992), *Visible Fictions: Cinema, Television, Video*. London: Routledge.

Geraghty, L. (2014), *Cult Collectors: Nostalgia, Fandom and Collecting Popular Culture*. London: Routledge.

Gray, J. (2010), *Show Sold Separately: Promos, Spoilers and Other Media Paratexts*. New York: New York University Press.

Guins, R. (2005), "Blood and Black Gloves on Shiny Discs: New Media, Old Tastes, and the Remediation of Italian Horror Films in the United States." In J. Schneider and T. Williams, eds., *Horror International*. Detroit: Wayne State University Press, pp. 15–32.

Hawkins, J. (2000), *Cutting Edge: Art Horror and the Horrific Avant Garde*. Minneapolis: University of Minnesota Press.

Hutchings, P. (2008), "Monster Legacies: Memory, Technology, and Horror History." In L. Geraghty and M. Jancovich, eds., *The Shifting Definitions of Genre: Essays on Labelling Films, Television Shows and Media*. Jefferson, NC: McFarland and Company, pp. 216–228.

Jackson, N, (2002), "*Cannibal Holocaust*, Realist Horror, and Reflexivity." *Post Script*, 21(3), 32–45.

Jauregui, C.G. (2004), " 'Eat it Alive and Swallow it Whole!': Resavoring Cannibal Holocaust as a Mockumentary." *Invisible Culture*, 7.

Jenkins, H. (2006), *Fans, Bloggers and Gamers: Exploring Participatory Culture*. New York: New York University Press.

Kattelman, B. (2011), " 'We Dare You to See This': Ballyhoo and the 1970s Horror Film." *The Journal of Horror Studies*, 2(1), 61–74.

Klinger, B. (2006), *Beyond the Multiplex: Cinema, New Technologies, and the Home*. Berkeley, CA: University of California Press.

McDonald, P. (2007), *Video and DVD Industries*. London: BFI Publishing.

Mendik, X. (2011), *The Long Road Back from Hell*. UK: Cine-Excess.

Metz, C. (1977), *The Imaginary Signifier: Psychoanalysis and the Cinema*. Bloomington: Indiana University Press.

Morgan, E. (2006), "Cannibal Holocaust: Digesting and Re-Digesting Law and Film." *Southern California Interdisciplinary*, 16, 555–570.

Petley, J. (1984), "A Nasty Story." *Screen*, 25(2), 68–75.

Petley, J. (2005), "*Cannibal Holocaust and the Pornography of Death*." In G. King, ed., *Spectacle of the Real: From Hollywood to Reality TV & Beyond*. Bristol: Intellect, pp. 173–185.

Petley, J. (2011), *Film and Video Censorship in Modern Britain*. Edinburgh: Edinburgh University Press.

Petley, J. (2013), Personal Interview. London.

Sconce, J. (1995), " 'Trashing' the Academy: Taste, Excess and an Emerging Politics of Cinematic Style." *Screen*, 36(4), 371–393.

Spivak, G. (1976), "Translators Preface." In J. Derrida, ed., *Of Grammatology*. Baltimore: The John Hopkins University Press, pp. ix–xc.

Thornton, S. (1995), *Club Cultures: Music, Media and Subcultural Capital*. Cambridge: Polity Press.

Thrower, S. (2007), *Nightmare USA: The Untold Story of the Exploitation Independents*. Godalming: FAB Press.

van Ooijen, E. (2011), "Cinematic Shots and Cuts: On the Ethics and Semiotics of Real Violence in Film Fiction." *Journal of Aesthetics & Culture*, 3, 1–15.

Walker, J. (2011), "Nasty Visions: Violent Spectacle in Contemporary British Horror Cinema." *Horror Studies*, 2(1), 115–130.

Part III
From Spoiler to Fan Activist

7
From *Angel* to *Much Ado*: Cross-Textual Catharsis, Kinesthetic Empathy and Whedonverse Fandom

Tanya R. Cochran

"Don't give people what they want, give them what they need," media auteur Joss Whedon has famously stated (Whedon in Robinson, 2011: 31). To fans of his many texts – from television series *Buffy the Vampire Slayer* (1997–2003) to web series *Dr. Horrible's Sing-Along Blog* (2008), from graphic novel *Fray* (2003) to film *Serenity* (2005) – his principle of offering them what is necessary rather than what is desired has become a justification for emotionally destroying them by "killing" beloved characters, such as *Buffy*'s Joyce Summers and *Serenity*'s Hoban "Wash" Washburne, among others. Like real life, these character losses can be profoundly affective for viewers and take months or years for them to recover from. In some cases, gaping emotional wounds remain open for a fan's lifetime. Unlike real life, the death of a character does not usually mean the death of an actor. As a result, it is striking that some fans have read across two of Whedon's texts – one an original creation, one an adaptation – to create their own sense of catharsis and narrative resolution in the aftermath of two major characters' deaths on the *Buffy* spin-off *Angel* (1999–2004), characters played by the same actors. To examine this occasion of cross-textual catharsis, I first provide a context for the relationship between *Angel* characters Winifred Burkle, played by Amy Acker, and Wesley Wyndam-Pryce, played by Alexis Denisof. Next, I comment on Whedon's adaptation of Shakespeare's *Much Ado about Nothing* (2013), especially noting the casting of Acker as Beatrice and Denisof as Benedick. Then I touch on catharsis and the purpose that it serves in art, highlighting how it is facilitated for

Angel fans through the actors' bodies and kinesthetic empathy. Finally, I turn to the significance of fans reading across *Angel* and *Much Ado* to achieve emotional resolution. Understanding in particular this screen-reading strategy among Whedonverse enthusiasts offers in general a deeper insight into the meaning of media consumption, spectatorship and fandom.

Most *Angel* viewers know Wesley Wyndam-Pryce from *Buffy the Vampire Slayer*. He first arrives in Sunnydale, California, at the direction of the Watcher's Council to replace Rupert Giles as Buffy and Faith's Watcher after Giles is fired. Wesley is quite annoying to Buffy and her friends, the Scoobies, as he is all ineffectual business and no play, right through his attempt to help defeat the third season's "Big Bad" Mayor Wilkins in the two-part "Graduation Day" (1999). Of course, Wesley goes through many changes, both off-screen between *Buffy* and *Angel* and onscreen during *Angel*. Fired by the Watcher's Council for incompetence, he leaves Sunnydale and later resurfaces in Los Angeles in the middle of *Angel*'s first season, declaring himself a rogue demon hunter in "Parting Gifts" (1999). This declaration is laughable to the characters and the viewing audience, but he eventually proves his usefulness and loyalty to Angel and is accepted into the fold of Angel Investigations.

Audiences first meet Winifred "Fred" Burkle towards the end of *Angel*'s second season when the team of Angel, Wesley and James Gunn must travel between worlds to rescue their friend and partner Cordelia Chase from Pylea in "Belonging" (2001). There they find Fred, dishevelled and scribbling complex mathematical formulas on the walls of her dwelling where she is being kept as a slave. Viewers later learn that, like Cordelia, someone has sent Fred to Pylea through a portal, and that someone in Fred's case is her graduate professor who has banished more than one promising physics student to Pylea. Apparently, Prof. Seidel, when threatened by the high intelligence and great promise of particular students, exiles them to another world and a life of slavery to preserve his own power and prestige.

In addition to Cordelia, the team brings Fred back to Los Angeles, a place that she had come to believe was only a figment of her imagination, where she begins to recover from her ordeal and gradually becomes an important member of Angel Investigations. She develops a particular fondness for Gunn and fairly quickly begins dating him, much to Wesley's disappointment because he admires her ardently. The two date for about a year before their relationship changes. Just before Fred and Gunn end their attachment, Fred and Wesley share a kiss, a kiss that fans cheering for the pairing of – or those "shipping" – the two characters had long desired and awaited. However, Fred learns that Wesley has been in an intimate relationship with Lilah Morgan, who works for the evil law practice and Team Angel's corporate nemesis, Wolfram & Hart. The potential coupling is thus derailed before it can begin.

In a bizarre twist of events later in the series, Team Angel reluctantly but necessarily assumes leadership of Wolfram & Hart, and Fred receives her own laboratory as the head of the organisation's Science Division. In "A Hole in the World" (2004), two-thirds of the way through the fifth and final season of the series on television, Fred begins to examine a sarcophagus that has been brought to her lab. During her inspection, she triggers an opening in the top of the container that releases a fateful gush of air, which is later discovered to be the essence of the ancient, pure demon Illyria, who has been bound in the sarcophagus. Slowly, the essence of Illyria begins to devour Fred from within, carving out her very soul to make room for Illyria's full being. It is revealed that Knox, Fred's co-worker and someone with whom she has gone out on several dates, has actually chosen Fred, because of his affection for her, to be Illyria's vessel. Knox, the audience learns, worships Illyria and has been instrumental in recovering her sarcophagus and preparing the way for her resurrection. Immediately prior to this goal being achieved, Fred and Wesley finally admit their romantic feelings for each other in the episode "Smile Time" (2004). At the time of broadcast, the gasps and cheers of shippers were heard around the world. Of course, another kind of gasp was only a few breaths and one episode away. As Fred quickly grows weaker, Team Angel frantically looks for a cure, but to no avail. The only way to save Fred would involve the deaths of thousands of other people, something that she would never want or agree to. As Fred fades away, Wesley cradles her in his arms. With her last inhalations, she asks: "Wesley, why can't I stay?" Then she is gone.

Not long after Fred's death and Illyria's possession of Fred's body, the series ends darkly in the season finale, "Not Fade Away" (2004). Team Angel plots an assault on the Circle of the Black Thorn, the most powerful demon alliance in the human realm. On the morning of the attack, Angel tells the team to live as if this were their last day. Wesley, attending to wounds that Illyria has suffered in a fight, explains why he does not follow Angel's directions:

Wesley: There is no perfect day for me, Illyria. There is no sunset or painting or finely aged scotch that's going to sum up my life and make tonight any... There is nothing that I want.

Illyria: You want to be with Fred.
Wesley: Yes. Yes, that's where I'd be if I could.

Illyria offers to take Fred's form but in the same breath acknowledges that Wesley would never ask her to do so. No, he would not ask such a thing. As Wesley explains,

> The first lesson a Watcher learns is to separate truth from illusion. Because in the world of magics, it's the hardest thing to do. The truth is that Fred is gone. To pretend anything else would be a lie. And since I don't actually intend to die tonight, I won't accept a lie.

Later, however, Wesley battles with the powerful warlock Cyrus Vail and suffers a mortal wound. As he lies dying, Illyria comes to his side and cradles him, much like Wesley held Fred:

Illyria: Would you like me to lie to you now?
Wesley: Yes. Thank you. Yes.

The camera tightly focuses on Wesley's face. He closes his eyes slowly, and as he opens them again, a small, human hand enters the screen and begins to stroke Wesley's cheek. A wide camera shot reveals Fred rather than Illyria cradling Wesley:

Wesley: Hello there.
Fred: Oh, Wesley. My Wesley.
Wesley: Fred. I've missed you.
Fred: [Through tears, she kisses him on the mouth and then forehead.] It's gonna be okay. It won't hurt much longer, and then you'll be where I am. We'll be together.
Wesley: I – I love you.
Fred: I love you. My love. Oh, my love.

Audience members cannot help but recall Fred's death at this moment. It is as if the two lovers have simply traded places; now Wesley takes his last breath. As soon as Wesley is gone, Illyria in the form of Fred gently lays his head on the floor and rises from her sitting position. Behind her, the warlock also rises from the floor, having been deterred but not arrested by Wesley. Approaching Illyria, still in Fred's form, Vail exclaims, "How very touching his meaningless death was, but this fight was never for mortals." Seeing an angry, red-faced Fred rather than Illyria, he chuckles: "Take your best shot, little girl." Filmed in slow motion, Fred pulls back to punch Vail, and as she follows through, the visage of Fred transforms back into Illyria. Illyria's fist strikes Vail's face, shattering his very skull into hundreds of pieces. Wesley is avenged. Nevertheless, *Angel* finales with the brutal loss of both Fred and Wesley.

It is important to understand the intensity of emotion, especially for shipping viewers, of Fred and Wesley's history of repeated magnetism and repellence and magnetism to also understand the desire and need for some sense of release or resolution, for any semblance of catharsis. Arguably, some release is achieved in "Not Fade Away", first when Illyria as Fred tells the dying Wesley that they will soon be together again and then when Illyria annihilates Vail. However, as Wesley himself explains earlier in the episode, Illyria as Fred as well as everything she says to Wesley is an illusion – a lie. The truth of the narrative is that both Fred and Wesley are dead, and there is no evidence that they will be reunited beyond death. Thus, for many Fred and Wesley shippers, true catharsis was not realised and their emotional turmoil outlived the television series. Considering the online fan investment in and collective grief about the ill-fated couple, it is surprising and even somewhat unbelievable that Whedon did not anticipate jubilant reactions from fans when Beatrice and Benedick in the bodies of Acker and Denisof kiss at the end of *Much Ado about Nothing*, Whedon's film adaption of Shakespeare's play. Fans across the Internet exclaimed: "Fred and Wesley forever!" Yet in promotional interviews leading up to the release of the film, the lead actors as well as Whedon repeatedly denied thinking before or during filming about how *Angel* fans might respond.

In an interview with Acker for *Vulture*, Jennifer Vineyard noted that she appreciated the opening scene of *Much Ado*, one that without dialogue provides a romantic backstory for Beatrice and Benedick. Vineyard then stated: "And there's another history you guys have together. Fred and Wesley finally get a happy ending" (Vineyard, 2013). These two sentences are intriguing. The first – "And there's another history you guys have together" – lacks precise meaning and, therefore, has multiple meanings. What "history" does Vineyard mean? Who is the "you" she refers to? Does she mean the history of the actors Acker and Denisof or the characters Fred and Wesley? Does the "you" refer to the actors or the characters? Perhaps the pronoun refers to both. Additionally, the second sentence – "Fred and Wesley finally get a happy ending" – signals why this cross-textual event should draw attention: it represents a screen-reading strategy that certain fans have used to make meaning for themselves. Of course, the reason the strategy works is that the actors themselves, their very bodies, become a site for narrative transubstantiation. By "narrative transubstantiation" I mean that one substance (in this case the narratives of Fred and Wesley as well as Beatrice and Benedick) becomes another substance (catharsis) (Cochran, 2014). A more detailed discussion of the role of the human body in this screen-reading strategy is provided below. For now, I return to Acker's interview with *Vulture*.

In response to Vineyard's statement about Fred and Wesley's happy ending, Acker admits that she should have realised that *Angel* viewers would be thrilled, but insists that she did not think about that possibility until after the film was complete and people such as Vineyard began pointing it out. When she realised that followers of Whedon's work might be excited about Beatrice and Benedick as Fred and Wesley proxies, respectively, she became interested in fans' responses:

> I do think there's something special [about *Much Ado*] for people like me who were like, "Why can't they be together?" I always thought Fred was in love with Wesley from the beginning, and then one day, I got a script where all of a sudden I was making out with Gunn, and I was like, "Wait! What?" I feel like there are so many people who felt like they should have been together, and then of course, in true Joss fashion, it got yanked away.
>
> (Acker in Vineyard, 2013)

"yanked away" is an accurate if understated description. Interestingly, Acker places herself among shippers by acknowledging that she thought that the *Angel* characters were destined to be a romantic couple.

In another interview regarding the film, Christina Radish of *Collider* asked Acker a similar question: "Did you ever think about how *Angel* fans would react to getting to see you and Alexis Denisof together, in this way?" (Radish, 2013). Acker, again, stated that she did not do so before or during filming. In this interview, she explained that one reason she did not anticipate *Angel* fans' excitement was because she and Denisof had been friends since *Angel* and spend time with each other regularly. As a result of a long friendship and often seeing one another outside work, neither she nor he thought about themselves or Beatrice and Benedick as the conduits for resurrecting Fred and Wesley until they were screening the film; after all, they are actors by profession. Acting is their job. "But after we saw it on film," said Acker, "he [Denisof] turned to me and was like, 'This is like Fred and Wesley, all grown up. I think the fans are gonna really like that.' We had the realization, watching it, that that would be a fun thing for people who had seen those characters before" (Acker in Radish, 2013). Obviously, "a fun thing" was a major underestimation of how many fans experienced Acker and Denisof in *Much Ado.*

Though it is slightly difficult to believe that the actors portraying Fred and Wesley as well as Beatrice and Benedick did not early on make the connection between the *Angel* and *Much Ado* characters, it is extremely difficult to believe that Whedon – as a creator, writer, director and producer – did not foresee at the beginning of the film's production an excited, cathartic response from *Angel* enthusiasts, especially Fred and Wesley shippers. Yet Whedon has said: "It was a couple of months ago, screening it, I suddenly went, 'Oh, my God! Wesley and Fred went to Heaven and they got this! They're suddenly kissing and neither of them is dying! This is delightful!' " (Whedon, 2013: 20). Richard Albright has "explore[d] audience perception of actors' prior acting roles in general and the unique 'delight' that informs the fan experience of [*Much Ado*]" (Albright, 2014). Certainly, "delight" is an applicable word, but that delight, I argue, is only possible because it is experienced by shippers alongside catharsis.

By catharsis I mean the most straightforward understanding of the term: "the purging of the emotions or relieving of emotional tensions, especially through certain kinds of art" ("Catharsis", 2014). Of course, the term is also familiar because it comes with the average person's basic knowledge of psychotherapy. In that context, generally speaking, the goal of catharsis is to bring repressed, typically harmful emotions to the surface, address them and purge them. This purging or cleansing is meant to bring about emotional healing and, therefore, health. From an Aristotelian perspective, art provides a conduit through which audience members may experience catharsis. Specifically, some scholars argue that Aristotle promoted the use of tragedy to elicit and rid spectators of excess pity and fear. Thus art offers those who engage with it – both actors and spectators – an opportunity to acknowledge buried emotions, express them and attain restored emotional balance. In other words, the characters and their narrative allow actors and particularly spectators to express the pain of real-world tragedy. This release of feelings should, in turn, produce emotional equilibrium. Sufficient evidence from fan messageboards and blogs suggests that for many Fred and Wesley fans, catharsis was not fully experienced; rather, their strong emotions – particularly grief, including denial, anger, bargaining and depression – stayed with them for a long time. Five years after

Angel concluded on television, one fan who goes by the name SuperWes representatively stated about Fred's death:

> This one is high on the list [of most painful character deaths in the Whedonverse] because it was so drawn out and painful. Wes standing there completely helpless as her insides are slowly burning away is too freaking devastating. This set the depression that would linger over the entire last half of the season and beyond for me. And my god, has anything sadder than those last words ever been written? "Why can't I stay?"
>
> ("WHEDONesque", 2009)

Similar expressions are shared by fans about Wesley, particularly because many audience members understand his death in terms of the much longer and more elaborate story arc that the character has across both television series, *Buffy* and *Angel*. Also often mentioned by fans is the fact that Wesley's death – like the deaths of *Buffy*'s Joyce Summers and Tara Maclay and *Serenity*'s Shepherd Book and Hoban Washburne – is not supernatural. These characters are human through and through, and their deaths are natural, the result of medical complications and violence perpetrated against them. For a lot of fans, this fact makes losing these characters all the more real and, therefore, affective.

How does *Much Ado* mean, then, for many Fred and Wesley fans? I submit that how it means can be explored through considering embodied experience and expression, or what Dee Reynolds and Matthew Reason and their collection's contributors call "kinesthetic empathy". Even a basic understanding of the phrase as it relates to film and television spectatorship suffices for my purposes: "sensations of movement and position" (Reynolds and Reason, 2012: 18) that evoke in spectators a sense of feeling what the fictional character or filmic or televisual mind and body are feeling. In "Cinematic Empathy: Spectator Involvement in the Film Experience", Adriano D'Aloia put it this way:

> [My] fundamental argument is that, in the particular spatial and psychological situation of the cinema auditorium, and especially in respect of the main characters, the viewer's involvement entails both motor and emotional participation despite his/her consciousness of the fictional nature of the filmic events. This participation is mostly realised via the activation of empathy, a factor that reduces the psychological separation between the spectator and the characters.
>
> (2012: 93)

Cognitive psychologists such as Raymond A. Mar and Keith Oatley would explain this experience as a parallel one, a simulation (Mar and Oatley, 2008). I the spectator do not feel what the character feels, but I feel something akin to – that is, parallel to – what the character feels. Edith Stein expressed a similar notion in *On the Problem of Empathy* when she posited that film spectators do not empathise "with" the screen actors or characters; rather, they empathise "at" the actors or characters (D'Aloia, 2012: 94). In other words, the experience of what is happening on screen is a quasi one: "rather than a projection or a fusion, empathy is an accompaniment, in which the spectator's subjectivity is not 'one with' the [character's] subjectivity, but only 'with' " (D'Aloia, 2012: 94). To use an example from *Angel*'s "A Hole in the World", the emotional tumult that Wesley experiences as Fred suffers from Illyria's annexing of her body is heart-wrenching for many viewers. Fred fans do not want to lose her any more than Wesley does. Denisof's portrayal of Wesley allows audiences access to their own powerful and dark emotions, perhaps regarding someone that they themselves have lost. Yet Wesley's emotions, feelings brought to life through the actor, are not perfectly replicated in spectators; they may sense his anger, frustration and grief, but what they themselves feel are those same emotions in quasi or virtual form. The important point here is that what makes filmic empathy possible is the human body in motion. The empathy is kinesthetically generated. Notably, even a still shot or screen capture can elicit a sense of motion that can just as easily produce empathy. Understandably, certain movements of screen- or quasi-bodies – such as exaggerated or unusual ones – have greater potential than others to evoke empathy in viewers, which is not surprising when one considers that memory, too, is impacted by intense emotions. For example, the reason many people clearly recall where they were and what they were doing when Princess Diana was killed or the Twin Towers were hit is that these types of event are accompanied by primitive or instinctive emotions, such as fear and anger. Thus it makes sense that "the situations [on screen] with most potential for empathy are those in which a strong kinesthetic intensification is invited (for instance, acrobatics, falling, sports performance, dance, etc.)" (D'Aloia, 2012: 95). This fact is interesting in light of Amy Acker's roles in both *Angel* and *Much Ado*.

While rewatching *Angel*'s "A Hole in the World" a year after viewing *Much Ado*, I was immediately struck by a kind of reverse-image embodied movement, one of falling. As many *Angel* fans probably remember, after Fred's initial encounter with Illyria's sarcophagus, she is examined by Wolfram & Hart's medical department, which clears her to go back to work. Returning to her lab with friend and colleague Lorne, Fred crosses paths with Wesley on the staircase of the main lobby. The two begin to talk sweetly about finding excuses to visit one another and planning surprise dates. As he passes by the lovers to descend the staircase, Lorne exclaims: "Oh, sheesh. Get a balcony, you two, huh?" Fred calls after him: "You'll find me after lunch, though, right?" From several steps below, Lorne turns to face her and says, "I'll just look where the sun shines" and begins singing: " 'You are my sunshine, my only sunshine...' ". Fred smiles and looks into Wesley's eyes as she continues: " 'You make me happy...' ". Before she can finish the stanza, though, she coughs, spewing blood into Wesley's face, and falls violently backward as if being thrown. Lorne and Wesley lunge to catch her, and it is at this moment that everyone – including the audience – realises that all is tragically unwell.

Juxtaposed with this scene is one of Beatrice in her uncle's house being so startled by overhearing the mention of Benedick's love for her that, with a basket of laundry in hand, she trips and falls face-first down a set of stairs. All three times I watched *Much Ado* in the theatre, audience members had a visceral response – audible gasps and then giggles – to this act of physical comedy. These two scenes – one tragic, the other comedic – stand out as perfect examples of what is meant by kinesthetic empathy. For fans of *Angel* viewing *Much Ado*, Acker's body and its exaggerated movements bind the roles of Fred and Beatrice. Said another way, the falling scenes visually reverberate with each other chiefly because the two characters – Fred and Beatrice – are portrayed by the same actor. "Not only are the bodies on screen experienced as fictional bodies (those of the characters)," notes D'Aloia, "but they are also inseparable from the performers' bodies (those of the actors). Hence the film experience is a quasi-intersubjective relationship in which the spectator, under certain conditions, can empathise with the character" (2012: 95). This concept relates to *Angel*, *Much Ado* and fandom in that fans' sense of catharsis or emotional purging could not have come about without Acker and Denisof playing the fated lovers in both visual texts. The human body – of the character, the actor and the spectator – plays an essential role in this fan-generated screen-reading strategy. This idea directly relates to Alyson R. Buckman's argument regarding "hyperdiegetic casting". She states: "within a particular hyperdiegesis, an actor may play multiple roles and accrue meaning that may slide and build across those roles" (Buckman, 2014). She goes on to say: "Other than the element of relationships, however, the collection of Whedonverse actors in *Much Ado* works mainly to create the pleasure of recognition rather than deeper meanings." On this last point I will respectfully disagree. Rather than the pleasure of the text being at most about the delight of recognition, it is only at least about that. Much more than the delight of recognition, *Much Ado* – precisely because of the casting of Acker and Denisof, precisely because of, in other words, their bodies – taps into deep meaning by engaging through movement spectators' own bodies, allowing, at least for some fans, catharsis to fully occur.

How might fandom scholars understand the importance of this occasion of cross-textual catharsis? While there are certainly other ways of explaining significance, several concepts offered by Jeffrey Bussolini, Alyson Buckman and Matt Hills provide key insights into the question. Namely, an understanding of Bussolini's "intertextuality of casting" (2013), Buckman's "hyperdiegetic casting" (2012, 2014) and Hills' "endlessly deferred narrative" (2002) greatly illuminate why this screen-reading strategy by fans matters.

In his article "Television Intertextuality after *Buffy*," Bussolini (2013) defines "intertextuality of casting" as "the often intentional crossover of actors . . . between and among different shows, and the way in which bringing along recognizable faces and styles serves to cross-pollinate televisual texts and create a larger televisual intertext". In other words, it can be very pleasurable for fans to map the careers of favoured actors, following them from role to role, series to series, medium to medium, and to detect actor and past character styles or traits in current and future characters. Casting not only an actor but also, in a sense, a previous character understandably has the potential and even the likelihood "to shape the 'Verses' of the artworks at hand," says Bussolini. In turn, "a larger televisual intertext" is created. Whereas this type of casting may sometimes occur unintentionally, it can obviously be done on purpose. In this sense, intertextual casting may be seen as one of many tools at the disposal of media creators. For instance, Summer Glau played the role of River Tam in Whedon's *Firefly* (2002–2003) and *Serenity* (2005). It is difficult for Whedon fans watching the CW's *Arrow* (2012 – present) not to think of River's traits – particularly her combat skills – when *Arrow*'s Isabel Rochev, also portrayed by Glau, breaks character as a reserved corporate executive to engage in a hand-to-hand fight with Oliver Queen, aka The Arrow. This type of casting across texts helmed by different showrunners or creators is what Bussolini largely refers to.

However, as he also notes and fans know well, Whedon is known for casting the same actors – people with whom he is friends, with whom he spends time – in roles across his many texts, in auteur-related if not narratively related storyworlds. Therefore, a slightly different effect is created for fans of Whedon when he uses the same actors repeatedly in his own works. For example, Amy Acker played Fred in *Angel*, Dr Claire Saunders and Whiskey in *Dollhouse* (2009–2010) and Beatrice in *Much Ado* – all texts with Whedon in the writing and/or directing chair. Although all film-goers understand that *Much Ado*'s author is Shakespeare, certain film-goers – those who are Whedon admirers – understand the film to be his adaptation in very distinct ways, including its casting. Perhaps, then, a better phrase for the effect of repeated casting within one creator's storyworlds is one coined by Alyson Buckman: "hyperdiegetic casting". As she defines it, this form of casting refers to "the way in which meaning is created through the use and reuse of actors solely and specifically within a particular, cohesive narrative space" (Buckman, 2012). Again, Buckman argues that hyperdiegetic casting brings with it the pleasure of recognition. She additionally suggests that pleasure is derived from the fact that "Whedon has built a collective, specialized fund of knowledge available specifically to those who have watched (and rewatched) his fictions, although certainly one may bring additional subtext" (Buckman, 2012). Put another way, the narrative space within which Whedon enthusiasts play is expansive – much like the universe. Thus the expression often used by fans as well as scholars to refer to Whedon's many texts is the Whedonverse. These concepts of ever-expanding narrative space and hyperdiegetic casting intentionally echo Matt Hills' discussion of the interaction among auteurism, endlessly deferred narratives and hyperdiegesis.

In a note to his *Fan Cultures* chapter "Media Cults: Between the 'Textual' and the 'Extratextual' ", Hills writes:

> Cult films are often marked by fans' emphasis on their *auteurs*. This creates a situation where a "series" of films can be produced out of titles which, diegetically, may be unrelated, and where each film may offer narrative closure. Through the figure of the *auteur* a type of "endlessly deferred narrative" can be produced by cult film fans which focuses on the *autuer*'s unfolding career.
>
> (2002: 194)

Though it addresses the medium of film, this passage can just as well refer to the medium of television and to Whedon as an auteur who works across media. This following of a media creator's career seems a fitting parallel to following the careers of beloved actors. The difference, though, resides in the ability of someone such as Whedon to be conscious and deliberate about creating an infinite story, even if made up of many different stories. Hills goes on to explain the "endlessly deferred narrative" in the context of what he calls "family resemblances" among texts. These resemblances can be "produced through fan reading strategies... as well as through 'textual' attributes" (2002: 194). Certainly, fans of *Angel* generally and Fred and Wesley in particular have practised such a reading strategy, one facilitated in large part if not wholly by the casting of the same actors for both *Angel*'s and *Much Ado*'s lovers. With regard to textual attributes, one common among cult texts is that of hyperdiegesis, which Hills defines as "the creation of a vast and detailed narrative space, only a fraction of which is ever directly seen or encountered within the text, but which nevertheless appears to operate according to principles of internal logic and extension" (2002: 137). As Buckman, among others, has noted, the "vast and detailed narrative space" that Hills speaks of aptly describes, as mentioned above, what fans and scholars refer to as the Whedonverse. Once more, *Much Ado* represents an adaptation rather than an original creation. However, Whedon has marked it as his own interpretation in many ways – from editing the script to directing a film instead of a play, from casting actors and friends whom he has worked with previously to shooting the film in his own home. Therefore, rather than being bound to a finite narrative space, the Whedonverse grand narrative continues to expand through intertextual as well as hyperdiegetic casting; the embodied actors become the site of the endlessly deferred Whedon metanarrative.

In sum, the cross-textual catharsis created for and by *Angel* fans, and Fred and Wesley shippers, provides much fodder for thought about media, audience and fandom studies. It highlights the deep emotional impact of narratives, fans' desire and even the need for catharsis, the convergent nature of storytelling in our time, and the role of the human body – the actor's as well as the spectator's body – in enabling the existence of endlessly deferred narratives. All of these points are demonstrated in fan ShiningArmor's response to the announcement that Whedon would be adapting *Much Ado* and casting Acker and Denisof as Beatrice and Benedick: "YAY! Fred and Wesley back together again as the leads! The little nerd romantic inside of me is going bezerk right now" (cited in Zutter, 2011). It is noteworthy that reading across the texts via the actors' bodies to achieve emotional resolution might still be considered an illusion or lie, as Wesley explains to Illyria in "A Hole in the World". After all, just as Illyria is not Fred, Fred is not Beatrice or vice versa; Wesley is not Benedick; and the actors Acker and Denisof are not any of these characters. Yet, somehow, they are. Therefore, we might call this screen-reading strategy a form of fantasy, the feel-good kind, and what Whedon might determine to be what audiences desire but should not be given. Sherryl Vint observes that Whedon's texts have "extraordinary value" because "what we need [as audience members] ... is a hybrid of myth and metaphor with real-world problems, a potent combination that allows us to both take pleasure from [his] series and also take seriously [their] themes" – themes such as the deaths of loved ones (Vint, 2014).

In the *Buffy* episode "Normal Again" (2002), Buffy finds herself moving between two apparent realties: Sunnydale, where she is a vampire slayer by night, a fast-food worker by day and a caregiver to her sister all the time; and an institution somewhere in California, where she is a mentally disturbed young woman who has a loving set of parents who support her and desperately want to see her well and whole. Vint notes that the "fantasy" of Sunnydale is far more real than the "reality" of the mental institution in that Sunnydale represents – despite its location on a hellmouth – a life that viewers recognise as authentic, including very human, everyday struggles of negotiating romantic relationships, learning to love others and oneself, paying bills, and dealing with loss and its attendant depression (Vint, 2014). Is *Much Ado*, then, the fantasy to *Angel*'s reality? In an intriguing and uncharacteristic turn, Whedon, even if subconsciously, may have provided for some fans – and perhaps even himself – a chance to experience what they want rather than what they need.

References

Albright, R. (2014), " 'Wesley and Fred Went to Heaven and They Got This!': Fred, Wesley, Mal, Simon, Topher, Dominic, Andrew, and Agent Phil do the Bard at Joss's House: The Whedon Coterie, the Fans, and *Much Ado*." Sixth Biennial Slayage Conference on the Whedonverses, 19–22 June, Sacramento, California.
Buckman, A.R. (2012), " 'Didn't Get the Memo? Hero of the People Now': Joss Whedon, Hat Tricks, and the Complication of Viewer Responses." Fifth Biennial Slayage Conference on the Whedonverses, 12–15 July, Vancouver, British Columbia.
Buckman, A.R. (2014), " 'We are not what we are': Hyperdiegesis in the Whedonverse." Sixth Biennial Slayage Conference on the Whedonverses. 19–22 June, Sacramento, California.
Bussolini, J. (2013), "Television Intertextuality after *Buffy*: Intertextuality of Casting and Constitutive Intertextuality." *Slayage: The Journal of the Whedon Studies Association*, Winter 10(1).
"Catharsis" (2014), *Dictionary.com Unabridged*. Available from http://dictionary.reference.com/browse/catharsis.

Cochran, T.R. (2014), "By Beholding, We Become Changed: Narrative Transubstantiation and the Whedonverses." *Slayage: The Journal of the Whedon Studies Association*, Summer 11(2)/12(1).

D'Aloia, A. (2012), "Cinematic Empathy: Spectator Involvement in the Film Experience." In D. Reynolds and M. Reason, eds., *Kinesthetic Empathy in Creative and Cultural Practices*. Chicago, IL: The University of Chicago Press, 2012, pp. 93–107.

Hills, M. (2002), *Fan Cultures*. London: Routledge.

Mar, R.A. and Oatley, K. (2008), "The Function of Fiction Is the Abstraction and Simulation of Social Experience." *Perspectives on Psychological Science*, 3(3), 173–192.

Radish, C. (2013), "Amy Acker Talks *Much Ado about Nothing* Blu-ray/DVD, Working with Joss Whedon Since *Angel*, and *Person of Interest*." Collider.com. Available 10 April 2014 from http://collider.com/amy-acker-much-ado-about -nothing-interview/.

Reynolds, D. and Reason, M. (2012), "Introduction." In D. Reynolds and M. Reason, eds., *Kinesthetic Empathy in Creative and Cultural Practices*. Chicago, IL: The University of Chicago Press, 2012, pp. 17–28.

Robinson, T. (2011), "*The Onion A.V. Club* Interview with Joss Whedon." In D. Lavery and C. Burkhead, eds., *Joss Whedon: Conversations*. Jackson, MS: University Press of Mississippi, pp. 23–33.

Vineyard, J. (2013), "Amy Acker on *Much Ado about Nothing* and Joss Whedon's Dance Parties." Available 10 April 2014 from http://www.vulture.com/2013/ 06/much-ado-about-nothing-amy-acker-interview.html.

Vint, S. (2014), "Difficult Men, Powerful Women: *Buffy the Vampire Slayer* and Quality Television." Sixth Biennial *Slayage* Conference on the Whedonverses, 19–22 June, Sacramento, California.

WHEDONesque. (2009), "Joss Whedon's 16 Most Painful Character Deaths." Available 28 May 2014 from http://whedonesque.com/comments/19106.

Whedon, J. (2013), *Much Ado about Nothing: A Film by Joss Whedon*. London: Titan Books.

Zutter, T. (2011), "Joss Whedon Might Be Adapting Shakespeare's *Much Ado about Nothing* with Whedonverse Alums." Available 10 April 2014 from http://www .tor.com/blogs/2011/10/joss-whedon-might-be-adapting-shakespeares-much -ado-about-nothing-with-whedonverse-alums.

8
Location, Location, Location: Citizen-Fan Journalists' "Set Reporting" and Info-War in the Digital Age

Matt Hills

> **What should I photograph?** Everything... Even with plenty of background research, details of the plot are limited. That burnt piece of plastic...may have a hitherto unexpected yet important role in the story. **Why Visit a Location Shoot?** It is often said that watching a film being shot is as interesting as watching paint dry. But if the painting is a Rembrandt or a Picasso that's pretty interesting indeed.
>
> (Robins and Mount, 2004: 12)

Recent work on popular media cultures has emphasised the growth in "film-induced tourism", both on-location and off-location – that is, at theme parks (see Beeton, 2005). However, such work has typically focused on practices of fan pilgrimage, which follow on from the broadcast and consumption of specific media texts (see Hills, 2002). This approach is resolutely "post-textual" in terms of seeking to consider how some audiences re-enact favoured media images (see Kim, 2010), and thus it misses the significance of pre-textual audience engagements with popular media (Gray, 2010: 120), such as the advice for fans given above. In the case of pre-textual interactions with media space, fans enjoy following details of filming in miniscule detail, as well as staking out and visiting locations while filming is in progress, along with following reports and images of this filming disseminated online via social media and forums. Fans of popular media are thus no longer just reactive to official news of film and television franchises. Instead, they now proactively seek out filming locations and wider information about production activities – for example, scouring agents' websites for unannounced casting news or details of production staff.

In this chapter I will focus on fans' pre-textual engagements with popular movie and television filming. I'll argue that this technologically facilitated but also culturally historicised fan activity has opened up a new front in ongoing producer/fan struggles between "official knowledge" and "popular knowledges" (See Fiske, 1993). After introducing the issues underpinning this contemporary "info-war" (Hills, 2010: 72), I will then move on to consider how fan "set reporting" might complicate theoretical accounts of "grassroots journalism" (see Gillmor, 2006) and "citizen witnessing" (see Allan, 2013). To what extent can fans who track information about filming, sharing this via social media, be considered as citizen-fan journalists serving an imagined "public"? I will suggest that the emphasis on citizenship in journalism studies debates has typically marginalised the range of (sub)cultural identities and modalities which can be articulated with notions of amateur journalism, such as the emergent figure of the fan reporter. First, though, how has the phenomenon of "location reporting" shifted the dynamic between media fans and producers?

"I know this is probably asking a lot": The rise of the pre-textual poacher

Perhaps surprisingly, relatively little scholarship has brought together concerns with how audiences relate to media(ted) space and how they use social media. Production designer David Brisbin has addressed this specific meeting point:

> What I am arguing here is that on [*Twilight:*] *New Moon* (and presumably other projects shot in 2009) these two strands converged on the back of the current wave of tech tools in the hands of fans. The result is something new: instant fan-made media, and instant...is a lot faster than movie production.
>
> (Brisbin, 2009/10: 56–57)

In *Spreadable Media*, Henry Jenkins et al. consider the development of such fan-made material in passing, noting the media industry's potential "discomfort about the public's expanded communication capacities" (2013: 300). The real-time fan monitoring of *Twilight: New Moon*'s art department as it set up sites for location filming meant that fans were questioning design decisions by drawing on their knowledge of source texts:

> The fans were not simply spoilers, seeking to reconstruct what happened on the set or to anticipate what would be in the movie. Nor were they simply helping to create buzz and public awareness. They were also sharp critics who ... leaked details in relation to firm expectations forged through their close and intimate engagement with the novel.
>
> (Jenkins et al., 2013: 301)

In Brisbin's personal account, he feels that "film production gets pushed in this moment toward something akin to live stage performance. Sure, in a stage performance you can choose to be deaf and blind to your real-time audience, but it is a whopper of a choice" (Brisbin, 2009/10: 57). Production teams working on projects that are likely to have a dedicated fandom are hence called upon to consider whether, and in what ways, their on-location practices might be under fan surveillance. Brisbin suggests that returning to the studio offered a welcome respite from playing cat and mouse with fans on location, eventually even installing a "twelve-foot-high barrier" around the property where they were filming (Brisbin, 2009/10: 55). By contrast,

> moving onto soundstages spelled relief for us all. We ... were well hidden from fans deep inside the studio. It felt almost luxurious to be able to execute this part of the project exclusively among the paid filmmakers, and to know that the public debut of this material would be fully controlled by our own publicity plan.
>
> (Brisbin, 2009/10: 58–59)

What I have termed an "info-war" between fans and producers with regard to the acquisition and circulation of spoilers means that fans can act as pre-textual poachers (Hills, 2010: 72), opposing the publicity plans of media organisations by breaking production (and textual) news ahead of official schedules and promotional strategies. Such pre-textual poaching, preceding the release of the film or television text concerned, is likely to be post-textual in another sense, of course, insofar as the fans who are committed to tracking production are already intensely and affectively invested in the pop cultural franchise concerned, whether this is *Twilight*, *Doctor Who* or *Sherlock*. As Lee Broughton has remarked, the "intriguing form of fan culture practice, wherein fan discourse leads to travel experiences which in turn provoke further discourse and further travel, demands more detailed research" (Broughton, 2011: 316). However, fans' location reporting, sometimes dubbed "set reporting" within fandom (Aimee, 2013), has developed rapidly in the past few years given the rise of mobile social media and smartphones, or what John Urry and Anthony Elliott term "miniaturised mobilities" (Elliott and Urry, 2010: 33). For instance, when BBC Wales' *Doctor Who* began filming in 2004, it made sense for commercial fan magazine *Starburst* to run a story about "setiquette", offering advice on how fans could legally stake out and follow *Doctor Who's* filming locations (Robins and Mount, 2004: 12). However, less than a decade later, series three of *Sherlock* – filmed in 2013 – had a dedicated Twitter hashtag, #setlock, which official production staff and fans both contributed to in differing ways, along with curatorial compilations of filming pictures and tweets via Storify (Richardson et al., 2013: 100). *Sherlock's* producer, Sue Vertue, even appealed directly to fans not to reveal filming locations and spoilers via social media:

> What I am nervous about is that our London shooting schedule is punishing and will really give us very little time to interact with you. The actors really hope you understand that. Also, and I know this is probably asking a lot, the majority of fans and indeed ourselves would REALLY appreciate it if you didn't post pictures or spoilers or ideally our daily locations. Thanks for your understanding. Sue x.
>
> (Sherlockology, 2013)

Meanwhile, in the period between 2004 and 2013, *Doctor Who* fans scored a palpable "set reporting" success by uncovering the true identity of the character River Song during principal photography for series six (26 April 2011), well ahead of the UK premiere of "A Good Man Goes To War" on 1 October 2011. However, what might be dubbed "Rivergate" did not make its way into official media such as tabloid newspapers, presumably as a result of pressure from the *Doctor Who* production office. Consequently, this spoiler only circulated online at fan news sites and forums, without the wider dissemination of professional media publications. This demonstrates the extent to which researching popular media cultures might now call for aspects of participant observation or fannish immersion. For, if writers have not followed real-time tweets, groups on Facebook or fan news sites, the record of a popular media text that they offer up may be strongly indebted to official sources rather than the counterknowledges circulating within (spoiler-oriented) sections of fandom. For instance, *Doctor Who* archivist and historian Stephen James Walker notes that in

> an interview with a BBC Radio 5 Live reporter...Moffat made some outspoken remarks about certain of the show's fans. This was reported by the BBC News website on 11 May [2011] in an item headed "*Doctor Who* boss 'hates' fans who spoil show's secrets."
>
> (Walker, 2013: 28)

But Walker then goes on to discuss how

> these comments seemed particularly surprising. The fact was that, contrary to Moffat's implication, detailed plot information about "The Impossible Astronaut"/"Day of the Moon" had not been widely available online prior to transmission...Nor had any such information leaked from fan websites into the press...The showrunner himself later characterised his remarks as a grumpy outburst.
>
> (Walker, 2013: 29)

Failing to consider the exact context in which these statements were made – that the production team would certainly have been aware that details of the 26 April filming at 14 Archer Road, Penarth, had leaked to fan sites, and hence that River's identity had not been kept secret – leaves Walker surprised by Moffat's symbolic attack on *Doctor Who* fandom. By contrast, I would say that the showrunner's outburst was wholly understandable – and readable as such by spoiler-oriented fans – as a reaction to "Rivergate", albeit in coded terms, since Moffat could hardly go public about the production team's failure to safeguard the major narrative "reveal" of a then forthcoming series. Instead, Moffat appeared to perform a kind of transformative work, shaping his response to the non-secret of River's identity into an alternative attack on spoilers surrounding "The Impossible Astronaut" and "Day of the Moon" (both 2011).

Another major cultural historian of *Doctor Who*, James Chapman, also reflects official paratexts rather than fans' secluded counterknowledges when he suggests that the "revelation of River's true identity – at the end of 'A Good Man Goes To War' – was one of the series' best-kept secrets and was filmed under conditions of high security" (Chapman, 2013: 277). Though this particular scene may have been successfully kept secret, River's identity most certainly was not, with production security being circumvented by dedicated fans ("River Song is...",

2011). Yet neither Walker nor Chapman fully integrate spoiler-oriented paratexts and practices of set reporting into their accounts, with fan news-gatherers thus being exnominated and rendered invisible. In such accounts, popular media cultures are reduced to their official meanings and practices, with the counterknowledges of "viewer-created paratexts" (Gray, 2010: 143) being silenced in favour of BBC publicity, while real-time processes of "info-war" are also problematically displaced by retrospective and reductive narratives of *Doctor Who's* production/reception.

The phenomenon of set reporting offers something innovative within fan practices. By utilising the likes of Twitter, Facebook groups and Flickr galleries, fan discussions and analyses of "set pics" participate in an ideology of "presentism" (Williams, 2013: 163). Here, "cameraphone photographs...travel 'timelessly' so...receivers can gaze upon events unfolding more or less in real time...Digital photography is typified by...the 'power of now'" (Urry and Larsen, 2011: 181). Rather than being an "unfolding text", the production of *Doctor Who*, say, thus becomes a sort of "*unfolding event* marked by fans' social media-intensified...valorization of liveness, and desired interaction with the show's various personnel" (Williams, 2013: 170). At the same time, as David Brisbin observes, "already the fan-to-production space has condensed" in response to fans staking out location filming, such that now you "can follow events on...set via Twitter" (Brisbin, 2009/10: 59), thanks to the official accounts of directors, designers and so on. This reaction from producers arguably represents one attempt to trump unofficial pictures with official information, hence redirecting fan energies. In reality, although official production tweets may be retweeted and favourited many times – for example, Sue Vertue's Twitpic of the final production slate of *Sherlock* series three filming retweeted 2,203 times – these become just one source viewed by fans within the real-time flow of reports and photographs.

Furthermore, as hashtags such as #setlock and #dwsr (short for *Doctor Who* set reports) indicate, a group identity can also form around fans' set reporting. Nancy Baym has reflected on this in the context of fan studies: "Groups sometimes develop a sense of themselves as a group, a social identity or schema of who they are that is shared amongst them...Groups may [also] develop names for themselves" (Baym, 2010: 88). *Doctor Who* fans have adopted a label from the BBC Wales series itself, suspecting that their activity of tracking production was being referenced in "The End of Time" (2009) by a diegetic group called the Silver Cloak. These OAPs tracked the Doctor's whereabouts by

sharing sightings of him, phoning one another and passing on information. Thereafter, the real-world fan group committed to tracking filming
locations – composed of many Cardiff-based fans – took on the identity of the Silver Cloak, and a Twitter account sharing location sightings
continues to run under this name.

In *Time On TV*, Paul Booth argues that a range of contemporary "complex" television narratives have been marked by the "networkization
of television" (Booth, 2012: 180). By this, Booth means that television
shows such as *Lost* and *Doctor Who* have represented "sprawling casts
of characters linked by... diegetic interconnections" where audiences'
"social networking... saliently mirrors the characteristics and specifics
of networked sociality in television" (2012: 186). For Booth, then,

> This networking function of contemporary television can be seen
> across complex television. For example, both the characters and nar-
> rative of *Doctor Who* are inherently networked, as the Doctor and
> River Song intersect in a variety of ways throughout time.
>
> (Booth, 2012: 185)

Although it may be tempting to suggest that by "recogniz-
ing... characters in a social network, audience members can then see
themselves within that network as well" (Booth, 2012: 187), Booth's
argument runs the risk of overly generalising. We might wonder what
distinguishes "networkized" television drama from longer traditions –
far pre-dating social media – of using ensemble casts. Many television
dramas involve sprawling casts of characters that are marked by diegetic
interconnection: indeed, soap opera as a television genre has been doing
this for many years, without any sense of somehow "mirroring" contemporary social media, or even changing to more closely approximate
the social media context that Booth posits (current UK soaps continue
to follow linear narrative traditions while remaining popular). It seems
likely that Booth thus overstates his case – constructing the "mirroring" relationship that he discerns – but in the case of the Silver Cloak
this articulation between fans' social networking and a diegetic network of (old media) OAPs has been specifically and actively co-produced
within fandom. Showrunner Russell T. Davies seems likely to have
been acknowledging real-world fan activities, albeit in his final screen-
play and in a humorous manner, while in turn *Doctor Who* fans have
embraced this wry depiction, converting the Silver Cloak into a badge of
identity, regardless of age. The key connotation threaded through both
diegesis and fan activity is the sense that (extra)textual Silver Cloaks are
highly effective at tracking down the Doctor.

However, the Silver Cloak fan group is engaged in a constant tussle for information with the production team, such as seeking to determine what initials are in use for the series' production base and location signage. At the time of writing, these signs deploy "MW" after producer Marcus Wilson, although early filming in 2004 made less effort to disguise its identity as *Doctor Who* work, with initial production being identified simply by "BBC WALES LOC" signs. Fan accounts on Twitter also retweet information from members of the public, bringing this into fan-cultural circulation, and the Facebook group Doctor Who Filming has also been known to share evidence of BBC filming information sent to Cardiff residents (another typical source of filming information). Such activity tackles "the ongoing informational problem fans face of never being able to know enough about that which they love" (Baym, 2010: 86).

Through the ongoing accumulation of filming information, specific groups and individual fans can build up a reputation over time. For example, when "Rivergate" broke, and what proved to be entirely accurate script dialogue was overheard, the news site *Doctor Who TV* referred to the story's source as somebody who had "provided many reliable *Doctor Who* filming reports" in the past ("River Song is...", 2011). However, the nature of a Twitter hashtag means that this material cannot always be verified, and #dwsr has been subjected to periodic hoaxing and trolling – something which fans tend to counter by using alternative online spaces (Facebook or Gallifrey Base) to warn when a hoaxer has been identified. Pessimistic views of social media, such as Geert Lovink's account – characterising "comment culture" as "mass hermeneutics... merely signs of life of individual users, special effects of... interactive systems that aren't worth noticing" (Lovink, 2011: 53) – might view this constant flow of information as a problem. Yet fandom represents a context in which rather than "better recommendation and reputation tools" requiring a technical, software fix (Gillmor, 2006: 190), reputation can solidify (both positively or negatively) as a result of ongoing fan activity. In this case, "mass hermeneutics" are displaced by communal hermeneutics.

The fan gaze of those who gather to watch and record filming is partly akin to the tourist gaze theorised by Urry and Larsen (2011) in that it too forms part of a collective experience. As Teresa Forde has noted in her discussion of "The *Doctor Who Experience*",

John Urry proposes that the tourist gaze is performed as part of a social experience: "Gazing is an interactive, communal game where individual gazes are mediated and affected by the presence and gazes of others". Existing in a public space, the *Doctor Who Experience* enables interaction and negotiation of groups of fans and visitors within the participatory culture of... fandom. The act of "negotiated gazing", and one could add listening... remains a crucial and active performative strategy.

(Forde, 2013: 69)

However, this "performative strategy" is not limited to the commercial space of the *Experience* (see Beattie, 2013). Watching location filming can similarly combine fans and "visitors" (i.e. more casual, curious spectators who aren't motivated by fan investment or identity). Gazing – and listening – are similarly "negotiated", but here the negotiation continues via social media. For example, fans do not only pool their photos – taken from different positions and angles, as well as with varied technology, competence and luck – they also debate exactly what can be heard on low-fidelity, snatched video of filming ("Doctor Who Spoilers", 2013).

Such "negotiated gazing/listening" (physically and via social media) means that spoilerhounds can utilise an expanded sense of proximity to the media text and the fan community:

Social media has expanded the "proximity" of social proximity – thanks to Twitter, chatting with the world about television... has become more common... The network doesn't just link the individual and the collective, but enacts a number of other linkages across... media and cultural boundaries [blurring... producer and consumer, spectacle and spectator, representation and information].

(Booth, 2012: 183)

Posting "set reports" is one way in which fans can become consumers and producers, but, more than this, such reporting both conveys an immediacy – "being there" and seeing filming happen in front of one's own eyes – and relies on hypermediation – that is, the ability of multiple fans to capture and circulate photos, videos and written reports. By fusing ideologies of immediacy with practices of hypermediation, these fans approach a state of "demediation" in Paul Booth's terms. By this he means that "the ubiquity of mediation hides that selfsame mediation," resulting in an " 'undecidable' position that mashes up... hypermediate and immediate conceptions of mediation" (2010: 181).

However, at the same time as it offers something innovative within fan practices – real-time demediation of fan and public sources on filming – set reporting continues in the vein of other long-established fan activities. As such, the binary explored by Paul Booth and Peter Kelly, where *Doctor Who* fans either exercise "entirely new fan practices using digital technology" or "augment old practices" (Booth and Kelly, 2013: 64), doesn't quite correspond to the complexity of set reporting. Unofficial reports gathered from filming represent pre-textual material that is somewhat akin to the counterknowledges which circulated via print fanzines in earlier decades: "Fanzine publishing in the 1970s and 1980s was our 'internet' " declares fan writer Peter Anghelides (cited in O'Day, 2013: 31). Within his cultural history of *Doctor Who* fandom, Andrew O'Day notes that

> the monthly news publication *Doctor Who Bulletin*...began life in 1983...While...[*Celestial Toyroom*], like *Doctor Who Monthly*, had to follow guidelines for news reporting set out by the *Doctor Who* production office, limiting what could be said, *DWB* was under no such restrictions, and quickly resembled a tabloid newspaper, with sensationalistic stories on the front cover.
>
> (2013: 32)

Events such as "Rivergate" thus form part of a lineage which goes back to 1980s fanzines in the UK, representing a distinctive mode of fan poaching which challenges production authority not by rereading texts or reworking diegetic universes but rather by challenging producers' control over "official" flows of information and publicity. Such adversarial fan paratexts attempt to frame franchises and television shows in radically different ways to official accounts:

> By issue three [of *DWB*, niche fan store] Forbidden Planet had received a formal letter from Christopher Crouch in BBC Enterprises asking them to "cease and desist" selling...[*Doctor Who Bulletin*]. "That was my main outlet so it really looked like the nail was in the coffin," says [editor Gary] Leigh..."I was banned from Forbidden Planet till issue 53 – they felt that they had to comply with Enterprises".
>
> (Marson, 2013: 134–135)

Fan-created paratexts are not alone in this pursuit of informational autonomy, with fans seeking to get beyond officially sanctioned versions of "the truth" about media production which are themselves typically driven by commercial, brand-protecting logics. Tabloid newspapers or publications such as *Private Eye* enact similar challenges to the cultural authority of producers, although their capacity to break stories tends to surpass the capabilities of "set reporters" who are limited to what can be observed on-location rather than reaching into the institutional contexts of media production. *Private Eye's* intervention may have led to "you are erased from *Doctor Who!*" becoming a fan meme ("Media News", 2013: 10), but it is usually the case that official narratives of media production remain culturally powerful and paratextually iterated, whereas counterdiscourses are marginalised or erased, just as "Rivergate" is already threatening to dematerialise from *Doctor Who's* published histories. Counterknowledges sometimes creep back in posthumously, when the careers of producers no longer need to be protected, but it remains to be seen whether fan knowledge circulating via social media will retain this longer-term efficacy, given the speed with which tweets, postings and YouTube videos can be lost from the historical record.

Although producers seek to co-opt hashtags and fan "buzz" to reinforce brand value, they also appeal to fans not to share filming-derived spoilers. However, since it is increasingly impossible to control the flow of information coming from fan groups such as the Silver Cloak or #setlock devotees, as well as those using Storify, producers have engaged in a further strategy to control fans' "popular knowledges". This involves casting doubt on the veracity of what fans have witnessed by suggesting that fake scenes have been filmed:

> There's a lot of people who follow you around. We did a few false shots. There will be things that people saw that have got nothing to do with it. That's the way we handled it (Jeremy Lovering, director of *Sherlock* series 3, episode 1).
>
> (Connelly, 2013)

Given the costs and tight timeframes involved in location shoots, it seems unlikely that fake scenes would actually be carried out. However, even raising the possibility in production discourse destabilises fan accounts of filming, attempting to shift "objective" fan descriptions into a limbo of pre-textual speculation. In this way, producer/fan "info-war" moves beyond controlling the flow of information (or not), and instead into the characterisation, by producers, of fans' popular knowledge as undecidably (in)valid. We therefore need to complicate the binary that John Fiske sets out between official knowledge, which is "uni-accentual", and "popular knowledges", which resist official forms of knowledge, acting as "multiaccentual" rumour or gossip rather than "valid", rational information (Fiske, 1993: 182). As Claire Birchall has more recently argued in *Knowledge Goes Pop*,

> Fiske's concentration on the oppositional nature of his version of popular knowledge...belies the way in which popular knowledges borrow from more established discourses in the attempt to legitimate themselves. (Why else would gossips appeal to direct knowledge of the event being relayed...?).
>
> (Birchall, 2006: 21)

Furthermore, Birchall suggests that "popular knowledges are not only dependent upon the 'official' discourses that might seek to repress them in various ways, as Fiske claims, but...'official' discourses are also 'reliant' upon popular knowledges" (Birchall, 2006: 19). Hence this info-war is never a zero-sum game where one side can triumph: even when fans secure spoilers against the wishes of the production team, producers can counter by attempting to shift the status of fan knowledge (and this attempt, in turn, can be resisted or dismissed by sections of fandom). Fiske's account gives "official" and "popular" knowledge an essential character, whereas the info-war surrounding popular film and television production demonstrates that "popular" knowledge can seek to "borrow from more established discourses", such as the objectivity and authority of professional journalism; these are "fan reporters", after all, often with reputations to protect. Simultaneously, supposedly authoritative, "official" and monological discourse can itself become multivalent, appropriating fannish circulation of rumours by developing rumours of its own. Indeed, despite fan worries that "Rivergate" spoilers might have been based on a false scene designed to mislead ("River Song is...", 2011), these accounts proved to be wholly accurate as fan reportage, even down to correctly capturing dialogue from "The Wedding of River Song" (2011).

Theorising "set reporting" as a form of popular knowledge that is nevertheless intertwined with established, legitimate cultural discourses of objective, trustworthy journalism raises the question of whether these emergent fan practices might be linked to debates surrounding "citizen witnessing" (Allan, 2013). In the next section I want to develop this approach, suggesting that the emphasis on citizen journalism and user-generated content in journalism studies misses how journalistic discourses have been adopted by fans as "eyewitness picture producers" (Mortensen, 2011: 68). Can we assume that "citizen" and "fan" form a binary here, or can "instant fan-made media" be thought of as hybridised citizen-fan journalism?

"The storyline is in no way derogatory": Freedom of information and affective intelligence

Fans who are engaged in "set reporting" frequently legitimate their practices via a sense of journalistic authority. Indeed, when *Doctor Who* first returned to production in 2004, not only did fans write "setiquette" guides (Robins and Mount, 2004: 12) but fan reports and photographs – along with those of press agencies – were also run professionally as news by the commercial fan magazine *Starburst* (Mount and Robins, 2004: 92–97).

Spoiler-hunting fans who want to get closer to productions in unauthorised ways are thus integrated into journalism culture via co-option by sectors of the press, as well as tweeting, blogging and posting at fan sites. It could be suggested that these fannish popular knowledges offer a good example of the "grassroots journalism" celebrated by Dan Gillmor in *We the Media*:

> What excites me in this context...is that the growing number of blogs written by people who want to talk intelligently about an area of expertise is a sign of something vital. Blogs can be...better...than the professionals who face the standard limitations of reporting time and available space... for what they learn.
>
> (2006: 139)

Fan reporting is evidently "better" than professional set reporting from a fannish point of view: it focuses on production for the entire duration of a shoot, sharing information in real time. By contrast, although professional journalists who are covering a shoot are likely to be granted access to high-status "backstage areas" that are denied to fans (Beeton, 2005: 194) – for example, interviewing cast and crew or being in studio as well as out on location – their reports are generally timed to coincide with bursts of planned publicity (Midgley, 2010: 40–45), usually appearing in the immediate build-up to a series premiere (Moran, 2011: 26–31). Sanctioned professional media coverage may be limited by space – a few pages in a glossy magazine – but it is also limited in terms of how it can write about a series (adopting a positive, celebratory tone) and when this story will be run. Even unauthorised tabloid coverage, such as that of *Sherlock* series three, remains restricted to major spoilers that are deemed "newsworthy" (e.g. how did Sherlock survive the end of series two?) (Gritt, 2013), whereas fans will build up a far more detailed and ongoing sense of production. As Cornel Sandvoss has rightly noted, while "in our popular imagination the Internet ... is often envisioned as a space it primarily functions not as a space, but as an archive that allows ... access to the multitude of ... paratexts across time and space" (2011: 66). Even if these archives may perish within a year or two, while they persist – in forum threads or Storify collections – they represent the focused collection of multiple sources whose filming reports can be sifted, evaluated and debated in real time by participating fans.

Fans' set reports form part of the "active ambient news environment", which has been fostered by social media such as Twitter (Murthy, 2013: 63). Using hashtags which combine fan sightings with retweeted comments and contributions from people outside fandom, even where "individuals tweet without journalism in mind, it may be that a 'journalistic community' surrounding a hashtag topic nonetheless emerges" (Murthy, 2013: 63). Forming such a "community", fans are dedicated to the "active investigation" of sightings and rumours (Duffett, 2013: 170), working to counter the fact that one "limitation of Twitter is the issue of information integrity. Tweets ... can be misleading, incorrect, or even fraudulent ... It is impossible to monitor the integrity of information flowing on Twitter" (Murthy, 2013: 65). Contra this presumed impossibility, fans do their best to check tweets, sometimes by visiting locations only to find that they've been misled by a hoaxer, sometimes by testing tweeted information against working theories that have already been established by fan reporting.

Dan Gillmor's "grassroots journalism" is specifically championed as a "civic engagement" (2006: 139), and fan reporting does not appear, on the face of it, to represent this: it does not serve the "public" or a notion of "public interest", instead being structured by the value systems of specific fan cultures. Nor is fan reporting linked to particular notions of the citizen – that is, somebody positioned by and in relation to the state as having certain obligations or responsibilities. As such, Mette Mortensen's argument that "citizen journalism" has been bandied about as a term without any real sense of its specificity would appear to be more accurate: "'citizen journalist' ... [is] used indiscriminately ... [yet] many of the picture producers in question do not qualify as ordinary 'citizens' ... I propose the term 'eyewitness picture producer' ... shunning the problematic designation 'citizen'" (Mortensen, 2011: 65, 68).

And yet, things may not be as clear-cut as this, where "fan" identity as part of an audience can straightforwardly be contrasted with "citizen" identity as part of a public. Both Liesbet van Zoonen and Sonia Livingstone have challenged the premature separation of audiences and publics. Van Zoonen writes that "rather than construing fan activities as an embryonic step to acquire more relevant civic qualities and virtues, I would argue for the equivalence of fan practices and political practices" (van Zoonen, 2005: 63), contesting any distinction between affective relations of fandom and cognitive processes of citizenship. Although not as strongly arguing for equivalence – and thus that both fans and citizens display "affective intelligence" (van Zoonen, 2005: 53) – Livingstone suggests the need for an intermediate realm between audiences and publics. Introducing a third term would avoid the "woolly expansion of the normative public sphere concept to encompass all forms of (...ambivalently) public discourse and participation" while recognising "ambiguous phenomena, grounded in...civil society and the lifeworld" (Livingstone, 2005: 32).

Both van Zoonen's call to address the "affective intelligence" of fandom and Livingstone's consideration of a position between audience and public resonate with Michael Saler's recent adaptation of Habermasian theory. He argues that emotional investments in fictional characters and their imaginary worlds can lead to "public spheres of the imagination" (Saler, 2012: 98). These are necessarily plural since each focuses on different characters – for example, Sherlock Holmes – but they share attributes of the Habermasian public sphere, engaging audiences in debates over plural meaning, tolerance of difference, and social and political concerns (emerging out of, or articulated with, investments in a specific fiction). However, Saler suggests that public spheres of the imagination, unlike "the" public sphere, draw on "an alternative to instrumental reason, one that was capable of reconciling modernity with enchantment. This more expansive definition of rationality...I call *animistic reason*" (Saler, 2012: 16). Akin to affective intelligence, this also conjoins "reason with imagination, analysis with intuition, thought with feeling" (16). Of particular relevance to my focus here, he notes that the "advent of the Internet has resulted in a vast proliferation of public spheres of the imagination, including newsgroups, blogs, web pages, and social networking sites" (101). And in Saler's terms, public spheres of imagination are dual focused, investigating the "mechanics" of fiction – for instance, media production processes in this instance – while simultaneously "enhancing the 'reality effects' of fantasy:...mak[ing] the imaginary world more virtually 'real' by probing its details, reconciling its apparent contradictions, and filling in its lacunae" (17–18). Yet by stressing animistic reason, he makes clear that this public participation is both enchanted – perceived as magical, heightened or wondrous by participants – and a matter of rationality. And although it may be difficult to argue that fans' set reporting necessarily relates "imaginary worlds to the real world . . . [so that] imaginary worlds . . . [become] 'good to think with' about topical social and political concerns" (99), it may be that Saler makes this connection too directly and bluntly. Animistic reason and the wonderment of set reporting's "synergy of multiple minds . . . as the [imaginary] world . . . [becomes] a shared, ongoing project" imply that any "social concerns" involved here may be less a matter of capital-P politics and more a matter of learning as much as possible about the unfolding fictional world (18). As such, I suspect that pre-textual public spheres of the imagination most frequently focus on how fans' pursuit of information can be successfully enacted, and how producers' attempts to control flows of information can be circumvented. Saler's potent concept is somewhat restricted by his post-textual focus, where audiences are once again theorised as responding to and reworking imaginary worlds rather than pursuing "popular knowledge" about their forthcoming developments.

Despite these caveats, I would say that amateur fan journalism readily meets calls to deconstruct fan/citizen and audience/public binaries. Although fans may not be writing on behalf of a generalised public or citizenry, "affective intelligence" is certainly deployed in the checking of information, as well as in the discovery of data from outside fan circles, and the sifting of theories and speculation posted as a result of filming reports or photos. Fans are just as attentive to the minutiae of film and television production processes as an obsessively blogging "political anorak" is to details of national politics (Richardson et al., 2013: 79). And although UK fan reportage may not directly serve the "public interest", it intersects fuzzily with civil society via an implicit cultural politics which desires, and pursues, the transparency of public service broadcasters. Such fan reporting does not simply generate diegetic spoilers; it also observes profilmic material that never makes it to the screen, speculating over production decisions that receive no official commentary. For instance, an elaborate stunt sequence was witnessed during *Doctor Who*'s filming of "Rose" (2005) – involving a sofa being dropped from a height – but this did not feature in the finished text, nor has its absence been fully discussed in promotional paratexts. Citizen-fan "eyewitness picture producers" therefore refuse to accept production discourses, supplementing the official record by rendering productions more transparent and open to scrutiny than they would otherwise be.

Stuart Allan's observations about "citizen witnessing" can help to capture the hybrid quality of citizen-fan reportage, where fans combine fact-checking and investigation with their emotional commitment to a media text, working on behalf of a wider community and establishing relationships of trust, such as the Silver Cloak in *Doctor Who* fandom. Allan notes that "Discourses of witnessing...recurrently stretch to encompass multiple modalities" (2013: 174). Consequently there is a need to address the "emergent ecology of citizen witnessing...[where] myriad modes of reportorial form, practice and epistemology – all too often obscured by apparent 'revolutions' in technology – have been crafted" (Allan, 2013: 176). This cautions us not to root "citizen-fan journalism" merely in new media developments (or social media fetishisation), but rather to see how specific cultures and histories – here, fandom's "popular knowledges" of unofficial, tabloidesque rumour – can feed into newer forms of counterknowledge.

In the UK context, freedom of information (FOI) requests have become a common legal tool within practices of critical journalism, facilitating the capacity of professional journalists to uncover wrongdoing in public office. A further sign that media fandoms are appropriating the legitimacy (and practices) of professional journalists came when an FOI request was submitted to the Greater London Authority (GLA) for details of exchanges with the BBC regarding 2013 *Doctor Who* filming in Trafalgar Square. A redacted document was duly released by the GLA and circulated within fandom (Mann, 2013). Although the filming had already been detailed and discussed within *Doctor Who* fandom, this FOI request gave citizen-fan journalists further access to the internal workings of the show's production. Again, the transparency of production processes was heightened, allowing fans to pore over requests to film in Trafalgar Square (*Doctor Who* Unit Manager, 2013a) and scrutinise the BBC's £15 million insurance. This documentation also made public the cost of filming (£6,000), exposing information about *Doctor Who*'s budgeting which has otherwise always been vague in official paratexts.

Such an FOI request also demonstrates the relationships in play between broadcasters such as the BBC and organisations such as the GLA, with the BBC's production team offering the following assurance: "For the purpose of our story the National Gallery is portrayed as the National Gallery but any interior scenes are to be shot elsewhere. The storyline is in no way derogatory to the Gallery" (*Doctor Who*

Unit Manager, 2013b). The initial, part-completed application to film in Trafalgar Square for "The Day of the Doctor" (2013) also noted that filming would involve "Dr Who being met by other characters from the episode (all human)" (*Doctor Who* Unit Manager, 2013a), as if to reassure the GLA that its landmarks would not be connected with threatening monsters. Such exchanges indicate an awareness on BBC Wales' part that recognisable landmarks should be represented in a broadly positive light. Within *Doctor Who* filming, then,

> Place...acquires an ambassadorial role, one which the BBC's charter acknowledges as "bringing the UK to the world and the world to the UK". The selectivity of the place image is valued because it both enhances the representation's capacity to look good and appealing, and to be familiar.
>
> (McElroy, 2011: 181)

Trafalgar Square and the National Gallery are hence subjected to a kind of metatourist gaze within production processes. The value of place-as-brand is self-reflexively reinforced, with non-derogatory representations being pledged by the BBC. At the same time that *Doctor Who* promises to iterate the image value of Trafalgar Square, fans perform a kind of "digital possessive spectatorship" (Gordon, 2010: 175) by acquiring and storing personalised images of the media(ted) location:

> the database city is not a pastiche or a schizophrenic collection of unrelated surfaces...In the database city, the user is not lost to an avalanche of signifiers; she is given the authority, motivation, and framework to filter them.
>
> (Gordon, 2010: 199)

And fandom acts as one such filter, with signifiers linked to the fans' object of devotion cutting through the "hypermap" of mediated sites that can accumulate around repeatedly filmed/televised locations (Collins, 2013: 2) – for example, Central London – but also places such as Hollywood or Vancouver (see Brooker, 2007). For Gordon, the "digital possessive" reinforces an allure of "accessibility" where the overarching "ideology of digital media...is accessibility" (Gordon, 2011: 206). But to dismiss this as simply ideological fails to note how fans' desire to possess images of filming represents a quasijournalistic and hence uneasily legitimated pursuit of production transparency. Production designers, and even unit managers, can suddenly find themselves caught up in public performances of professional identity (van Dijck, 2013: 7). Fans don't just want "access"; rather, they seek greater alignment between "official" and "popular knowledges" through the application of affective intelligence, given that these knowledges usually interact in "a contest between...fans and...producers, one group trying to get their hands on...knowledge the other is trying to protect" (Jenkins, 2006: 43).

Greater attention needs to be paid to fans' pre-textual interactions with location filming (see Hills, 2012). Amateur fan reporters appropriate the legitimacy of professional journalists, serving fan communities while seeking to occupy (public) media spaces, or what would usually be "deep backstage" regions of production (Beeton, 2005: 194). By operating as citizen-fan journalists – verifying reports of filming, building up relations of trust with the wider fandom and deploying affective intelligence to investigate location filming – these fan reporters hybridise "popular" and "official" knowledges within public spheres of the imagination. Ultimately, though, their wish for greater transparency in film/television production is blocked by industry practices of information control rather than freedom, leaving an ongoing "info-war" in play.

References

Aimee. (2013), "She-goat: #Setlock – A Normal Set Reporting Day." Blogger. Available 10 February 2015 from http://tlchimera.blogspot.co.uk/2013/03/setlock-normal-set-reporting-day.html.

Allan, S. (2013), *Citizen Witnessing*. Cambridge and Malden: Polity Press.

Baym, N. (2010), *Personal Connections in the Digital Age*. Cambridge and Malden: Polity Press.

Beattie, M. (2013), "The 'Doctor Who Experience' (2012–) and the Commodification of Cardiff Bay." In M. Hills, ed., *New Dimensions of Doctor Who*. London and New York: I.B. Tauris, pp. 177–191.

Beeton, S. (2005), *Film-Induced Tourism*. Clevedon: Channel View Publications.

Birchall, C. (2006), *Knowledge Goes Pop*. Oxford and New York: Berg.

Brisbin, D. (2009/10), "Instant Fan-Made Media." *Perspective*, 27 (December–January), 54–59.

Booth, P. (2010), *Digital Fandom: New Media Studies*. New York: Peter Lang.

Booth, P. (2012), *Time on TV: Temporal Displacement and Mashup Television*. New York: Peter Lang.

Booth, P. and Kelly, P. (2013), "The Changing Faces of *Doctor Who* Fandom: New Fans, New Technologies, Old Practices?" *Participations: Journal of Audience and Reception Studies*, May, 10(1), 56–72.

Brooker, W. (2007), "Everywhere and Nowhere: Vancouver, Fan Pilgrimage and the Urban Imaginary." *International Journal of Cultural Studies*, 10(4), 423–444.

Broughton, L. (2011), "Crossing Borders Virtual and Real: A Transnational Internet-Based Community of Spaghetti Western Fans Finally Meet Each Other Face to Face on the Wild Plains of Almeria, Spain." *Language and Intercultural Communication*, 11(4), 304–318.

Chapman, J. (2013), *Inside the TARDIS: The Worlds of Doctor Who* (2nd edition). London and New York: I.B. Tauris.

Collins, G. (2013), "New to the Scene: The Emerging Paradigm of Geographic Hypermedia and Its Applications in St. Louis Film Tourism." *Polymath: An Interdisciplinary Arts and Sciences Journal*, 3(1), 1–18.

Connelly, B. (2013), "Sherlock Director Claims That Fake Scenes Have Been Shot to Mislead Us All." *Bleeding Cool*. Available 10 February 2015 from http://www.bleedingcool.com/2013/08/27/sherlock-director-claims-that -fake-scenes-have-been-shot-to-mislead-us-all/.

Doctor Who Spoilers. (2013), "Video from Christmas Filming – 13 September." Available 10 February 2015 from http://www.doctorwhospoilers.com/2013/09 /video-from-christmas-filming-13th.html.

Doctor Who Unit Manager. (2013a), "Redacted Email." BBC. Available 10 February 2015 from http://www.london.gov.uk/sites/default/files/0210-attachment -redacted.pdf%5B1%5D.pdf.

Doctor Who Unit Manager. (2013b), "Redacted Email." BBC. Available 10 February 2015 from http://www.london.gov.uk/sites/default/files/0210-attachment -redacted.pdf%5B1%5D.pdf.

Duffett, M. (2013), *Understanding Fandom*. New York and London: Bloomsbury.

Elliott, A. and Urry, J. (2010), *Mobile Lives*. Abingdon and New York: Routledge.

Fiske, J. (1993), *Power Plays, Power Works*. London and New York: Verso.

Forde, T. (2013), " 'You Anorak!' The *Doctor Who* Experience and Experiencing *Doctor Who*." In P. Booth, ed., *Fan Phenomena: Doctor Who*. Bristol: Intellect, pp. 62–71.

Gillmor, D. (2006), *We the Media: Grassroots Journalism by the People, For the People*. Sebastopol: O'Reilly Media Inc.

Gordon, E. (2010), *The Urban Spectator*. Hanover: Dartmouth College Press.

Gray, J. (2010), *Show Sold Separately: Promos, Spoilers and Other Media Paratexts*. New York: New York University Press.

Gritt, E. (2013), "A More Fearful Adversary than Moriarty?" *Mail Online*. Available 10 February 2015 from http://www.dailymail.co.uk/tvshowbiz/ article-2309243/Derren-Brown-seen-Sherlock-Holmes-set-hypnotizing-Martin -Freemans-Dr-Watson.html.

Hills, M. (2002), *Fan Cultures*. London and New York: Routledge.

Hills, M. (2010), *Triumph of a Time Lord: Regenerating Doctor Who in the Twenty-First Century*. London and New York: I.B. Tauris.

Hills, M. (2012), "Psychoanalysis and Digital Fandom: Theorizing Spoilers and Fans' Self-Narratives." In R.A Lind, ed., *Produsing Theory in a Digital World: The Intersection of Audiences and Production in Contemporary Theory*. New York: Peter Lang, pp. 105–122.

Jenkins, H. (2006), *Convergence Culture: Where Old and New Media Collide*. New York: New York University Press.

Jenkins, H., Ford, S., and Green, J. (2013), *Spreadable Media: Creating Value and Meaning in a Networked Culture*. New York: New York University Press.

Kim, S. (2010), "Extraordinary Experience: Re-enacting and Photographing at Screen Tourism Locations." *Tourism and Hospitality Planning & Development*, 7(1), 59–75.

Livingstone, S. (2005), "On the Relation between Audiences and Publics." In S. Livingstone, ed., *Audiences and Publics: When Cultural Engagement Matters for the Public Sphere*. Bristol: Intellect, pp. 17–41.

Lovink, G. (2011), *Networks Without a Cause: A Critique of Social Media*. Cambridge and Malden: Polity Press.

Mann, S. (2013), "City Hall Publishes Spoiler-Ridden Doctor Who Special Correspondence." *London24*. Available 10 February 2015 from http://www.london24.com/entertainment/around-the-web/city_hall_publishes_spoiler_ridden_doctor_who_special_correspondence_1_2371725.

Marson, R. (2013), *JN-T: The Life and Scandalous Times of John Nathan-Turner*. Tadworth: Miwk Publishing.

McElroy, R. (2011), "'Putting the Landmark Back into Television': Producing Place and Cultural Value in Cardiff." *Place Branding and Public Diplomacy*, 7(3), 175–184.

"Media News" (2013), *Private Eye*, 22 March – 4 April, 1336, 10.

Midgley, N. (2010), "Crunch Time." *Telegraph Magazine*, 13 March, 40–45.

Moran, C. (2011), "'I Bounce on Sherlock's Bed. I feel I Owe All of Womankind This Action. I Refrain from Sniffing the Pillow. That Feels Undignified'." *The Times Magazine*, 24 December, 26–31.

Mortensen, M. (2011), "The Eyewitness in the Age of Digital Transformation." In K. Anden-Papadopoulos and M. Pantti, eds., *Amateur Images and Global News*. Bristol: Intellect, pp. 63–75.

Mount, P. and Robins, T. (2004), "On Location with Doctor Who." *Starburst*, 315, 92–97.

Murthy, D. (2013), *Twitter*. Cambridge and Malden: Polity Press.

O'Day, A. (2013), "Social Spaces: British Fandom to the Present." In G.I. Leitch, ed., *Doctor Who in Time and Space: Essays on Themes, Characters, History and Fandom, 1963–2012*. Jefferson: McFarland, pp. 25–43.

Richardson, K., Parry, K., and Corner, J. (2013), *Political Culture and Media Genre: Beyond the News*. Basingstoke and New York: Palgrave Macmillan.

Robins, T. and Mount, P. (2004), "Lights, Camera, Legal Action!" *Starburst*, 317, 12.

"River Song is . . .", (2011), *Doctor Who TV*. Available 10 February 2015 from http://www.doctorwhotv.co.uk/river-song-is-18856.htm.

Saler, M. (2012), *As If: Modern Enchantment and the Literary Prehistory of Virtual Reality*. Oxford: Oxford University Press.

Sandvoss, C. (2011), "Fans Online: Affective Media Consumption and Production in the Age of Convergence." In M. Christensen, A. Jansson, and C. Christensen, eds., *Online Territories: Globalization, Mediated Practice and Social Space*. New York: Peter Lang, pp. 49–74.

Sherlockology, (2013), "Sherlock in London: A Message from Sue Vertue." Available 10 February 2015 from http://www.sherlockology.com/news/2013/4/9/message-from-sue-vertue-090413.

Urry, J. and Larsen, J. (2011), *The Tourist Gaze 3.0*. London: Sage.

van Dijck, J. (2013), *The Culture of Connectivity: A Critical History of Social Media*. Oxford: Oxford University Press.

van Zoonen, L. (2005), *Entertaining the Citizen: When Politics and Popular Culture Converge.* Oxford: Rowman and Littlefield.

Walker, S.J. (2013), *River's Run: The Unofficial and Unauthorised Guide to Doctor Who 2011.* UK: Telos Publishing.

Williams, R. (2013), "Tweeting the TARDIS: Interaction, Liveness and Social Media in *Doctor Who* Fandom." In M. Hills, ed., *New Dimensions of Doctor Who.* London and New York: I.B. Tauris, pp. 154–173.

9
Sherlock Holmes, the *De Facto* Franchise

Roberta Pearson

In May 2012 *The Guinness Book of World Records* announced that

> Having been depicted on screen 254 times...Sherlock Holmes, Sir
> Arthur Conan Doyle's fictional detective, has been awarded a world
> record for the most portrayed literary human character in film &
> TV...Through a combination of films, television series, dramas
> and documentaries, Sherlock's appearances beat the character of
> Shakespeare's Hamlet by 48 portrayals to claim the record.
> (see "Sherlock Holmes Awarded Title", 2012)

The 254 film and television paratexts derived from Conan Doyle's urtext
of 56 short stories and 4 novels constitute a mere fraction of the mas-
sive Sherlockian paratextual surround that, in addition to the screen
adaptations, includes profic and fanfic, video games and mobile apps,
museums and pubs, and much, much more.[1] This paratextual proliferation makes Holmes an ideal case study for addressing what the
editor, in his proposal for this volume, refers to as "the prominent
position of...media paratexts". This chapter first discusses what I term
the "Holmes franchise" and some of its myriad paratexts. In his proposal, the editor also speaks of "the related cultural practices that add to
and expand the narrative worlds with which fans engage". The chapter
follows on from discussing the franchise by addressing cultural practices, specifically that of copyright, the legal assertion of authorship by
writers and their heirs. I discuss a case that was recently ruled upon
in the US federal courts that may have profound implications for the
Holmes franchise as well as for other derivative works related to serial
characters.

The Sherlock Holmes franchise

Does it make sense to refer to a Sherlock Holmes franchise? Most scholars agree that the contemporary media franchise emerged in the New Hollywood of the 1980s as studios sought to minimise risk and maximise profits by dispersing their intellectual property (IP) across multiple platforms.[2] Indeed, Henry Jenkins defines franchising as the "coordinated effort to brand and market fictional content within the context of media conglomeration"; this leads to a "more integrated approach to franchise development" (Jenkins, 2006: 326, 334). Hence it might not make sense to speak of a Holmes franchise because there is no central corporate holder of the IP and no integrated approach to branding and marketing. However, as Derek Johnson says, the term "franchise" has become "cultural shorthand for understanding the expansion of cultural production across different media and industry sectors" (2013: 27). Hence it might make sense to speak of a Holmes franchise, as does indeed Robert Doherty, executive producer of the US television adaptation *Elementary* (2012 – present): "I've seen Sherlock in other novels, in comic books, in television shows, in movies, in TV movies. Some are better than others, but nobody has managed to ruin the franchise" (cited in Memmott, 2012). Sherlockian paratexts resemble those that have been generated by media franchises such as *Star Trek* and *The Lord of the Rings*. They appear in different media and across different industry sectors, they target both general and niche audiences and various age cohorts, and they have a large and active fan base.

Accepting Johnson's cultural shorthand understanding, we can distinguish between three types of franchise or mode of paratextual proliferation differentiated by ownership of IP:

- Corporate author: The urtext originated within a corporation, which may subsequently have become part of a media conglomerate. For example, Batman first appeared in *Detective Comics* copyrighted by DC Comics. As a result of corporate mergers, Time Warner now holds the rights to the character and coordinates its dispersion across media platforms.
- Individual author: The urtext was copyrighted by an author who licenses another party to produce derivative works. For example, Warner Bros acquired the rights to film the Harry Potter books from J.K. Rowling. In the case of a deceased author, the heirs may grant the rights. The Conan Doyle Estate licensed Warner Bros to film

the Holmes stories. The corporation rather than the author or heirs coordinates the dispersion of the subsequent derivative works across media platforms.

- Public domain: The urtext originated before IP laws – for example, Shakespeare, Robin Hood – or has entered the public domain, as 87% of the Sherlockian urtext has now as a result of the legal case mentioned above. There is no coordinated dispersion across media platforms for all paratexts, although such coordinated dispersion can occur for paratexts that are related to copyrighted derivative works, such as a Sherlock Holmes film or television series.

Paratexts proliferate in all three cases, but the IP status of the urtext may determine the nature of that proliferation. Writing in 2007, I argued:

> Fully kitted-out, narrativized virtual worlds such as *Star Trek, The Lord of the Rings,* and Sherlock Holmes seem to produce the widest range of commodities, but there's a distinction even here between copyrights vested in a single media franchise and those not; as a result, the first two examples give rise to more centralized production of commodities than the third.
>
> (Pearson, 2007: 105)

Writing in 2012, Matt Hills expanded on this point:

> Working very differently, the likes of Sherlock might be thought of as de facto transmedia where there is no guiding (corporate) hand compelling any unity across media and across narrative iterations, precisely because there is no singular franchise, but rather a network of intertextualities – some disavowed, others privileged – which contingently coalesce into the reinventions and extensions of cultural myth.... Textual pathways through de facto transmedia are far more plural and decentered than the possibilities offered by de jure transmedia, with its legally- bound authenticities of rights-owning franchise maintenance.
>
> (Hills, 2012: 38)

A full exploration of the *de jure* (controlling rights holder) versus the *de facto* (no controlling rights holder) transmedia proliferation of paratexts would require a book. However, as an indication of these complexities, I briefly consider

- how the Holmes franchise differs from most *de jure* franchises by looking at the most high-profile current instantiations of the Holmes urtext;
- how the Holmes franchise resembles a *de jure* franchise by looking at the range of professionally produced printed paratexts.

Three recent screen adaptations have enjoyed great success at the box office, in the ratings and in social media buzz. The Warner Bros film *Sherlock Holmes*, directed by Guy Ritchie and starring Robert Downey and Jude Law, premiered in 2009 with the sequel, *A Game of Shadows*, appearing in 2011 and the third instalment in the series due soon. The BBC television series *Sherlock*, created by Steven Moffat and Mark Gatiss and starring Benedict Cumberbatch and Martin Freeman, premiered in 2010, and the CBS television series, *Elementary*, created by Rob Doherty and starring Jonny Lee Miller and Lucy Liu, launched in 2012. While the former has been more lauded by fans and reviewers, both have achieved critical and commercial success and both are, at the time of writing, approaching their fourth series. The Hollywood blockbuster films, UK public service television programme and US commercial television programme all adapt the character to their specific needs, resulting in distinctive interpretations of the urtext. All three update the character to some extent: the film series turns him into an action hero suited to a big screen spectacular, *Sherlock* transports him to 21st-century London, and *Elementary* moves him to 21st-century New York City, while also transforming Watson into a woman.[3] *Sherlock* showrunner Steven Moffat said of *Elementary*: "They've got three big changes: it's Sherlock Holmes in America, it's Sherlock Holmes updated and it's Sherlock Holmes with a female Watson. I wonder if he's Sherlock Holmes in any sense other than he's called Sherlock Holmes?" (cited in Jeffery, 2012).

The central characters in all three adaptations share the name of Sherlock Holmes but differ significantly from each other and from the urtext. This degree of divergence is relatively uncommon when a *de jure* franchise exercises coordinated control of branding and marketing. For example, as a result of a complicated corporate restructuring of Paramount Viacom in late 2005, two previous divisions of the mega media conglomerate split the *Star Trek* rights between them, with Paramount Pictures holding the rights to *Star Trek* cinema and CBS those to *Star Trek* television. However, since Paramount Pictures and CBS continue to coordinate the exploitation of the *Star Trek* IP, it is unlikely that a new *Star Trek* television series, particularly one featuring the characters from the original television show, will emerge while the rebooted film series featuring those same characters remains in production (see Pearson and Messenger Davies, 2014). When it comes to their copyrighted characters, concern for the bottom line causes corporations to err on the safe side of the balance between standardisation and differentiation.[4]

Radical character divergence also occurs among professionally produced printed Sherlockian paratexts, with those that are aimed at the long-established Sherlockian fan market generally adhering more closely to the urtext than those that are aimed at a more general market. However, this very targeting of a range of consumers, from casual readers to hard-core fans, resembles a *de jure* franchise's paratextual circulation, although Sherlockian paratexts may cross cultural hierarchies and audience segments to a greater extent. At the top of the cultural hierarchy are two novels that are aimed at a general readership, both featuring an elderly (and in one case unnamed) Holmes in retirement. Mitch Cullin's *A Slight Trick of the Mind* (2006) has front-of-book blurbs from the *New York Times*, the *Chicago Tribune*, *Newsday*, the *Boston Globe* and the *Christian Science Monitor* among others (a film based on the novel, directed by Bill Condon and starring Sir Ian McKellan, will be released in 2015). Amazon describes the book as "A novel of exceptional grace and literary sensitivity, *A Slight Trick of the Mind* is a brilliant imagining of our greatest fictional detective and a stunning inquiry into the mysteries of human connection" ("*A Slight Trick of the Mind*", n.d.). Michael Chabon's *The Final Solution* (2006) has cover blurbs from the *New York Times*, the *Washington Post* and *New York* magazine. The paperback edition front material says: "This brilliant homage, which won the 2004 Aga Khan Prize for fiction, is the work of a master storyteller at the height of his powers." The books' paratexts disassociate them from the popular mystery genre by stressing their status as serious literary novels that are penned by accomplished authors. By contrast, Lyndsey Faye's *Dust and Shadow*, issued by publishing giant Simon and Schuster and also aimed at a general audience, is explicitly linked both with Holmes and with the mystery genre. The subtitle, "An account of the Ripper Killings by Dr. John H. Watson", accords with the Sherlockian conceit that Watson, rather than Conan Doyle, actually wrote the Holmes tales. The cover blurb by author Caleb Carr refers to the author's "thorough, enthusiastic knowledge of the Sherlock Holmes canon". Carr is a well-known writer of 19th-century historical mysteries as well as of the Holmes pastiche novel *The Italian Secretary*, so his endorsement serves to widen the book's appeal beyond Sherlockian fandom to a more general, but undoubtedly overlapping, audience of readers of historical mysteries.

Holmes paratexts also target younger audiences. For example, Andrew Lane's young adult series features a teenage Holmes fighting crime in the 1860s. In 2010 the comics publisher Boom!Studios issued a four-part Muppet Sherlock Holmes series that was written by Patrick Storck, each title reworking a Conan Doyle story, with Gonzo as Holmes, Fozzie Bear as Dr Watson and Miss Piggy as Irene Adler and other female characters. Well-known comics writer Ian Edginton penned versions of *A Study in Scarlet* and *The Hound of the Baskervilles* for comics publisher Sterling as well as the steam-punk *The Victorian Undead* for DC, in which Holmes and Watson fight zombies. While the readership of comics and graphic novels extends beyond children and young adults, this audience segment probably skews younger than the readership for the high-end "literary" novels and perhaps for *Dust and Shadow* as well.

Fans may consume some or all of the above depending on their degree of enthusiasm, but there are also publishers that are dedicated in part or in whole to Sherlockian imprints that are targeted specifically at the fan community. Among the former are an important player within several fan communities, Titan Books, which has been republishing old Sherlockian pastiches (the Sherlockian term for professionally produced fanfic) and commissioning new ones, and MX Publishers, which in addition to publishing materials about coaching and therapy includes Sherlockian texts in its series on Victorian history and literature. Wessex Press, through its Gasogene Books imprint, is almost entirely dedicated to publishing Sherlockian materials. Its homepage describes the press as the "premiere publisher of books about Sherlock Holmes and his world", with books suitable for both "seasoned Sherlockians" and those who've "just discovered the Great Detective" (Review, n.d.).

The franchise business model seeks to minimise risk and maximise profits through market saturation that is achieved by dispersing its core IP across multiple platforms and targeting different audience segments. This brief look at the circulation of printed paratexts has demonstrated that the *de facto* Holmes franchise perhaps more successfully exploits the business model than some *de jure* franchises, but, as noted above, does so in the absence of centrally held IP. In *de jure* franchises the holder of the IP constructs an intertextual network that is held together by storyworld or brand, and encourages consumers to move through that network in what Jenkins refers to as "the migratory behavior of media audiences" (Jenkins, 2006: 2). This migratory behaviour undoubtedly takes place within the *de facto* Holmes franchise; keen newbies who have just discovered the Great Detective through a high-profile instantiation such as *Sherlock* may eventually wend their way through the intertextual network of paratexts to the Wessex Press website. However, it's not the owners of the Holmes character but Holmes himself, or rather a common cultural understanding and recognition of the Holmes character, who encourages the migration. Like some other literary characters, such as Dracula and James Bond, Holmes has escaped from his originating author and urtext. Michael Saler tells us that at the turn of the 20th century, "The economic logic of mass-production created a situation in which fictional characters began to overshadow their corporeal authors, as publishers increasingly promoted lucrative, brand name characters whose public visibility overshadowed that of their authors" (Saler, 2012: 47). Holmes was among the foremost of those lucrative brandname characters at the time and is one of the few who has maintained a high-profile brand at the turn of the 21st century. Today, as Benjamin Poore puts it, "The iconography of the Sherlock Holmes industry – erroneous deerstalker, calabash pipe, and all – is the language that is understood worldwide, not Conan Doyle's words" (Poore, 2013: 160). Sometimes not even the iconography is necessary; recall Stephen Moffat's questioning whether the lead character in *Elementary* is Sherlock Holmes in anything but name. The most basic signifiers of the Holmes character can serve to link paratexts into the Holmes franchise's intertextual network; it's not the hand of a corporate rights holder but the hand and sometimes just the name of the globally recognised cultural icon that points audiences from paratext to paratext and across media platforms.

In discussing transmedia storytelling, Jenkins says that narrative is not only the "transmedia logic... shaping the contemporary entertainment realm. We might identify a range of others – including branding, spectacle, performance, games, perhaps others...." (Jenkins, 2009). I would add character and author to the list, although both could be seen as elements of branding. The Holmes franchise's intertextual network privileges character logic over author logic, but some franchise paratexts, or at least their surrounding discourses, do foreground Conan Doyle in conformance with what Foucault terms the "author function". According to Foucault, an author's name "is functional in that it serves as a means of classification. A name can group together a number of texts and thus differentiate them from others" (Foucault, 1977: 123). Perhaps seeking to differentiate his own paratext from an increasingly crowded field, the *Sherlock* showrunner frequently invokes Conan Doyle. Responding to the news that the first episode of series three had attracted almost 10 million viewers, Steven Moffat said that the ratings were "A tribute to the team who work so hard, and with such pride, on the show, and of course to the genius of Sir Arthur Conan Doyle" (cited in Westbrooke, 2014). From the outset, both Moffat and writer/actor Mark Gatiss repeatedly stressed their shared Sherlockian fandom and their respect for Conan Doyle. For example, a BBC press release at the time of the series premiere quoted Moffat: "On our many train journeys from London to Cardiff, we talked about our love for Sherlock Holmes, how brilliantly modern Arthur Conan Doyle's writing was and how someone should do a contemporary version." Gatiss said: "Arthur Conan Doyle was a writer of genius and it's worth trumpeting that point... His short stories, particularly, are thrilling, funny, lurid, silly, strange, wonderful pieces of exciting adventure..." (Press Release, 2010). Moffat and Gatiss may cite Conan Doyle's authorial authority to mark out their programme from the competition, but the Conan Doyle Estate represents itself as the primary enactor of the classification of which Foucault speaks: it differentiates Sherlockian paratexts through both licensing and endorsement.

The Conan Doyle Estate, copyright and the author function

Subsequent to Conan Doyle's death in 1930, the Holmes copyright has had a long and complicated history, involving disputes among the author's descendants as well as a rival claimant whom the courts have repeatedly rebuffed (see Itzkoff, 2010). Holmes entered the public domain in the UK when the last copyright on Conan Doyle's work expired in 1980. However, the character still remains under copyright in the US where the 1976 Copyright Act allowed Dame Jean Conan Doyle, the author's last surviving child, to recapture the rights to Holmes stories that had previously entered the public domain in that country. Taking advantage of this opportunity, Dame Jean and her legal advisors established the estate in 1981; subsequent to Dame Jean's death in 1997, control of the estate passed to nine indirect descendants of the author. A year after Dame Jean's death, the US Copyright Term Extension Act of 1998 extended copyright for individually authored works that were published prior to 1 January 1978 by 20 years to a total of 95 years from their publication. As a result, the estate's copyright on the last ten Sherlock Holmes stories expires in January 2023. As discussed below, the estate has contended that holding the copyright for these ten stories equates to holding the copyright for the Holmes character. Those holding the US copyright exercise control over the global circulation of Sherlockian paratexts, which must comply with US IP laws to enter that country. No producer of Sherlockian texts wishes to be debarred from the large and lucrative US market, so, until recently, there has been a strong incentive for producers based both in the USA and overseas to comply with the estate's demands for licence fees. The estate licensed all three current high-profile screen incarnations of the great detective, *Sherlock*, *Elementary* and the Warner Bros films.

The estate's website says that "we manage the literary, merchandising, and advertising rights in Sir Arthur Conan Doyle's works and characters, including Sherlock Holmes, Dr Watson, Professor Challenger, and many others". This management has consisted primarily of demanding licence fees for derivative works based upon the Holmes and Watson characters but has sometimes extended to endorsing particular paratexts. The website continues: "we can arrange to provide our unique trademark and seal of approval for contemporary projects" (ConandoyleEstate, n.d). The estate has commissioned two authors to produce new Sherlock Holmes stories. Anthony Horowitz's *House of Silk* (2011) bears on its cover the estate's logo, a white silhouette of Holmes' profile tellingly superimposed upon and partially obscuring a black silhouette of Conan Doyle's profile, both profiles within a circle with the words "Sherlock Holmes" at the top and "Conan Doyle Estate Ltd." at the bottom. *The Guardian*'s reviewer reported that

> *The House of Silk* is in a class of its own: Horowitz's novel is the first Sherlock Holmes addition to have been written with the endorsement of the Conan Doyle Estate. It is not a pastiche. It is not an update. It is, as its cover proudly declares, "the new Sherlock Holmes novel". Horowitz is the anointed successor.
>
> (Sansom, 2011)

The field of contemporary Sherlockian pastiches is a crowded one – Titan Books alone offers 27 new Holmes novels and short story collections, with more on the way. However, the estate's endorsement marked *House of Silk* out from the field, garnering it not only *The Guardian* review but much more widespread publicity than pastiches, usually aimed primarily at the fan market, warrant. Clearly the estate's unique trademark and seal of approval has value, differentiating the *House of Silk* from the competition and making its publication a notable event. A *New York Times* editorial, however, questioned the actual literary value of the estate's endorsement: "there is no reason why an 'official' 21st-century Holmes story will be any better or more authentic – whatever that means in this case – than an 'unofficial' one". But an "unofficial" story almost certainly wouldn't have warranted a *New York Times* editorial, while the "official" one did. This was a paradoxical confirmation of the estate's enactment of the author function (Editorial, 2011).

The estate also commissioned Andrew Lane to write a series of young adult novels, Young Sherlock Holmes, mentioned above, which, says the website, stay "true to the stories written by Sir Arthur Conan Doyle". Tellingly, the estate's website reveals the motivation behind the series' origin: "In 2010, during a critical time in the history of Sherlock Holmes copyright, Conan Doyle Estate felt the time was right for a series that could be given unique authorisation from the Conan Doyle family" (ConandoyleEstate, n.d.). That critical time resulted from yet more squabbling among Conan Doyle's descendants, but 2013 was to be an even more critical time in the history of the Sherlock Holmes copyright. In that year, eminent Sherlockian scholar and editor Leslie Klinger filed a successful legal action against the estate in the US federal courts that resulted in all but those last ten Sherlock Holmes stories, still protected by the 1998 copyright extension, entering the public domain. This, in effect, meant that Sherlock Holmes himself, or most of him, entered the public domain, subject to free appropriation by anyone who wished to produce a derivative work for fun or for profit.

The case and its outcome attracted worldwide press coverage, from the USA, to the UK, China and India, attesting not only to Holmes's status as a global cultural icon but also to the increasing salience of IP laws in a networked society. The *New York Times* spoke to this latter point three years prior to Klinger's complaint in an editorial linking the 2010 dispute among Conan Doyle's descendants to Congress's tendency to repeatedly extend copyright protection: "The law gives an author and the author's descendants more than adequate control over creative work – a minimum of the author's life plus 70 years. The public is better served if copyrights have a reasonable limit. Sherlock Holmes should belong to us all right now" (Editorial, 2010). In saying that copyright limits best serve the public, the *New York Times* implicitly acknowledged the ongoing debate about copyright extension that began with the 1998 legislation. Copyright protection, together with the financial benefits that are derived from it, was initially meant to stimulate creativity, but repeated extensions of this protection, some would say, have had precisely the opposite effect, cutting off a society's store of ideas from those who would make creative use of them. Scholars such as Yochai Benkler (2006) and Jenkins et al. (2013) argue for a reconsideration of IP laws, believing that the heavy hand of copyright impedes the collaborative production and "spreadability" that are engendered by a networked society. For example, Benkler says that "What characterizes the networked information economy is that decentralized individual action – specifically, new and important cooperative and coordinate action carried out through radically distributed, nonmarket mechanisms that do not depend on proprietary strategies – plays a much greater role than it did, or could have, in the industrial information economy" (Benkler, 2006: 3). Benkler asserts that while those within the legal profession may cling to the proprietary strategies of IP laws that are appropriate to the older economic order, these very strategies impede the new and emerging economic order of the information age.

The ruling in *Leslie S. Klinger vs. Conan Doyle Estate* means that Sherlock Holmes, or 87% of him, now belongs to us all. Given the current salience of IP laws, the case's outcome has implications for debates about the extent and extension of copyright law and the resultant shrinking of the public domain, but these are outside the scope of this chapter. It also has implications for the copyright status of fictional characters, as briefly discussed in this chapter's conclusion. The case obviously has specific implications for the Holmes' franchise, rendering it ever more *de facto* than *de jure*, but the impact of this upon the production and circulation of Sherlockian paratexts will only become apparent over time. The estate may well continue to influence production and circulation, still enacting the author function through its endorsement of selected paratexts. Said one of the estate's press releases on the legal dispute: "The Doyle family intends to continue to foster creative new uses of the characters by others, as recent television and motion picture series, novels, and other programs demonstrate" (cited in Allison, 2014). Andrew Albanese, a writer for *Publishers Weekly*, argues that since the estate had never actually sued anyone for infringement, the licence fee itself was merely a version of an endorsement. The estate "tried to just get people to enter licensing agreements that would sanction their products. Whether Sherlock Holmes is under copyright or not, you can still offer value in being an official Sherlock Holmes product, something that is blessed by the Conan Doyle Estate" ("Sherlock Holmes, RIP", 2013). Certainly the majority response to *The House of Silk* would seem to confirm this. The estate also claims to have IP rights other than copyright in the form of the "United States trademark and common law rights in the name and image of Sherlock Holmes and other of Sir Arthur's characters". Trademark can be a very powerful protector of fictional characters and, unlike copyright, does not expire. But here, too, according to Klinger, the estate may face legal challenges to its ostensible IP (Klinger in Kleffel, 2013).

Rather than speculate about the future, however, the rest of this chapter briefly examines the documents in the case, outlining the arguments of the plaintiff, Klinger, and the defendant, the estate. Jonathan Kirsch, the lawyer representing Klinger, said: "Everyone is making the decision to pay for permission they don't need to avoid the costs and risks of litigation" (cited in Schuessler, 2013). It's simpler for a large and affluent media corporation to pay a relatively trivial amount for permission than it is for it to pay its very expensive lawyers to contest the estate's demand for a licence fee, with all of the attendant risks and delays of a legal proceeding. In fact, Random House did just that when publishing Klinger's edited collection of new Sherlock Holmes stories, *A Study in Sherlock*, in 2011. Klinger reported: "We told them no way, don't give them a nickel. Random House basically told us, 'it costs more to engage our lawyers [than] to pay the $5,000 license fee'" (cited in Suddath, 2013). Klinger asserts that Random House paid the fee "without conceding the legal or factual merits of the position asserted by [the estate] ... and for avoidance of litigation only" (*Leslie S. Klinger vs. Conan Doyle Estate*, 2013a: 14).

However, when Klinger wished to publish a sequel called *In the Company of Sherlock Holmes* with Pegasus Books, his new publishers took a different stance. The estate's US agent contacted them demanding a licence fee "under the implied threat of an infringement action" (*Leslie S. Klinger vs. Conan Doyle Estate*, 2013a: 12). Pegasus replied that there was no infringement because the new stories would use only "such character and story elements ... that have already passed into the public domain" and not characters and story elements from the ten stories still under copyright (*Leslie S. Klinger vs. Conan Doyle Estate*, 2013a: 12). The estate's US agent replied that there would be dire consequences if Pegasus refused to comply with the estate's demand:

If you proceed ... to bring out [the book] unlicensed, do not expect to see it offered for sale by Amazon, Barnes & Noble, and similar retailers. We work with those companies routinely to weed out unlicensed uses of Sherlock Holmes from their offerings, and will not hesitate to do so with your book as well.

(*Leslie S. Klinger vs. Conan Doyle Estate*, 2013a: 13)

Pegasus then told Klinger that it would publish the book only if he was "successful in adjudicating the public domain status of the Sherlock Holmes Story Elements" (*Leslie S. Klinger vs. Conan Doyle Estate*,

2013a: 14). Klinger filed a complaint against the estate, stating on his website Free Sherlock:

> This isn't the first time the Estate has put pressure on creators... It is the first time anyone has stood up to them. In the past, many simply couldn't afford to fight or to wait for approval, and have given in and paid off the Estate for "permission". I'm asking the Court to put a permanent stop to this kind of bullying. Holmes and Watson belong to the world, not to some distant relatives of Arthur Conan Doyle.
>
> (Free Sherlock, 2013)

Klinger argued that Holmes and Watson belong to the world because "the characteristics that people associate with Sherlock Holmes can all be found in the public domain stories. Arthur Conan Doyle didn't really add much to the character in terms of new attributes over the years since *A Study in Scarlet*" (cited in Kleffel, 2013). Since Holmes was fully developed in the stories written prior to 1923 – that is, those stories that are now in the public domain – any representation of the character that doesn't draw upon elements introduced in the still protected stories does not violate copyright, Klinger asserted. His complaint stated that "any member of the public, including Plaintiff, has the right in the United States to copy the expression embodied in these public domain works, and to create and exploit derivative works based on these public domain works, without infringing any right of Defendant [the estate] under copyright" (*Leslie S. Klinger vs. Conan Doyle Estate*, 2013a: 15). Klinger's argument drew on existing legal opinion and case law on copyright and fictional characters. For example, the Memorandum of Law supporting his complaint quotes the "leading copyright treatise", *Nimmer on Copyright*, regarding the protection of serial characters:

> What of the situation where an author has used the same character in a series of works, some of which works subsequently enter the public domain, while others remain protected by copyright? Clearly anyone may copy such elements as have entered the public domain, and no one may copy such elements as remain protected by copyright.
>
> (cited in *Leslie S. Klinger vs. Conan Doyle Estate*, 2013b: 6)

Klinger's "Sherlock Holmes Story Elements", a list of the key characters, their attributes and the particular stories in which each was mentioned, distinguishes between public domain and copyrighted elements. Holmes' birthdate, family background, lodgings in Baker Street, retirement, bohemian nature, erratic eating habits, schooling, smoking, patriotism, drug use and many other key attributes including his physical appearance are all established in the public domain stories, even if subsequently referred to in the still copyrighted stories. Only one of landlady Mrs Hudson's dozens of appearances takes place in a copyrighted story. However, Watson's second wife is mentioned only in copyrighted stories, so her inclusion in a derivative work requires the estate's permission until 2023 (see Exhibit A, n.d.).

The estate argued that the existing legal opinion and case law concerning copyright and serial characters don't apply to Holmes since, contra Klinger, the character was continually developed from the first story to the last and cannot be disaggregated into public domain and copyrighted elements. Therefore the character should enjoy full protection until the copyright on the last stories lapses in 2023. As Benjamin Allison, one of the estate's lawyers, put it, "Holmes is a unified literary character that wasn't completely developed until the author laid down his pen" (cited in Schuessler, 2013). The estate's response to Klinger states:

> Although Holmes and Watson were introduced in ... *A Study in Scarlet*, the characters were not fully created or disclosed in that novel. Sir Arthur continued to create Holmes's and Watson's characters throughout the Canon [Sherlockians' term for the complete works], adding attributes, dimensions, background, and both positive and negative changes in the characters until the last story.
>
> (cited in *Leslie S. Klinger vs. Conan Doyle Estate*, 2013c: 4)

Klinger, the estate says, denies the narrative significance of the developments in the copyrighted stories. For example, Watson's second marriage had consequences not only for his relationship with Holmes but also for Watson himself.

To differentiate Holmes from other serial characters, the estate called upon the opinions of two literary experts: Larry Woiwode, who has published numerous books and short stories, and served as Writer in Residence at the University of Wisconsin and Director of Creative Writing at the State University of New York, Binghamton, and novelist Valerie Sayers, Chair of the English Department at the University of Notre Dame and winner of the Pushcart Prize for Fiction. Both invoked the distinction in narrative theory between flat and rounded characters and asserted that while the former remain forever the same, the latter change over the course of a novel or series of related literary works.

In his affidavit, Woiwode quoted *The Harper Handbook of Literature* to the effect that a flat character "is two-dimensional, without the depth and complexity of a living person; the opposite of a *round character*". Crucially, said Woiwode, "Flat characters do not continue to change in each new story; they merely find themselves in different scenarios bringing about changes in dialogue, not character" (*Leslie S. Klinger vs. Conan Doyle Estate*, 2013d: 3–4). Sayers said that in works of "popular entertainment", characters "do not alter dramatically", which confirms readers' expectations, whereas in "literary fiction... characters continue to develop, thereby frequently upsetting or surprising a reader's expectations" (*Leslie S. Klinger vs. Conan Doyle Estate*, 2013e: 3). Woiwode acknowledged that Holmes is indeed a serial character, but argued that he is more akin to the rounded and developing characters in the serial novels of Updike, Faulkner, Roth and Cheever than he is to the flat and stable characters of Amos and Andy, the US radio characters that gave rise to some of the existing case law upon which Klinger bases his argument. Says Woiwode: "So many instances of rounded dimensional characters created progressively in continuing books and stories are present in so much of the best in American fiction..." (*Leslie S. Klinger vs. Conan Doyle Estate*, 2013d: 6). Sayers also equates the Canon with the "best" fiction, saying that her colleagues have frequently included Holmes novels and stories in their courses, exploring them as "rich literary texts open to multiple critical approaches and techniques" (*Leslie S. Klinger vs. Conan Doyle Estate*, 2013e: 2).

The estate's distinction between flat and round characters, and the testimony of its expert witnesses, valorised proponents of serious, literary fiction, somewhat disingenuously seek to elevate Holmes from popular to high culture, but the character's origins lie firmly within the former. Conan Doyle's first Holmes story, *A Study in Scarlet*, had been rejected by several publishers before the author decided to send it to Ward, Lock & Co., which he knew "made a specialty of cheap and often sensational literature...". The editor replied that he couldn't publish the story immediately as the market was "flooded at present with cheap fiction", but the novel did eventually appear in *Beeton's Christmas Annual* in 1887 (cited in "The Truth about Sherlock Holmes", 2012). Both Conan Doyle and his publisher judged the first Holmes adventure as cheap and sensational fiction, in the same category as the sensation novels of Wilkie Collins, Mary Elizabeth Braddon and Charles Reader, all of which were popular entertainments for the rapidly expanding audience of the literate middle classes. *The Strand Magazine*, in which Conan Doyle and Holmes achieved lasting success, was aimed at a similar audience; according to Christopher Pittard, *The Strand*'s clientele were educated, male, middle-class commuters who bought the magazine at railway newsstands (Pittard, 2010: 109).

In 1891, by which time Holmes stories were appearing regularly in *The Strand*, Conan Doyle wrote to his mother that his detective was taking his "mind from better things", those being his "historical dramas and military adventures" (cited in Pittard, 2007: 13). In 1893, Conan Doyle killed Holmes in "The Final Problem", yielding to his desire to give up the cheap and sensational literature that earned him a very good living in favour of those better things. But public and financial pressures caused the author to reboot his detective in *The Hound of the Baskervilles*, which was published serially in *The Strand* in 1901 and 1902. Conan Doyle resurrected Holmes but never reconciled with him, writing rather bitterly that "I believe that if I had never touched Holmes, my position in literature would at present be a more commanding one" (cited in "The Truth about Sherlock Holmes", 2012). Conan Doyle wrote the stories as if churning out ephemeral fiction that was valuable primarily for paying the bills, not as if crafting great literature for posterity. There are few indications in the stories of a concerted effort to continually develop and nuance the characters, and considerable indications of the relative indifference to character continuity: the location of Watson's wound (shoulder or leg), the number of his wives (anywhere from two to five), his first name (John or James) and numerous other examples. In other words, contra the estate's assertion that Holmes and Watson are unified literary characters that were not completed until Conan Doyle put down his pen, the author was frequently making it up as he went along without much concern for continuity or development.

The court rejected the estate's argument but dubbed it "novel", a word, says Klinger, that is "often used in legal circles to indicate that an argument is imaginative but unsupportable in the law" (News Release, 2014). As I have argued above, it's also unsupported by the extratextual and textual evidence. Nonetheless, in January 2014 the estate filed an appeal with the Seventh Circuit Court of Appeals against the lower court's ruling, its press release stating that "This important decision is likely to affect copyright protection for many other longstanding series characters" (cited in Allison, 2014). The estate implied that upholding the lower court's decision would result in many series characters suddenly entering the public domain, implicitly viewing this as a bad thing. By contrast, lawyer Mike Masnik, writing on the Techdirt blog, pointed out that the court's ruling in favour of the estate would be a bad thing because it would create perpetual copyright. If the estate is right in arguing that "at any given point in their fictional lives, the characters depend on copyrighted character development" then, "so long as you never 'complete' the character creation, they can never go into the public domain". Says Masnick:

> it basically presents a way to make copyright on characters perpetual. You just need to have someone continue to release new works that have some minor change to the character, and they get to pretend you have a new starting point for the public domain ticker. That can't be what the law intended.
>
> (Masnick, 2013)

In fact, the appeals court decided that it was indeed not what the law intended, both upholding the lower court's rejection of the estate's argument and requiring it to pay Klinger's legal fees, in yet another vindication of the plaintiff's action against the estate's copyright claims. The case has been hailed as a victory for the principle of the public domain, which permits the unrestricted production of derivative works based on properties that are no longer under copyright. Alyssa Rosenberg, blogger for *The Washington Post*, contrasted the multiple iterations of Holmes with those of the characters owned by corporate authors:

> The long-running "House," whose painkiller-addicted main character owes a heavy debt to the famous sleuth and his cocaine dependency, focused on the relationship between brilliance and substance abuse. Robert Downey Jr.'s turn as Holmes in Guy Ritchie's films gave the detective a more active relish for the London underworld, with the addition of a talent for bareknuckle boxing. And "Sherlock," a co-production of the BBC and Boston's WGBH public television station, explores the intimacy of friendship between men with a tenderness and emotional intelligence that is rare in popular culture.
>
> (Rosenberg, 2014)

But, says Rosenberg, Spider-Man's reoccurences exhibit a depressing similarity – Sony must repeatedly trot out the same version of the character in order to retain the copyright, which would otherwise revert to Marvel Studios. To use the terms that I set out at this chapter's beginning, Holmes is a *de facto* franchise with no central rights holder, while Spider-Man is a corporate franchise with a central rights holder. Rosenberg is suggesting that while a *de jure* franchise might produce the better corporate balance sheet, a *de facto* franchise might produce better content, with the collective intelligence of the public domain trumping the corporate intelligence of IP. From that perspective, the Klinger case has implications not only for the Holmes franchise but for arguments such as those made by Benkler (2006) against the stranglehold of IP laws.

Notes

1. For a survey of recent Holmes adaptations across media, see Porter (2012).
2. See, for example, Thompson (2007), Johnson (2013) and Meehan (2008).
3. In a recent essay I attribute the differences between *Sherlock* and *Elementary* to the roles that they play in their respective national broadcasting contexts. See Pearson (2015).
4. There are exceptions that prove the rule. Warner Bros has licensed Fox to produce the Batman-prequel television programme, *Gotham* (2014 – present) but made it clear that the show's continuity will not affect that of the ongoing feature film series.

References

Allison, B. (2014), "Conan Doyle Estate Appeals Sherlock Holmes Copyright Decision." Available 10 February 2015 from http://www.conandoyleestate.co.uk/index.php/category/arthur-conan-doyle-news/.

"*A Slight Trick of the Mind.*" (n.d.). Available 10 February 2015 from http://www.amazon.co.uk/Slight-Trick-Mind-Mitch-Cullin/dp/1400078229/ref=sr_1_1?ie=UTF8&qid=1385997235&sr=8-1&keywords=a+slight+trick+of+the+mind.

Benkler, Y. (2006), *The Wealth of Networks: How Social Production Transforms Markets and Freedom.* New Haven, CT: Yale University Press.

Editorial. (2010), *New York Times.* Available 10 February 2015 from http://www.nytimes.com/2010/01/24/opinion/24sun4.html?_r=1&.

Editorial. (2011), *New York Times.* Available 10 February 2015 from http://www.nytimes.com/2011/01/28/opinion/28fri4.html.

Exhibit A. (n.d.), Sherlock Holmes Story Elements, Klinger v. Conan Doyle, Complaint.

Foucault, M. (1977), "What Is an Author?" In D.F. Bouchard, ed., *Language, Counter-Memory, Practice: Selected Essays and Interviews.* Ithaca: Cornell, pp. 113–138.

"Free Sherlock". (2013), Available 10 February 2015 from www.Free-sherlock.com.

Hills, M. (2012), "*Sherlock*'s Epistemological Economy and the Value of 'Fan' Knowledge: How Producer-Fans Play the (Great) Game of Fandom." In L.E. Stein and K. Busse, eds., *Sherlock and Transmedia Fandom: Essays on the BBC Series.* Jefferson, NC: McFarland & Company, Inc., pp. 27–40.

Itzkoff, D. (2010), "For the Heirs to Holmes, a Tangled Web." *New York Times.* Available 10 February 2015 from http://www.nytimes.com/2010/01/19/books/19sherlock.html?pagewanted=all&_r=0.

Jeffery, M. (2012), "Steven Moffat on *Elementary*: 'CBS have Change Sherlock too Much'." *Digitalspy.co.uk*. Available 10 February 2015 from http://www .digitalspy.co.uk/ustv/news/a381974/steven-moffat-on-elementary-cbs-have -changed-sherlock-too-much.html.

Jenkins, H. (2006), *Convergence Culture: Where Old and New Media Collide*. New York: New York University Press.

Jenkins, H. (2009), "The Revenge of the Origami Unicorn: Seven Principles of Transmedia Storytelling." *Convergenceculture.org*. Available 10 February 2015 from http://www.convergenceculture.org/weblog/2009/12/the_revenge _of_the_origami_uni.php.

Jenkins, H., Ford, S., and Green, J. (2013), *Spreadable Media: Creating Value and Meaning in a Networked Culture*. New York: New York University Press.

Johnson, D. (2013), *Media Franchising: Creative License and Collaboration in the Culture Industries*. New York: New York University Press.

Kleffel, R. (2013), The Agony Column: A 2013 Interview with Leslie Klinger. Available 10 February 2015 from http://bookotron.com/agony/news/2013/ 02-18-13-podcast.htm#podcast022113.

Kleffel, R. (2013b). Memorandum of Law in Support of Plantiff's Motion for Summary Judgment Pursuant to FRCP, United States District Court for the Northern District of Illinois, Eastern Division, July.

Kleffel, R. (2013c). Conan Doyle's Response in Opposition to Plantiff's Motion for Summary Judgment Pursuant to FRCP56, United States District Court for the Northern District of Illinois, Eastern Division, 9 October.

Kleffel, R. (2013d). Affidavit of Larry Woiwode, United States District Court for the Northern District of Illinois, Eastern Division, 10 October.

Kleffel, R. (2013e). Affidavit of Valerie Sayers, United States District Court for the Northern District of Illinois, Eastern Division, 10 October.

Leslie S. Klinger v. Conan Doyle Estate, Ltd. (2013a). Complaint for Declaratory Judgment, United States District Court for the Northern District of Illinois, Eastern Division, February.

Masnick, M. (2013), "Conan Doyle Estate Is Horrified That the Public Domain Might Create 'Multiple Personalities' of Sherlock Holmes." *Culture*. Available 10 February 2015 from http://www.techdirt.com/articles/20130915/ 00291924523.shtml.

Meehan, E.R. (2008), "Ancillary Markets – Television: From Challenge to Safe Haven." In P. McDonald and J. Wasko, eds., *The Contemporary Hollywood Film Industry*. London: Blackwell Publishing, pp. 106–119.

Memmott, C. (2012), "Sherlock Holmes Gets Modern Treatment in Two TV Shows." *USA Today*. Available 10 February 2015 from http:// usatoday30.usatoday.com/life/television/news/story/2012-08-27/sherlock- holmes-elementary/57356504/1.

News Release. (2014), Available 10 February 2015 from www.Free-sherlock.com.

Pearson, R. (2007), "Bachies, Bardies, Trekkies and Sherlockians." In J. Gray, C.L. Harrington, and C. Sandvoss, eds., *Fandom: Identities and Communities in a Mediated World*. New York: New York University Press, pp. 98–109.

Pearson, R. (2015), "A Case of Identity: *Sherlock*, *Elementary* and Their National Broadcasting Systems." In R. Pearson and A.N. Smith, eds., *Storytelling in the Media Convergence Age: Exploring Screen Narratives*. London: Palgrave MacMillan, pp. 122–148.

Pearson, R. and Messenger Davies, M. (2014), *Star Trek and American Television*. Berkeley, CA: University of California Press.

Pittard, C. (2007), " 'Cheap, Healthful Literature': The Strand Magazine, Fictions of Crime, and Purified Reading Communities." *Victorian Periodicals Review*, 40(1), 1–23.

Pittard, C. (2010), "From Sensation to the Strand." In C.J. Rzepka and L. Horsley, eds., *A Companion to Crime Fiction*. Chichester: Wiley-Blackwell, pp. 105–116.

Poore, B. (2013), "Sherlock Holmes and the Leap of Faith: The Forces of Fandom and Convergence in Adaptations of the Holmes and Watson Stories." *Adaptation*, 6(2), 158–171.

Porter, L. ed., (2012), *Sherlock Holmes for the 21st Century: Essays on New Adaptations*. Jefferson, NC: McFarland.

Press Release, (2010). Available 10 February 2015 from http://www.bbc.co.uk/pressoffice/pressreleases/stories/2010/07_july/12/sherlock2.shtml.

Review. (n.d.). Available 10 February 2015 from http://www.wessexpress.com.

Rosenberg, A. (2014), "The Fight Over Sherlock Holmes and How Copyright Changes Pop Culture." *The Washington Post*. Available 10 February 2015 from http://www.washingtonpost.com/news/act-four/wp/2014/08/05/the-fight-over-sherlock-holmes-and-how-copyright-changes-pop-culture/.

Saler, M. (2012), *As If: Modern Enchantment and the Literary Prehistory of Virtual Reality*. Oxford: Oxford University Press.

Sansom, I. (2011), "*The House of Silk* by Anthony Horowitz – Review." *The Guardian*. Available 10 February 2015 from http://www.theguardian.com/books/2011/oct/27/house-silk-anthony-horowitz-sherlock-holmes.

Schuessler, J. (2013), "Suit Says Sherlock Belongs to the Ages." *New York Times*. Available 10 February 2015 from http://www.nytimes.com/2013/03/07/books/suit-says-sherlock-belongs-to-the-ages.html?pagewanted=all.

"Sherlock Holmes Awarded Title For Most Portrayed Literary Human Character In Film & TV." (2012), Guinness World Records. Available 10 February 2015 from http://www.guinnessworldrecords.com/news/2012/5/sherlock-holmes-awarded-title-for-most-portrayedrary-human-character-in-film-tv-41743/.

"Sherlock Holmes, RIP." (2013), Beyond the Book: A Podcast Series on the Business of Writing and Publishing. Available 10 February 2015 from http://beyondthebookcast.com/sherlock-holmes-rip/.

Suddath, C. (2013), "The Man Who's Trying to Free Sherlock Holmes." *Business Week*. Available 10 February 2015 from www.businessweek.com.

Thompson, K. (2007), *The Frodo Franchise: The Lord of the Rings and Modern Hollywood*. Berkeley, CA: University of California Press.

"The Truth about Sherlock Holmes." (2012), The Sherlock Holmes Archives Altenmunster Jazzybee Verlag.

Westbrooke, C. (2014), "Stephen Moffatt Hails 'thrilling' Debut for Sherlock Series Three after Almost 10m Viewers Tune in." *The Metro*. Available 10 February 2015 from http://metro.co.uk/2014/01/02/steven-moffat-hails-thrilling-debut-for-sherlock-series-three-after-almost-10m-viewers-tune-in-4247294/.

10
"Cultural Acupuncture": Fan Activism and the Harry Potter Alliance

Henry Jenkins

> The teenage girl fan of Madonna who fantasizes her own empowerment can translate this fantasy into behavior, and can act in a more empowered way socially, thus winning more social territory for herself. When she meets others who share her fantasies and freedom there is the beginning of a sense of solidarity, of a shared resistance, that can support and encourage progressive action on the micro-social level.
>
> John Fiske, *Reading the Popular* (1989)

> By translating some of the world's most pressing issues into the framework of *Harry Potter*, [the Harry Potter Alliance (HPA)] makes activism something easier to grasp and less intimidating. Often we show them fun and accessible ways that they can take action and express their passion to make the world better by working with one of our partner NGO's [non-governmental organisations].
>
> Andrew Slack, Harry Potter Alliance (2009)

Written two decades apart, these statements by Fiske and Slack illustrate shifts in how fan activity connects the popular imagination and real-world politics. Both claim that fandom's "sense of solidarity ... [and] shared resistance" empowers individuals to make decisive steps towards collective action. Fiske sees fandom as an informal set of everyday practices and personal identities, while Slack describes organisations with institutional ties to NGOs. In Fiske's view, participants' fantasies shape how they see themselves and the world, while Slack describes a conscious rhetorical strategy mapping fictional content worlds onto real-world concerns – what he calls "cultural acupuncture". Slack notes how dispersed members of fannish communities are connected into a networked public that is capable of coordinated action.

While Fiske's concepts of resistance, fan discrimination and semiotic productivity shaped the early evolution of fan studies, his claims that fan participation might lead to enhanced political agency and civic engagement have been less explored. Nonetheless, they seem to offer a starting point for more contemporary work on fan activism. Some 20 years ago, the relationship between the micropolitics of everyday life that Fiske describes and the macropolitics of public policy was the subject of debate between critical and cultural studies. Jim McGuigan (1992), for example, singles out Fiske's claims about Madonna fans as indicative of a tendency to substitute meaning-making for "material" politics. Adopting a position closer to Fiske's, David Buckingham (2000: 29) warns: " 'Micro-politics' should not come to be seen as a substitute for 'macro-politics.' On the contrary, the challenge is surely to find ways of building connections between the two." Slack offers us a much more fully articulated theory of how fan activism can bridge the micro and macro, one tested by the HPA's successful mobilisation of fans in human rights campaigns.

Fiske's Madonna fans, however far-fetched his claims may have seemed at the time, were among the forerunners of Third Wave feminism, much as Riot Grrls moved from being fans of popular music to producers of their own DIY culture (Conti, 2001). The Riot Grrls performed as fans, as cultural producers, as activists and as ideological critics, helping to map potential links between these roles and activities. Third Wave feminism has, in turn, provided models for subsequent forms of fan activism. For example, Clan PMS and the Game Grrls movement challenged hurtful gender stereotypes in computer games and the surrounding culture (Jenkins, 2000). The Sequential Tarts (DeVries, 2002) confronted representational and retail practices that were hostile to female comics readers. In both cases, participants' claims of fan status gave them credibility for critical interventions that were focused on pop culture industries.

Some might still dismiss these activities as not fully political in that they direct their energies at changing corporate practices rather than governmental policies. Yet attempts to shape policies, institutions and values are increasingly recognised as political, even if they are not directly tied to parties or governments. Lizabeth Cohen (2003) argues that throughout the 20th century, many groups – among them, women and racial and ethnic minorities – have sought to reform or transform dominant practices through coordinated efforts as consumers. In the digital world, the forums for expressing political concerns, and the policies and infrastructures that shape our capacities to do so, are controlled by private interests. Our political struggles often take place through languages and contexts that are heavily shaped by commercial culture, making fan and consumer activism central to contemporary social movements.

A striking feature of post-millennial politics is the ways in which pop culture references are shaping political rhetoric and movement practices, while at the same time, as Earl and Kimport (2009: 223–225) suggest, the characteristics of social and political movements are "perpetual" and "ubiquitous" features of everyday lives. Accordingly, fan activism has moved from a crisis response to, for example, programme cancellations into a consistent, ongoing engagement with real-world concerns.

For the purposes of this discussion, "fan activism" refers to forms of civic engagement and political participation that emerge from within fan culture itself, often in response to the shared interests of fans, often conducted through the infrastructure of existing fan practices and relationships, and often framed through metaphors that are drawn from popular and participatory culture. I am describing as "civic" those practices that are designed to improve the quality of life and strengthen social ties within a community, whether defined in geographically local or dispersed terms. As we seek to better understand the logics of fan activism, we may need to explore points of overlap between it and other, closely related forms of cultural politics. How, for example, might we describe groups that deploy practices from participatory culture, seek to construct their own media content worlds, and adopt a more playful approach to activism, but do not originate in a pre-existing fan community? Or how might we characterise efforts to mobilise specific images from popular culture within more conventional partisan or activist campaigns (see Brough and Shesthrova 2012)?

Following a brief history of fan activism, I will explore the HPA, a sustained effort to mobilise a network of fans of J.K. Rowling's fantasy books around an array of different issues and concerns, ranging from human rights in Africa to rights to equal marriage, from labour rights to media concentration and net neutrality. My focus will be on the HPA as an organisation, addressing its tactics, rhetoric and underlying theory of cultural activism, rather than on how individual members develop greater agency and efficacy (see Kligler-Vilenchik et al., 2012). The HPA embraces a politics of "cultural acupuncture", mapping fictional content worlds onto real-world concerns. A content world is the network of characters, settings, situations and values that forms the basis for the generation of a range of stories, in the hands of either a commercial producer or a grassroots community. So the content world around Harry Potter includes characters such as Snape and Dumbledore, settings such as Hogwarts, situations such as the sorting of students into houses by the Sorting Hat, and values such as friendship and maternal love, any or all of which can be used to generate new narratives or to tap into the meanings that are associated with the original stories. What Slack calls cultural acupuncture is a means of deploying elements of the content world (and their accumulated meanings) as metaphors for making sense of contemporary issues. The HPA speaks of the "eighth book" in the Harry Potter series (which canonically has only seven) to describe how participants extend the story through their choices and practices as fan activists.

A brief history of fan activism

Fans often entered civic discourse when they assert their collective rights as the most active and engaged segments of the media audience. The fan identity is often an embattled one, and efforts to save shows from cancellation or to rally support for a film project have helped to cement social ties between fans, define their shared interests, and shape their public status. The 1969 effort to "save *Star Trek*", led by Bjo and John Trimble, was the defining early example of fan activism (Lichtenberg et al., 1975). Having run the art show at the annual World Science Fiction Convention for more than 15 years, the Trimbles were deeply immersed in fandom's infrastructure, practices, rhetoric and values (Trimble, 1999). Through ties to Gene Roddenberry and his long-time secretary Susan Sackett, the Trimbles identified strategies for intervening in NBC's decision-making process to ensure the series' survival. Bjo Trimble's "Do's and Don'ts of Letter-Writing" (n.d.) still informs more recent "save our show" campaigns. The spread of these practices across different fan communities illustrates a complex, interlocking history, with fans forging collective identities sometimes around specific texts and sometimes around genres or subgenres. The resulting structure has sustained itself over decades of shifting tastes and its traditions are handed down to subsequent generations. Such a structure means that fans of a particular franchise have a more extensive set of allies for more localised campaigns through cross-fan alliances – fandom's latent capacity.

More recent campaigns innovate practices that are designed for an era of networked communication. For example, fans of *Stargate SG-1* (1997–2008) responded rapidly to news of the series' cancellation (Jenkins, 2006b). Affiliated websites included sophisticated analyses of how networks make decisions about shows and provided arguments in *Stargate*'s favour, contact information for key decision-makers, a range of potential tactics to gain their attention, and, perhaps most significantly, sample letters in multiple languages. *Stargate*'s declining ratings in the USA were not matched in other markets, and thus its fans sought to mobilise international affiliates to keep the series in production. In another case, the campaign to save *Chuck* (2007–2012) used social media to get supporters to buy foot-long sandwiches from Subway, a series sponsor (Seles, 2010). Subway's increased sponsorship, inspired by this show of support, tipped the scale for *Chuck*'s renewal.

Whether such efforts constitute activism according to traditional political criteria is an interesting question. Political scientists recognise some forms of cultural activism, such as rallying to protest budget cuts for public broadcasting, to protect local arts institutions or to save public landmarks. Functionally, fan attempts to protect texts that they see as meaningful represent similar efforts to shape the cultural environment, though they rarely get taken seriously in literature about activism, suggesting a residual distinction between high and low culture. Gene Roddenberry's efforts to link science fiction with a utopian and humanist philosophy, which included support for racial and gender equality (Fern, 1996), helped to fuel the Save *Star Trek* efforts. Martin Luther King Jr allegedly urged Nichelle Nichols to remain on *Star Trek* because Uhura's presence on the bridge was a statement that his dream might be realised. Nichols in turn redirected support for *Star Trek* to promote female and minority participation in NASA's manned space programme. Barbara Adams, an alternative juror in the 1996 Whitewater trial, made fan activism more visible when she wore a Star Fleet uniform into the courtroom, citing *Star Trek*'s idealism as an alternative set of virtues against which to position the trial's legal and political struggles.

Andrew Ross (1991) recounts how science fiction fan organisations such as the Futurians and the Committee for the Political Advancement of Science Fiction functioned in the 1930s and 1940s as spaces for debating radical political ideas, recruiting fans into larger labour and social movements, and paving the way for more socially conscious forms of science fiction. The female-led fandom of *Star Trek* was closely affiliated with larger movements to promote feminist themes through science fiction (Tulloch and Jenkins, 1995), and discussions of the Vulcan philosophy of "Infinite Diversity in Infinite Combinations" anticipated more recent fan debates about the genre's representation of racial diversity (e.g. the extended online discussion within the science fiction community which became known as "Racefail '09"). These recent debates have spawned activism around the "white-casting" of genre films (Racebending.com) and the formation of an alternative press focused on publishing genre fiction by people of colour (Verb Noire) (Klink, 2010).

Such utopianism also empowered a group of queer fans, the Gaylaxians, to organise their own letter-writing campaign to get a gay or lesbian character added to *Star Trek: The Next Generation* (1987–1994) (Tulloch and Jenkins, 1995: 237–266). While the first letter-writing campaign partnered with Roddenberry against the networks, the Gaylaxians put pressure on *Star Trek's* producers to remain true to Roddenberry's ideological commitments, seeing the inclusion of same-sex couples as following the same logic that had led to the inclusion of female officers and a multiracial crew. The Gaylaxians sought to reach queer youth at risk because of our homophobic climate, as does Dan Savage's more recent It Gets Better campaign. The producers dismissed the Gaylaxians as "activists" or "interest groups", but they asserted their status as "fans" with a deep investment in *Star Trek*. This rhetorical move hints at fans' sense of entitlement, based on their emotional engagement with and extended support for "their" series. These fans, collectively and individually, defined themselves in opposition to commercial interests while supporting the values that are embodied within these content worlds, even against the worlds' own producers.

By the time these fan groups had defined an issue, identified decision-makers, developed tactics, and educated and mobilised supporters, they had completed all of the steps required for activism. Those who participated in such efforts had built the infrastructure and acquired the personal and organisational skills to take meaningful action. Those who succeed in such efforts might also find their civic voices and be more likely to take such action in the future. In *Entertaining the Citizen*, Liesbet van Zoonen concludes that fan practices embody, "in abstract terms, the customs that have been laid out as essential for democratic politics: information, discussion, and activism" (2005: 63). All of this suggests that fandom may represent a particularly powerful training ground for future activists and community organisers.

Other well-established forms of fan activism centre on efforts to resist censorship or to defend participatory practices against threats from commercial rights holders. Muggles for Harry Potter was organised by the American Library Association, the American Civil Liberties Union and the Electronic Frontier Foundation in response to efforts by the Christian right to ban Rowling's books from schools and public libraries. Alternatively, Defense against the Dark Arts arose when Warner Bros sent take-down notices to fan websites that the studio claimed infringed franchise materials, and the group helped to reshape the company's policies for dealing with fan participation (Jenkins, 2006a). Both efforts moved from a desire to defend fan practices towards a more critical perspective on constraints on participatory culture, from specific crises to a critique of current IP regimes. The Organization for Transformative Works, which publishes *Transformative Works and Cultures*, represents a concerted effort by fans to defend participatory culture, including by developing new platforms for distributing fan-produced materials outside the commodity logic of Web 2.0 and new academic and legal defences of fan cultural practices.

As this brief account suggests, fan activism includes many different kinds of mobilisation, some directed at promoting the interests of the fan community (lobbying to protect series from cancellation, organising against censorship or cease and desist orders), some involving struggles over representation (such as the Gaylaxians' efforts to get a queer character on *Star Trek*) and some involving commenting on public policy (whether Adams' personal statement or the HPA's collective action). All tap into fandom's communication infrastructure and social networks, and all deploy fictional content worlds and fan rituals, practices and rhetoric to motivate participation.

John Tulloch (Tulloch and Jenkins, 1995: 143–172) characterised *Doctor Who* fans as a "powerless elite" who cannot influence the decisions that most impact their cultural pursuits, but who exert considerable discursive power in shaping the popular memory of favourite texts. Fans leverage that discursive power to extend their voices beyond their own community, forming alliances with other invested groups, attracting mainstream coverage and increasing their persuasiveness. Lori Kido Lopez (2011) reaches a similar conclusion in her account of Racebending.com, an organisation that was launched to protest against the "white-casting" of characters who are presumed to be Asian when the animated series *Avatar: The Last Airbender* (2005–2008) was made into a live-action feature film:

> Some of the organization's strongest and most effective tactics rely on the skills developed as members of the fan community: honing their arguments through community discussions, producing and editing

multimedia creations, educating themselves about every facet of their issue, and relying on their trusted networks to provide a database of information.

Enter the HPA

The experience of reading, debating, performing and rewriting Harry Potter has been shared by many in the millennial generation (Anelli, 2008). Rowling's stories of the boy wizard, the remarkable school Hogwarts, and the battle against the Dark Lord became global best-sellers. Emerging alongside the popular embrace of the Internet, Harry Potter fandom has developed new media platforms and practices (Scott, 2010). The community was among the first to use podcasting and blogs, to develop beta reading practices to improve fan fiction, to distribute mp3 files (such as those of Wizard Rock) through social networking sites, and to use machinima production practices to construct fan vids. Over the coming decade, Harry Potter fandom will function as the feeder for many subsequent fan communities, much as *Star Trek* fandom modelled Baby Boom fan practices and politics. The HPA needs to be understood as yet another example of innovative practices emerging from this fan community.

Started by Andrew Slack, a twentysomething trained community organiser who has a background in working with troubled youth, the HPA is fan activism on a previously unimagined scale. The group currently has more than 100,000 members in more than 70 active chapters across the world, organised and mobilised by Slack and his 40-person staff, both volunteer and paid. The group collaborates with more traditional activist and charity organisations, such as Doctors for Health, Mass Equity, Free Press, The Gay-Straight Alliance and Wal-Mart Watch. When the HPA takes action, the results can be staggering. For instance, it raised $123,000 to fund five cargo planes transporting medical supplies to Haiti after the earthquake. Its Accio Books! Campaign has collected over 55,000 books for communities around the world. HPA members called 3,597 residents of Maine in just one day, encouraging them to vote against Proposition 9, which would deny equal marriage rights to gay and lesbian couples. Wizard Rock the Vote registered more than 1,000 voters.

Fan communities have long supported favourite charities, including efforts on behalf of the homeless (popular among fans of *Beauty and the Beast* (1987–1990)), the Elizabeth Glaser Pediatric AIDS Foundation (*Starsky and Hutch* (1975–1979)), and Equality Now and Kids

Need to Read (*Serenity* (2005) and *Firefly* (2002–2003) fans, known as Browncoats). Fans of a particular franchise often choose to support specific causes because they perceive them as being tied to the theme of the franchise or because key actors or producers are involved. The HPA links members to a range of such charity and relief efforts, but it also promotes activism around structural changes. As Slack explains,

> We do want people to both volunteer with people at a local AIDS clinic as well as advocate for better treatment of AIDS victims in Africa. We want our young people tutoring underprivileged kids and helping them read, getting them engaged in the Internet and learning those things, but then also challenging the rules of the game that are making it possible for kids to go without food.
>
> (Jenkins, 2009)

Running the HPA from his living room in Somerville, Massachusetts, Slack is a charismatic leader who inspires his volunteer army and part-time paid staff, but also embraces more dispersed and decentralised power structures that allow members a greater voice in the organisation's decisions. Local chapters participate in national campaigns but also initiate their own activities that reflect their own agendas (e.g. veterans' rights) and solicit participation by other chapters. The HPA's regular online exchanges become places to negotiate the group's sometimes competing priorities. Unlike most activist groups and charities, the HPA is not defined around a single mission; rather, it embraces a flexible framework that is inspired by Rowling's content world, enabling it to respond quickly to any crisis or opportunity and to its dispersed members. This mixture of strong leadership, dispersed membership, social networks and flexible structures informs many contemporary forms of activism, ranging from the US Tea Party movement to youth uprisings in the Arab world. The HPA demonstrates how the pop culture worlds that are central to fandom offer particularly rich resources for supporting collective action and reaching young people who have not yet embraced political identities.

Among Slack's first moves was to join forces with prominent fans, directly courting Wizard Rock stars, podcast producers, fan fiction editors and writers, high-profile bloggers and convention organisers. Paul DeGeorge, who, together with his brother Joe, fronts Harry and the Potters was an early and important HPA supporter, recruiting other performers to participate in Wizard Rock the Vote, Rock Out against Voldemedia and other HPA campaigns (Scott, 2010: 263–264). Paul

DeGeorge helped to spearhead the Wizard Rock EP of the Month Club, which for two years raised money for literacy-related non-profits by offering members exclusive CDs by groups such as the Whomping Willows, the Moaning Myrtles, Tonks and the Aurors, Danny Dementor, MC Kreacher and the Shrieking Shack Disco Gang. Many groups wrote songs that are tied to specific HPA campaigns and the HPA uses their concerts as major recruiting sites.

While Slack was relatively new to fandom, support from other prominent fans helped to establish his credibility and broaden his reach. In July 2007 the group worked with the Leaky Cauldron, one of the most popular fan news sites, to organise house parties around the country that were focused on increasing awareness of the Sudanese genocide. Participants listened to and discussed a podcast that featured real-world political experts, such as Joseph C. Wilson, former US ambassador to Gabon, and John Prendergast, senior advisor to the International Crisis Group, alongside performances by Wizard Rock groups. While some fans contested his allegiances, Slack's own mastery of the Harry Potter texts helped to overcome any lingering perceptions that he was an "outside agitator", a concern that echoed the reality of Communist Party interventions in the science fiction fan world in the 1930s.

Instead, Slack worked within the structures of fandom, using such things as the House Cup competition. Hogwarts is organised around four houses – Gryffindor, Slytherin, Ravenclaw and Hufflepuff – each of which embodies different ideals and virtues. Harry Potter fans deploy many different "sorting" mechanisms to place members into appropriate houses, and many feel a strong sense of identification and affiliation with their house. (I am, for the record, a loyal member of the House of Ravenclaw.) The HPA recruits high-profile heads for each house who encourage members to take action for the cause. (Ravenclaw's house has been headed by Evanna Lynch, the actress who plays Luna Lovegood, the best-known Ravenclaw character, and by young adult author Maureen Johnson.) For example, Wrock4Equality was a House Cup competition, where members earned points for each person whom they contacted in the effort to rally voters against Maine's Proposition 9. Such structures respect things that fans value, even as leaders sometimes nudge them beyond their comfort zones as budding young activists.

The HPA materials are not always as polished as those of some other activist groups, who work with professional media-makers and consultants. Rather, the HPA embraces fandom's own DIY ethos, lowering barriers to participation by respecting the work of novices and amateurs.

Many of the HPA's most effective videos simply depict students, in their bedrooms, speaking directly into the camera. The HPA has formed a strong partnership with the video blog community Nerdfighters, whose capacity to mobilise its members was a key factor in the HPA's success in a 2010 Chase Manhattan Bank online competition. Other HPA videos, such as a campaign supporting workers' rights that depicted Harry's battles against the Dark Lord, WaldeMart, involve broad parodies of the Rowling content world.

Imagine better

Speaking at the 2008 Harvard graduation, J.K. Rowling told a generation of young students who had come of age reading her books: "We do not need magic to change the world, we carry all the power we need inside ourselves already: we have the power to imagine better." Neither a generic celebration of the human creative capacity nor a simple defence of bedtime stories, Rowling's talk describes how her early experiences working with Amnesty International shaped the books. Linking imagination to empathy, she calls out to those who refuse to use their imaginations:

> They choose to remain comfortably within the bounds of their own experience, never troubling to wonder how it would feel to have been born other than they are. They can refuse to hear screams or to peer inside cages; they can close their minds and hearts to any suffering that does not touch them personally; they can refuse to know.
>
> (Rowling, 2011)

Rowling's speech has become a key source of inspiration for HPA members: her notion of the socially engaged imagination connects their love of her content world with their own campaigns for social justice. Slack has named a recent initiative to forge partnerships between the HPA and other fan communities Imagine Better.

Rowling's call to "imagine better" could describe a range of movements that are embracing "a politics that understands desire and speaks to the irrational; a politics that employs symbols and associations; a politics that tells good stories" (Duncombe, 2007: 9). Zoonen (2005: 63) has similarly questioned the divide between the affective commitments of fans and the cognitive processes that are associated with active citizenship: "Pleasure, fantasy, love, immersion, play, or impersonations are not concepts easily reconciled with civic virtues such as knowledge, rationality, detachment, learnedness, or leadership." For Duncombe, the way forward bridges this divide by means of "ethical spectacle" (124–175) – public performances that are pleasurable, participatory and playful, yet also confront reality. Whereas Mark Dery (1993) described 1990s cultural and political movements as "jamming" dominant culture, Duncombe alternatively suggests that activists surf the popular imagination, hitching themselves to Hollywood's publicity to reach a larger public.

Slack describes this new form of activism as "cultural acupuncture". Writing in the *Huffington Post*, he explained:

> Cultural acupuncture is finding where the psychological energy is in the culture, and moving that energy towards creating a healthier world... We activists may not have the same money as Nike and McDonald's but we have a message that actually means something... What we do not have is the luxury of keeping the issues we cover seemingly boring, technocratic, and inaccessible. With cultural acupuncture, we will usher in an era of activism that is fun, imaginative, and sexy, yet truly effective.
>
> (Slack, 2010)

Recognising that the news media were more apt to cover the launch of the next Harry Potter film than the genocide in Darfur, Slack saw the HPA as a way to identify key cultural pressure points, thus redirecting energy towards real-world problems. Pinning political and social causes to Harry Potter works because this content world has a large following, is familiar to an even larger number of people, has its own built-in mechanisms for generating publicity and is apt to attract many subsequent waves of media interest. Harry Potter constitutes a form of cultural currency that can carry the group's messages to many who would not otherwise hear them and that channels our emotional investments. Fans' previous attempts to tap the power of source material have been primarily focused on the source's power as a shared reference point within the fan community itself, whereas Slack's notion of cultural acupuncture also recognises and seeks to deploy the larger public's investments in these popular media to get under people's skin and prod them to take political action.

Unlike some political groups that dismiss popular culture as "bread and circuses" and "weapons of mass distraction", the HPA respects fans' existing emotional investments, seeing them as deeply meaningful and also as potential motivators for political change. Moving beyond fantasy, the HPA educates its community about issues that it should be concerned about, returning to the content world for powerful analogies. In that sense, we might draw parallels between the ways in which the HPA taps the Harry Potter mythos and the ways in which, say, the civil rights movement of the 1960s deployed Biblical allusions – such as the Promised Land and the River Jordan – that were familiar to its churchgoing supporters. Fandom is not a religion and does not depend on literal belief, but it recognises the power of great stories to move hearts and minds. Catherine L. Belcher and Becky Herr Stephenson's 2011 book, *Teaching Harry Potter*, describes how a range of educators have offered their students ways into Rowling's content world that reflect their lived experiences as undocumented immigrants, racial and ethnic minorities, special-needs kids and so forth, seeing it as offering many potential identifications and messages. Fandom represents a space where shared allusions become socially and politically meaningful.

Cultural acupuncture inspires civic participation by mapping content worlds onto real-world problems. Writing for *In These Times*, Slack describes Harry Potter in terms that resonate post-9/11:

> Imagine a world faced with unpredictable attacks that are carried out by a cult-like network. Led by a charismatic figure that is rarely ever seen or heard from, this network continues to claim responsibility for heinous acts that include random kidnappings, the destruction of bridges and mass murders. Stateless and living among the masses, its members have become so hard to track down that the government is at a loss. Officials have begun to focus more on the image of "looking tough" than on creating real safeguards to protect its citizens. The world has become haunted by fear.
>
> (Slack, 2007)

Against this backdrop of Death Eater terrorists, bungling or manipulative government officials, a deceptive press and repressive school authorities, Rowling tells how one young man organised his classmates into Dumbledore's Army, a loosely organised activist group, to go out and fight evil – sometimes working alone, sometimes collaborating with adult groups such as the Order of the Phoenix, but always carrying much of the burden of confronting Voldemort and his minions (Slack, 2010). Slack argues that the Harry Potter books take young people seriously as political agents and thus can inspire youth to change the world:

> Young people are depicted in the books as often smarter, more aware of what's happening in the world, than their elders, though there

are also some great examples where very wise adults have mentored and supported young people as they have taken action in the world... We are essentially asking young people the same question that Harry poses to his fellow members of Dumbledore's Army in the fifth movie, "Every great Wizard in history has started off as nothing more than we are now. If they can do it, why not us?" This is a question that we not only pose to our members, we show them how right now they can start working to be those "great Wizards" that can make a real difference in this world.

(Jenkins, 2009)

James Paul Gee (2007: 45–70) argues that games are effective tools for mobilising learning because they offer their players clearly defined roles and goals, offering compelling identities and new epistemic perspectives, the capacity to act in meaningful ways, and clear paths to success. The HPA similarly offers its participants roles within larger-than-life campaigns, roles that Slack sees as echoing the power of myth as described by Joseph Campbell and Carl Jung: "What if we gave our teenagers the opportunity to imagine themselves as the heroes that they have grown up watching, rather than treating their precious minds as nothing more than a way to line the pockets of some CEO?" (Slack, 2010). The HPA's playful deployment of terms like "Voldemedia" and "WaldeMart" maps the personalised embodiment of evil in the content world to an expanding understanding of real-world harms. Consequently, the HPA allows its young members to know who they are as activists, what they are fighting against and what they are fighting for – all key steps towards achieving social change.

Battling the Muggle mind-set

For the HPA, overcoming the "Muggle mind-set" and releasing the power of fantasy represent vital first steps in becoming an activist. When many Harry Potter fans think of Muggles, they think first of the narrow-minded Dursley family who keep Harry locked away in the cupboard under the stairs out of fear of and embarrassment about his magical capacities. Harry is literally closeted at the saga's start and emerges as a key political figure by the series' conclusion – a classic coming-out story. Building on Rowling's depiction, the HPA depicts Muggles as embodying racism, sexism and homophobia, as seeking to constrain cultural diversity through shame and fear: "The 'Muggle Mindset'... that pervades our culture is unimaginative and two-dimensional. It is a system based on fear that sets normalcy as one's aspiration" (Slack, 2007). The HPA uses the elastic concept of the "Muggle mind-set" as an all-purpose signifier for those forces that resist social justice, including many that are the targets of other kinds of activism, such as conformity, commercialisation, authoritarianism and the politics of terror. The term "Muggle mind-set" is as loose and as encompassing as, say, "neoliberalism" or "dominant ideology", and, like them, it links structures of belief, power and action. In challenging the Muggle mind-set, the HPA is able to link the personal and the political in ways that are inspired by feminist and queer activist groups. The Muggle mind-set is, of course, a simplification of the more complex representations of the politics of diversity within the Harry Potter books themselves, given the degree to which Rowling criticises the wizarding world for its own insensitivity to "mudbloods" and the rights of house elves, the ways in which she uses the Society for Protection of Elfian Welfare to spoof certain forms of student activism, and how Dumbledore himself defends the rights of Muggles (Carey, 2003; Horne, 2010).

In their final struggles with Voldemort, Harry, Hermione, Ron and their classmates had to seek out and destroy seven horcruxes – magic objects of supreme evil that contained hidden fragments of the Dark Lord's soul. In the months leading up to the release of the final movie, the HPA launched an ambitious campaign to identify and direct its collective energy against seven real-world horcruxes. Some, such as the Starvation Wages Horcrux, called attention to global human rights issues; HPA members who pursued it sought to get Warner Bros to commit to license Harry Potter candies only to fair trade companies. Others represented concerns in young people's lives. For the Dementor Horcrux, the HPA partnered with Reachout.com, an online support group for teens considering suicide: "Like Harry, many of us may feel debilitated by the dementor-like experiences of anxiety, depression, low body image, and lots of feelings, thoughts, and behaviours that knock us off balance" (Harry Potter Alliance, 2010a). The Body Bind Horcrux helped members to push back against distorted body images, while for the Bullying Horcrux the HPA joined forces with the Gay-Straight Alliance to battle homophobia in schools. Its efforts against bullying included both collecting signatures for the Make It Better Oath and making phone calls to voters in Rhode Island to urge them to support an equal marriage initiative there. Some of the HPA's horcruxes required concerted efforts on a national scale, while others encouraged personal reflection and localised action. While critics might see such short, focused efforts as token gestures, the overall horcrux campaign was designed to help participants to understand the links between campaigns for social justice, and the internalised fears and anxieties that block many from taking meaningful action. The horcruxes were peda-gogical devices that helped participants to see themselves and the world differently, much like the preparation that Hogwarts students under-went prior to their final confrontation with the gathering forces of evil. They were intended less to create immediate fixes than to map the terrain upon which social change must take place.

As they battle the Muggle mind-set, HPA members often draw sage advice from Hogwarts' headmaster, Albus Dumbledore. A 2009 cam-paign asked members to wonder: "What would Dumbledore do?" Slack refers often to the Dumbledore Doctrine – a loose set of ideas drawn from the books:

[Dumbledore] discusses how prevailing ideas of racial superiority for full-blood wizards must be transformed into curiosity and interest in people's differences. Half-giants, like Harry's friend Hagrid, shouldn't have to hide their identities. House elves in servile positions must be allowed freedom and respect. Indigenous populations, like the Centaurs and Merpeople, must be treated with the reverence and fairness they deserve. And unconventional marriages, such as the one between Lupin, the werewolf, and Tonks, the full-blood witch, should be welcomed so long as they bring more love into the world.

(Slack, 2007)

Dumbledore Doctrine provides a launching point for the group's efforts to support legalising gay marriage, because they see the acceptance and embrace of diversity as core values in the Harry Potter narratives. Slack sometimes compares Dumbledore with real-world political and philosophical leaders, such as Mahatma Gandhi, Martin Luther King and the Dalai Lama, on the basis of their shared philosophies of tol-erance and social justice. Some HPA members challenge this tendency to read Dumbledore as the moral centre of the books, arguing that Dumbledore's motives are not always pure or wise. Other critics have questioned whether the books offer a consistent or progressive focus for fan activism, pointing out that, like many other popular texts, the Harry Potter franchise is a contradictory blend of progressive impulses and retrograde elements. Such debates about character morality reflect fandom's existing interpretive practices, sustaining fan engagement as new members offer their own insights into core ethical and psychologi-cal dilemmas. Should fan activism in the future be understood as acting on a shared set of ideologies and dogmas that shape how fans read the world, or can we imagine a kind of politics that builds on the ongoing debates that fans have about how to interpret and how to evaluate the characters, actions and values that are depicted in a favourite text?

Empowering youth

While the HPA is open to members of all ages, the group has focused its energies on attracting young people who have grown up reading the books and on helping them to find a path towards political engagement. According to HPA chapter coordinator Sara Denver (personal communication, July 2011), of the organisation's 98 chapters, 24 are hosted by high schools and 33 by colleges and universities, suggesting strong student representation in the group. An informal survey conducted by Ben Stokes of the University of Southern California's Civic Paths research group found that the median age of members is 21, again suggesting a strong youth focus, which has also been borne out by the Civic Paths team's fieldwork and qualitative interviews with 27 members of the HPA. The fieldwork provides rich examples of young people who have assumed leadership roles in the organisation and who have come to embrace activism as a result of the HPA's rhetoric and practices. (For more on this fieldwork, see Kligler-Vilenchik et al., 2012.)

In starting with a fantasy about youth empowerment, the HPA addresses many prevailing concerns about young people and civic engagement. Current scholarship (Buckingham, 2000; Gibson, 2003; Levine, 2007; Bennett, 2008; Wattenberg, 2008) suggests that young people are rarely addressed as political agents, that they are not invited into the political process, and that they are not consulted in the political decision-making process, whether local, state, national or global. Existing literature suggests that young people are most apt to become politically involved if they come from families with a history of citizen participation and political activism; if they encounter teachers, especially in the civics classroom, who encourage them to reflect on and respond to current events; if they attend schools where they are allowed a voice in core decisions; and if they participate in extracurricular activities and volunteerism that give back to their community. Most forms of activism reach the same core group of participants, who are already politically engaged, and redirect them towards new issues. However, the HPA is targeting young people who are engaged culturally, who may already be producing and sharing fan culture, and it helps them to extend their engagement into politics, often deploying existing skills and capacities in new ways. Kahne et al. (2011: 2) discovered that involvement in online networks focused on shared interests (e.g. fandom) also shapes political identities: "online, nonpolitical, interest-driven activities serve as a gateway to participation in important aspects of civic and, at times, political life, including volunteering, engagement in community problem-solving, protest activities, and political voice".

As researchers such as David Buckingham (2000) have long argued, young people often feel excluded from the language and processes of adult politics. In most cases they are not invited to participate; their issues are often not addressed; and the debates are framed in a language that assumes familiarity with debates and policies. By contrast, the HPA's "cultural acupuncture" approach is imaginative and playful, offering an alternative set of metaphors and analogies that are already part of young people's lives, much as Fiske understood fans as transforming mass-media content into "cultural resources" for critiquing the dominant order (Jenkins, 2011: xxx–xxxi). The HPA embraces grassroots appropriation as a way of generating a new vocabulary for talking about political change.

HPA leaders and members may object to Fiske's characterisation of such practices as "resistance" (Jenkins, 2011: xxxiii) since they see themselves as building on the framework that Rowling, herself a human rights activist, provided. Nevertheless, they do prioritise the struggle for social justice ahead of those commercial motives that shape Warner Bros' management of the Harry Potter franchise, as is made clear by the HPA's November 2010 campaign to encourage the studio to contract with candy companies that observe fair trade policies. The effort defines HPA members as fans of the franchise and as consumers who are likely to buy affiliated products, but also mobilises content-world expertise to challenge studio decisions:

When Hermione Granger discovers that the food at Hogwarts, chocolate included, is being made by house elves – essentially unpaid, indentured servants – she immediately starts a campaign to replace exploitation with fairness... In Harry Potter's world, chocolate holds a unique place: it is a Muggle item with magical properties. Chocolate is featured prominently throughout the books as a powerful remedy for the chilling effects produced by contact with dementors, which are foul creatures that drain peace, hope and happiness from the world around them... It is doubtful that chocolate produced using questionable labor practices would have such a positive effect, both in Harry's world and ours.

(Harry Potter Alliance, 2010b)

Rather than seeing the licensed candies as mere commodities, the HPA evaluates them according to their meaningfulness in the content world and then links their "magical" powers to the ethics of how they are produced and sold: "As consumers of Harry Potter products, we are interested in supporting and purchasing products that are true to the spirit of the Harry Potter franchise." Throughout its campaign, the HPA holds open the prospect of a meaningful collaboration with corporate interests, but it also pledges to use boycotts and buycotts against the studio and its subcontractors.

In *The Future of Democracy*, Peter Levine argues, "There are limits to what adults and institutions can accomplish, given the opacity of youth culture and young people's resistance to being manipulated. Therefore, it is important that young people themselves have the skills and values they need to make their own sphere as constructive as possible" (2007: 76). In some ways, fan activism flies in the face of Levine's claims: fandom has historically been a space where youth and adults work together, outside the hierarchies that shape relations at school or home, because of their shared interests and mutual passions. Strikingly, though, Slack and many of the other core HPA leaders are in their 20s and early 30s – closer in age to the young activists than their parents and teachers, though experienced enough to mentor them and to help to negotiate with more adult-centred organisations.

Beyond the Potter franchise

The HPA has long hitched its campaigns to the release of the books and, more recently, the release of the feature films. Such moments offer a window of visibility as the news media go into a feeding frenzy around all things Harry. For example, the HPA drew coverage from mainstream media outlets through a bit of imaginative (if geeky) street theatre, staging an epic battle between the Death Eaters and the Order of the Phoenix in New York's Columbus Circle tied to the 2010 release of *Harry Potter and the Deathly Hallows: Part 1*. These releases also represent moments where new fans discover the series and old fans renew their commitment.

With the 2011 release of the final feature film, the HPA's leadership faced a crisis of sustainability. Would what they had built over the previous five years function in the absence of new waves of media attention? Many fan communities – including those centred on the *Star Trek* franchise, *Doctor Who*, *Star Wars*, *The Lord of the Rings*, and *Firefly* – have sustained creative energy and social ties over a decade or more of lapses in commercial output, although they have often retrenched, growing smaller but more intense, and taking greater ownership over the content world. Yet an activist group, by its very nature, needs to reach beyond its own community if it wants to make a difference. So, under the banner "Imagine Better," the HPA is now seeking to forge alliances with other fan communities (for *Firefly*, *True Blood*, *Lord of the Rings*, *Twilight* and *Glee*, among many others). However, as it does so, it may need to disconnect its goals and practices from the specifics of the Harry Potter content world. How far can it go, and remain Dumbledore's Army?

One factor working in its favour is that many fans are nomadic, moving across content worlds and sometimes genres in the course of a lifetime in fandom. Many fan conventions are organised around broader generic rather than franchise-specific categories – and some of these, such as slash, originate from fan reading and production practices rather than industry discourse. So perhaps the HPA's core themes can be grafted onto a broader range of popular myths that may also motivate young people to take political action. Linking together Harry Potter and *Twilight* seems, on the surface, a smaller step than bringing in *Glee* fans, since they are both fantasy worlds rather than mundane ones, but to see them in this way is to focus on only one dimension of these franchises, and not necessarily the one that is most relevant to fans. Perhaps further expansion will result in innovations in new media platforms and practices, new issues and tactics for reading and responding to real-world problems through acts of collective imagination. What happens next will tell us a lot about how much we can abstract from the HPA model to forge new theories of youth and civic engagement.

My focus here has been on the processes of cultural acupuncture, deploying popular culture metaphors and analogies to refresh political rhetoric. In the case of the HPA, such metaphors remain closely linked to fan culture. But what happens when fandom incubates new discursive frames that feed back into mainstream politics? For example, Whitney Phillips (2009) has written about how 4Chan, a controversial online community that started as a place to discuss manga and anime, has deliberately generated memes and spread them across the Internet. Among them, she argues, was the Obama Joker imagery deployed in the Tea Party's campaign against "Obamacare". Or consider how undocumented youth, organising in support of the DREAM Act, have claimed Superman as another "illegal alien" who has nevertheless contributed to truth, justice and the American way (Zimmerman, n.d.).

Such efforts deploy pop icons, already holding affective power, to grab media and public attention (see Brough and Shresthova, 2012). Such efforts defamiliarise the issues and offer a welcome sense of play and pleasure to struggles for social justice. As the Joker might put it, "Why so serious?" Writing about this larger movement to integrate pop culture and politics, John Hartley claims: "While it may not look very much like the Habermasian public sphere, it is clearly attracting the attention of those who are notoriously hard to reach by traditional technologies of citizenship" (2012: 147). Such efforts rely for their success on general knowledge rather than fan expertise: they deploy aspects of popular culture texts that are familiar even to those who have not encountered them directly.

Fan activism pushes deeper, dealing not with isolated references but with the full content world, recognising and rewarding fans who know more and imagine better. Certainly, some of the HPA's allusions are widely recognised – Dumbledore's Army, perhaps – facilitating meaningful partnership with non-fan organisations that value the creative energy that the Harry Potter books unleashed. Yet, as fan activists, the HPA members mobilise obscure characters and events, even quoting specific dialogue, and thus reward fan mastery. Fan activism works because of its fannishness. This fannishness extends beyond specific ways of reading texts to specific forms of fan participation (including cosplay, Wizard Rock, fan fiction and fan vidding), some of which may look strange outside the community. However, each contributes to fandom's ability to organise and mobilise quickly, to frame issues and educate supporters, to get the word out through every new media platform and channel. This ability is what ultimately distinguishes fan activism from the more casual deployment of pop culture references.

Acknowledgements

This chapter was informed by the ongoing conversations of the Civic Paths Research Group in the Annenberg School of Communications and Journalism, University of Southern California, and by the MacArthur Network on Youth and Participatory Politics. Our research on fan activism has been funded by the Spencer and MacArthur foundations.

The chapter was originally published in "Transformative Works and Fan Activism", edited by Henry Jenkins and Sangita Shresthova, a special issue of *Transformative Works and Cultures*, 10. doi:10.3983/twc.2012.0305.

References

Anelli, M. (2008), *Harry, A History*. New York: Pocket Books.
Belcher, C.L. and Stephenson, B.H. (2011), *Teaching Harry Potter: The Power of Imagination in Multicultural Classrooms*. New York: Palgrave.

Bennett, W.L. (2008), *Civic Life Online: Learning How Digital Media Can Engage Youth*. Cambridge: MIT Press.

Brough, M.M. and Shresthova, S. (2012), "Fandom Meets Activism: Rethinking Civic and Political Participation." *Transformative Works and Cultures*, 10.

Buckingham, D. (2000), *The Making of Citizens: Young People, News and Politics*. London: Routledge.

Carey, C. (2003), "Hermione and the House Elves: The Literary and Historical Context of J.K. Rowling's Antislavery Campaign." In G.L. Anatol, ed., *Reading Harry Potter: Critical Essays*. Westport, CT: Praeger, pp. 103–115.

Cohen, L. (2003), *A Consumers' Republic: The Politics of Mass Consumption in Postwar America*. New York: Knopf.

Conti, C. (2001), " 'Stepping Up to the Mic': Le Tigre Strategizes Third Wave Feminist Activism Through Music and Performance." MS Thesis, Massachusetts Institute of Technology.

Dery, M. (1993), *Culture Jamming: Hacking, Slashing and Sniping in the Empire of the Signs*. Open Magazine pamphlet series. Open Media.

DeVries, K.M. (2002), "A Tart Point of View: Building a Community of Resistance Online." Paper presented at "Media in Transition 2: Globalization and Convergence," Massachusetts Institute of Technology, Cambridge, 10–12 May.

Duncombe, S. (2007), *Dream: Re-imagining Progressive Politics in an Age of Fantasy*. New York: New Press.

Earl, J. and Kimport, K. (2009), "Movement Societies and Digital Protest: Fan Activism and Other Nonpolitical Protest Online." *Sociological Theory*, 27(3), 220–243.

Fern, Y. (1996), *Gene Roddenberry: The Last Conversation*, Rev. ed. New York: Pocket Books.

Fiske, J. (1989), *Reading the Popular*. London: Routledge.

Gee, J.P. (2007), *What Video Games Have to Teach Us about Learning and Literacy*. New York: Palgrave Macmillan.

Gibson, C. (2003), *The Civic Mission of Schools*. Report from Carnegie Foundation and CIRCLE: The Center for Information and Research on Civic Learning and Engagement.

Harry Potter Alliance (2010a), "Dementor Horcrux." Available from http://thehpalliance.org/action/campaigns/deathly-hallows/horcrux-2/.

Harry Potter Alliance (2010b), "Letter to Time Warner." Available from http://thehpalliance.org/action/campaigns/deathly-hallows/horcrux-1/letter-to-wb/.

Hartley, J. (2012), *Digital Futures for Cultural and Media Studies*. Malden: Wiley-Blackwell.

Horne, J. (2010), "Harry and the Other: Answering the Race Question in J.K. Rowling's *Harry Potter*." *The Lion and the Unicorn*, 34(1), 76–104.

Jenkins, H. (2000), "Voices from the Combat Zone: Game Grrls Talk Back." In J. Cassell and H. Jenkins, eds., *From Barbie to Mortal Kombat: Gender and Computer Games*. Cambridge: MIT Press, pp. 328–341.

Jenkins, H. (2006a), *Convergence Culture: Where Old and New Media Collide*. New York: New York University Press.

Jenkins, H. (2006b), "Fan Activism in a Networked Culture: The Case of *Stargate SG-1*." *Confessions of an Aca-Fan* (blog), 28 August. Available from http://www.henryjenkins.org/2006/08/fan_activism_in_a_networked_cu.html.

Jenkins, H. (2009), " 'How 'Dumbledore's Army' Is Transforming Our World: An Interview with the HP Alliance's Andrew Slack (Part One)." *Confessions of an Aca-Fan* (blog), 23 July. Available from http://henryjenkins.org/2009/07/how_dumbledores_army_is_transf.html.

Jenkins, H. (2011), "Why Fiske Still Matters." In J. Fiske, ed., *Television Culture.* (2nd edition), London: Routledge, pp. xv–xli.

Kahne, J., Lee, Nam-Jin, and Feezell, J.T. (2011), "The Civic and Political Significance of Online Participatory Cultures Among Youth Transitioning to Adulthood." DML Central Working Papers, Youth and Participatory Politics.

Kligler-Vilenchik, N., McVeigh-Schultz, J., Weitbrecht, C.,and Tokuhama, C. (2012), "Experiencing Fan Activism: Understanding the Power of Fan Activist Organizations through Members' Narratives." *Transformative Works and Cultures*, 10.

Klink, F. (2010), "Verb Noire." *From Participatory Culture to Public Participation.* Available from http://sites.google.com/site/participatorydemocracyproject/case-studies/verb-noire.

Levine, P. (2007), *The Future of Democracy: Developing the Next Generation of American Citizens.* Medford, MA: Tufts University Press.

Lichtenberg, J., Marshak, S., and Winston, J. (1975), *Star Trek Lives!* New York: Gorgi Childrens.

Lopez, L.K. (2011), "Fan Activists and the Politics of Race in *The Last Airbender.*" *International Journal of Cultural Studies*, 15(5), 431–445.

McGuigan, J. (1992), *Cultural Populism.* London: Routledge.

Phillips, W. (2009), "Unmasking the Joker." In " 'Why So Socialist?': Unmasking the Joker," by Henry Jenkins, *Confessions of an Aca-Fan* (blog), 14 August. Available from http://www.henryjenkins.org/2009/08/unmasking_the_joker.html.

Ross, A. (1991), *Strange Weather: Culture, Science and Technology in the Age of Limits.* London: Verso.

Rowling, J.K. (2011), "J.K. Rowling Speaks at Harvard Commencement." *Harvard Magazine*, 5 June 2008. Available from http://www.youtube.com/watch?v=wHGqp8lz36c.

Scott, S. (2010), "Revenge of the Fanboy: Convergence Culture and the Politics of Incorporation." PhD dissertation, University of Southern California.

Seles, S.M. (2010), "Audience Research for Fun and Profit: Rediscovering the Value of Television Audiences." MS thesis, Massachusetts Institute of Technology.

Slack, A. (2007), "Harry Potter and the Muggle Activists." *In These Times*, 26 October. Available from http://www.inthesetimes.com/article/3365/harry_potter_and_the_muggle_activists/.

Slack, A. (2010), "Cultural Acupuncture and a Future for Social Change." *Huffington Post*, 2 July. Available from http://www.huffingtonpost.com/andrew-slack/cultural-acupuncture-and_b_633824.html.

Trimble, B. (1999), Interview. *Trekplace.* Available from http://www.trekplace.com/bjotrimble.html.

Trimble, B. (n.d.), "Do's and Don'ts of Letter-Writing." *Bring Back Kirk Letter Campaign.* Available from http://www.bringbackkirk.com/bjo_tips.html.

Tulloch, J. and Jenkins, H. (1995), *Science Fiction Audiences: Watching "Doctor Who" and "Star Trek."* London: Routledge.

van Zoonen, L. (2005), *Entertaining the Citizen: When Politics and Popular Culture Converge*. Lanham, MD: Rowman and Littlefield.

Wattenberg, M.P. (2008), *Is Voting for Young People?* New York: Pearson Longman.

Zimmerman, A. (n.d.), "Dream Activism: New Media Strategies in the Undocumented Youth Movement." White paper under development for the USC Civic Paths Project.

Afterword: Studying Media with and without Paratexts

Jonathan Gray

In my 2010 book *Show Sold Separately: Promos, Spoilers, and Other Media Paratexts*, I argue that we need to examine paratexts more, not as some odd exercise in completionism, whereby we could then proclaim triumphantly that we'd studied everything, even the "outskirts" of a text, but rather because paratexts are regularly constitutive, central and absolutely important. They are, in short, part of the text. Thus to ignore them and yet still feel comfortable about making a declaration regarding a text's meaning, impact, power, effects or value would be an act akin to reading only the third and fourth chapters of a book and feeling that this suffices for a full analysis. Undoubtedly we can still engage in analysis with only part of the text in front of us. Indeed, it is a rare day when an analyst ever has access to the whole text, and we are instead always forced to analyse with only some of the picture. However, paratexts are as valuable a source of information about a text, and as important a site for the generation of text, as is the work itself. If we want to know about a text's place in the world, after all, asking the work alone is as limiting as it would be to study a person's legacy by consulting only that person. Texts can cast long shadows over society, and the sociocultural examination of textuality should be as much or more a process of sketching out these shadows, and hence of the text's interaction with its environment, as it should be a process of studying the work itself.

However, since writing *Show Sold Separately*, a large number of questions that I've fielded about the book are about where paratextuality begins and ends, and about what counts as a paratext. On a personal level, these questions can be rather amusing, as if I have magically become a high court judge of paratextuality, empowered with the right to determine for all what counts. I've also had to answer a lot of questions about terminology. Some answers to some of these questions might help to enlighten readers as to why the work in collections like this one is important, and where it might be leading our field of media and cultural studies. In this afterword, therefore, I will address some of them as an exercise not in narcissism but in elaboration on how paratexts and their audiences matter, and thus why this book takes us several steps forward in the analysis of textuality.

The most frustrating questions that I receive are those that posit a mutually exclusive distinction between text and paratext, often invoking "the text itself" as opposed to the paratextual surround. Let us be clear, though, that the paratext is always part of the text. Gerard Genette pronounced the opposite, yes, insisting of "paratexts without texts" that "The paratext is only an assistant, only an accessory of the text. And if the text without its paratext is sometimes like an elephant without a mahout, a power disabled, the paratext without its text is a mahout without an elephant, a silly show" (1997: 410). To Genette, then, it was absolutely possible to have a paratext without a text. I disagree. Vehemently. First, let us note in passing that Genette's desire for Orientalist spectacle and his metaphor's devaluation of an Indian man as meaningless without his elephant is the true "silly show" and is offensive. Any metaphor that posits a human being as irrelevant unless sitting atop an elephant screams out for us to disagree with it, so I will do exactly that. In positing the text and paratext as existing in two distinct bodies, Genette precludes the possibility of the paratext being part of the text (to him, it only sits on the text's back), much less therefore of it creating the text or even being the text. But surely even within Genette's terms, the spectacle – that which will be observed – and hence the text is not the elephant in and of itself (we can go to zoos or look in picture books for that spectacle) but the elephant performing. Here, surely the mahout could sit down with us and either illustrate or explain how that elephant moves, perhaps even delighting us, and hence create the text and spectacle even while the elephant sleeps unobserved in the other room. I do not mean to deny the elephant's size and grandeur, but the mahout can create a spectacle without that elephant. So too, then, is the paratext not apart from the text – it is apart from the work (in Barthes' (1977) conceptual schema of text and work) but very much a contributing, and at times constitutive, part of the text.

It may be worth discussing the tricky prefix that causes problems with paratexts: para. This commonly means "at or to one side of", and so it is understandable that some readers would be confused into thinking of the paratext as to the side of the text. However, if we explore further some of the words that use this prefix, we find a more complex relationship. A paramedic, for instance, isn't simply someone standing next to a medic who cheers their colleague's every move. If someone falls over in the street and a bystander calls emergency services, we will all be relieved to see the arrival of an ambulance, not because it will take the person to a medic but because the paramedics on board will hopefully be able to attend to whatever ails the person immediately. Granted, they do not have the same resources as the hospital to which they may likely transport their patient, and they may not have the same extensive training and expertise as the doctors who will greet the gurney as the patient arrives at the hospital, but they can do a lot, and many a life has been saved by a paramedic. Many a life, by contrast, has been ended by paramilitaries. Again, a member of a paramilitary does not simply stand next to a military, supplying ammo and words of encouragement: they too do the work of the military. They may even in some cases be an elite force, "better" at doing military work than the traditional, institutionalised armed forces. Once more, then, "para" becomes a more complicated prefix, and I hope the application to textuality is clear: a paratext is not simply to the side of a text. Rather, paratexts do the work of texts and are functional parts of them. Sometimes they will represent a smaller, specialised component of the text; sometimes they are its elite edge. Sometimes they do everything the rest of the text does; sometimes they are entrusted to conduct very particular tasks and to play very particular roles in the construction of the text.

So why bother with the word "paratext" at all, then? Why not just talk about different parts of the text? My answer here is a practical one: we need the word as a reminder – an insistence, even – to look at paratexts. As evidenced by the frequency with which many analysts refer to "the text itself" when they actually mean "the work itself", and hence the frequency with which scholars who in theory know Barthes' (1977) distinction between the work and the text still fail to use it in practice, it's all too easy to fall back on a mode of scholarship that is centred and isolated on the work itself even when we suggest we're studying "the text" instead. This can be dangerous scholarship if it effaces and erases so much of a text's imprint on the world, pretending or hoping instead that a film, television show or other work speaks itself. Impetuous directors and overzealous studio copyright lawyers may like to insist that they're doing everything themselves, but they're wrong, and our scholarship is weak and craven if we believe them. To talk of paratexts, though, is to remind ourselves how much more work is required to understand a text's role in society.

However, although I therefore believe that we still need the word "paratext", I also hope that consideration of paratexts becomes so commonplace that one day we can discard the word as a quaint remnant of a past mode of scholarship. When paratexts are no longer offered the analytical consolation prize or bronze medal of being considered "tertiary", in Fiske's words (1989), when studied at all, or of being considered in tack-on paragraphs in articles and books, or tack-on classes in courses that otherwise consider the work first, foremost, and almost only, then let us drop the word. When we all no longer feel comfortable saying that a text "does", "means" or "is" this or that without moving beyond the film, television show, game or other work, then great, let's agree that using the word "paratext" is redundant and self-defeating. Till then, I hope the word can serve to embarrass us by its presence, subtly reminding us always to attend to paratexts.

Towards this end, I am greatly encouraged by the approach to paratextuality that I see in this book. Some of the chapters use the language of "paratext", while in others the word itself is largely absent yet the importance of studying paratexts is still impressively illustrated. All show how much of media culture is generated in the paratextual surround, while also showing us different ways in which paratexts matter.

Thus, for instance, several chapters use paratexts to map out how texts, genres and authors have changed over time. If, as Rick Altman's (1999) and Jason Mittell's (2004) respective books on genre argue, genre is always discursively constructed, the contributions by Mark Jancovich and Stacey Abbott (chapters 4 and 5) form a helpful pairing that examine the impact of paratexts on the discursive construction and reconstruction of horror. Jancovich notes how numerous films that were considered horrors in the 1940s are now regarded as thrillers, as the shifting sands of generic classification have recoded the films and their stars over time. As a result, he argues, "understandings of them today are neither necessary nor inevitable but a product of our own historical context". To access that earlier context, though, Jancovich requires the paratext, and armed with it we can now make better sense of the films' meanings and genre's contingency and volatility. Abbott, meanwhile, shows how horror is discursively invoked by the paratexts of television title sequences. Even before we watch the shows beyond the title sequences, she illustrates, a genre is nominated and "it is left to the audience to choose to enter at their own peril", as we now know to expect a horror.

The discursive construction, positioning, and repositioning of specific texts – not just genres – within the public eye is the topic of

Simon Hobbs' exploration of *Cannibal Holocaust*'s paratextual meaning-making (Chapter 6). Hobbs takes the case of the notorious "video nasty" and shows how its public meaning has been so profoundly changed over time. For example, turning to special features on a DVD that use Julian Petley as academic expert to reframe the critical value of a text long derided in the popular press, he notes that these special features "seek to re-position the film and furnish it within the conventions of academic study. Here the paratext, operating externally from the main body of the film, has the capacity to alter the cultural perceptions of a narrative and re-apprise it within a previously unavailable and impenetrable cinematic environ." And thus, just as the moral panic surrounding the film's release onto VHS had earlier proved the power of paratexts to publicly reposition what a text is, what it stands for and what we should all think of it (regardless of whether we were to watch it or not), its subsequent DVD release once again allows for a reframing and discursive repositioning. Interestingly, though, Hobbs' interests in the chapter lie not "just" in what paratexts do to this text but in how they "influence the cinematic environ in general", as he argues for the potential for paratexts to frame film-viewing culture writ large.

Lincoln Geraghty (Chapter 3) uses another form of paratext, the fan letter, to read what *Star Trek* meant to those watching it. Audience research has long attempted to chart how audiences interact with texts, but it has always struggled with the tricky methodological challenge of how to access "authentic" responses, not just the response created on the spot to satisfy a researcher's rather odd line of questioning (see Morley, 1992; Ang, 1996). The allure of online fan forums has thus perhaps naturally attracted many an audience researcher who is keen to study individuals and communities unobserved or unannounced. However, fan letters offer another compelling resource, addressed to the creators or stars of a text instead of to fellow audiences, and characterised by different rhetorical goals. Of course, the perfectly "authentic" audience response will always be elusive – a chimera – as fan letters are performative in their own ways, but they are highly valuable tools in helping us to determine how a text's fans are using that text, and how they want it to be used and made. Michael O'Neill (Chapter 1), meanwhile, explores how producers have themselves responded to audience activity, and how they have tried to limit, direct and dictate the terms for textual and paratextual engagement. Studying the case of fan archives and social media, he shows how aware producers are of the power of paratexts, yet how much they struggle to control those powers. Certainly, as social media allow for all manner of commentary and activity to occur immediately and fleetingly, while fan archives may "threaten" a producer's distribution strategy with an unwanted perma-nence, we can witness a multiplication of the sites and temporality of paratextuality, and observe considerable concern and headache from producers who are trying to tame such sites, flow and overflow.

From genre to text to cinematic environs, we can also move to Roberta Pearson's explorations of the legal claims and counterclaims of authorship (Chapter 9). In examining the case of the Conan Doyle Estate's legal attempts to wrestle control of the exclusive right to make paratexts, she offers a clear view of just how important courts and policy will be in determining the future of paratexts. Indeed, it is worth considering how rarely paratexts enjoy the same legal protec-tions that many "works of art" do, as many countries' legal systems do not accord to most paratexts the status of being *bona fide* works of artistic expression. We should expect, then, and as Pearson shows, that paratexts will be a site for legal wrangling, wherein authorship is determined and fought over. Her contribution is an important inter-vention in paratextual studies, and an invitation for us to do a better job of exploring sites where paratextual, and hence textual, control is "settled".

It is this notion of contested meaning that also governs Matt Hills' superb contribution (Chapter 8) as he focuses on the ability of set reporting by fans to challenge the authority of the producers. The "pre-textual poachers", as he calls them, become a pain in many pro-ducers' sides as the latter find themselves unable to control completely the paratextual creation of textuality. Here an important reminder exists, that paratextuality is never just a game for producers to play, as fans and other audiences can always intervene in the production of meaning too. To even talk of "pre-textual" engagements with texts, moreover, Hills reminds us of the significant pleasures of any text that might exist before the work itself has been presented. If one reason that the work itself has so often been privileged in critical discus-sion, and that the paratext has been ignored, is that the work is seen to be the true site of engagement, Hills challenges this rudimentary knowledge of textuality and engagement to show how much audi-ence activity and industry involvement exist before a work is even released.

Henry Jenkins' challenge to notions of the work doing all the work is no less profound, as he turns his attention to the HPA's fan activism (Chapter 10). I have written above of studying a text's imprint on the world, and Jenkins shows that some of the Harry Potter stories' greatest imprint has been mediated, after the fact, by the HPA's savvy use of the world of Harry to pivot fans to imagine and work towards a better world outside the stories. As one important strand of media and cultural studies work has always looked to the media for the narratives of civic engagement on offer, hoping that the media could live up to its role in the public sphere, Jenkins' contribution shows how this process of engaging viewers can be aided and mediated by fan activists. Here the parallel of the paramedic listed above strikes me as relevant, as the HPA moves out from the work like teams of ambulances trying to address real-world problems in direct fashion.

Working both in tandem and in contrast to Jenkins' work is Cornel Sandvoss, Kelly Youngs and Joanne Hobbs' exploration of fan discussions and activities surrounding RSRDs (Chapter 2). The authors chart a starkly apolitical fandom, characterised in some cases by paratextual and transmedial creativity and productivity, but rarely by an attempt to engage wider scripts of civic importance. Theirs is a sobering reminder to my overly romantic metaphor of paratexts as paramedics: neither heroes nor paramilitaristic villains, RSRD fans are simply other motorists, the white lorry drivers of the textual motorway. To truly gauge the work's involvement in political, civic discourse, though, Sandvoss, Youngs and Hobbs need to engage the paratext.

Tanya R. Cochran (Chapter 7) looks at fans too, but in doing so finds an interesting instance in which paratexts and intertexts overlap. Her fascinating account of *Angel* fans finding narrative resolution for their beloved characters in creator Joss Whedon's much later film project *Much Ado about Nothing* indicates how personalised paratextuality and intertextuality can be. One person's *bona fide* "work" is another person's paratext, and it may be both to a third person. As a result, characters, plots and themes from one text can easily continue, develop and entertain across not only other texts in the same franchise or family, but tangentially in the shadows and traces of other texts with an author figure, cast member, storyline or theme in common. At times, then, we may find ourselves as analysts engaging in a different form of "textual poaching", hunting a text within another's preserve.

In sum, this collection offers multiple models for how to integrate the study of paratexts, ephemeralia, fan productions, trailers and all manner of other supposedly "secondary" or "tertiary" materials into the primary, and thereby constructs numerous pathways away from a mode of analysis that fetishises "the work of art" and towards a mode of analysis that studies textual imprints on society.

References

Altman, R. (1999), *Film/Genre*. London: BFI.
Ang, I. (1996), *Living Room Wars: Rethinking Media Audiences for a Postmodern World*. London: Routledge.
Barthes, R. (1977), "From Work to Text." In *Image/Music/Text*, trans. S. Heath. Glasgow: Fontana-Collins, pp. 155–164.
Fiske, J. (1989), "Moments of Television: Neither the Text Nor the Audience." In E. Seiter, H. Borchers, G. Kreutzner, and E. Warth, eds., *Remote Control: Television, Audiences, and Cultural Power*. London: Routledge, pp. 56–78.
Genette, G. (1997), *Paratexts: Thresholds of Interpretation*, trans. J.E. Lewin. Cambridge: Cambridge University Press.
Gray, J. (2010), *Show Sold Separately: Promos, Spoilers, and Other Media Paratexts*. New York: New York University Press.
Mittell, J. (2004), *Genre and Television: From Cop Shows to Cartoons in American Culture*. London: Routledge.
Morley, D. (1992), *Television, Audiences, and Cultural Studies*. London: Routledge.

Index

Note: The letter '*n*' following locators refers to notes.

Abbott, Stacey, 10, 114, 119, 233
Abominable, Doctor Phibes, The
 (film), 96
Acker, Amy, 149, 153–5, 158–61
acting, 103, 154, 155
Adam & Joe Show, The (TV), 17
adaptation, 67, 77, 100, 105, 149, 160,
 161, 178, 186, 187, 189, 203*n*1
Adler, Irene, 191
advertising, 32, 59, 78, 129, 136, 194
Alfred Hitchcock Presents (TV), 96
Alias Nick Beal (film), 93
Altman, Rick, 74–5, 233
Amazon, 12, 190, 197
AMC (channel), 113
American Civil Liberties Union, 212
American Horror Story (TV), 10, 117,
 121, 122–4
American Library Association, 212
Amityville Horror, The (film), 122
Angel (TV), 113, 115, 116, 149–58,
 160–2, 236
Arrow (TV), 159
Arsenic and Old Lace (film), 99, 100
Artificial Eye (film distributor), 133–4
Atwill, Lionel, 9, 91, 103
audiences, 1–2, 7–8, 10–12, 17–20, 23,
 33, 35, 42, 53, 57, 65, 67, 69*n*10,
 73, 75, 76, 78, 81, 95, 97, 105,
 110–19, 122–5, 131, 136, 150,
 151, 152, 155–8, 161–2, 164, 165,
 170, 178–9, 190–2, 200–1, 209,
 231, 233, 234, 235
 demographics, 8, 18, 19, 29, 33, 34,
  55, 68*n*2, 131, 134
 niche, 17, 40, 173, 187
 youth, 8, 17, 18–19, 24–31, 34, 41,
  52, 59, 66, 132, 211, 218,
  222, 224
authenticity, 12, 54–5, 57, 134, 137,
 139, 140, 188, 194, 234

authorship, 7, 12, 60, 111, 186, 235
Avatar: The Last Airbender (TV), 212
Awful Truth, The (film), 99

Badalamenti, Angelo, 112
Ball, Alan, 113
Barnes & Noble, 197
Barthes, Roland, 231, 232
Bass, Saul, 122
Battlefront (TV), 8, 19, 24–7
Baum, L. Frank, 76
Baym, Nancy, 169, 171
BBC, 12, 21, 26, 27, 30, 168, 169, 173,
 180, 189, 193, 202
BBC Wales, 167, 171, 181
Beau Geste (film), 93
Beauty and the Beast (TV), 213
Bebo (social media), 26
Beeton's Christmas Annual, 200
Bergman, Ingrid, 92, 97, 98, 101
Bernardi, Daniel, 74
Beverly Hills 90210 (TV), 40
BFI (British Film Institute), 134
Big Bang Theory, The (TV), 69*n*3
Big Brother (TV), 28, 40
Big Clock, The (film), 93, 95, 97
BitTorrent, 21, 22
Black Panthers, 83
blogging, 12, 25, 67, 155, 176, 178,
 179, 201, 202, 213, 214, 216
Bonanza (TV), 116
Bones (TV), 113
Booth, Paul, 170, 172, 173
Brackett, Charles, 94, 95
branding, 3, 6, 11, 13, 18, 21–2, 26–7,
 28, 31–5, 111, 121, 124, 133–6,
 138, 140, 173–4, 181, 187, 189,
 191–2
British Board of Film Classification
 (BBFC), 143–4

broadcasting, 6, 17–25, 28–30, 35, 40,
    57, 59–61, 65, 111–12, 114, 117,
    151, 164, 180, 203n3, 210
    public service, 18–19, 24, 26–7, 35,
    179, 189
Brooker, Will, 22, 59, 181
Buffy the Vampire Slayer (TV), 51, 113,
    114–15, 116, 149–50, 156,
    159, 162
Bulldog Drummond Escapes (film), 94

Caldwell, John, 32
Cameron, David, 41
Campbell, Joseph, 1, 219
Cannibal Holocaust (film), 10–11,
    127–30, 132–7, 139–44, 234
capitalism, 66, 67
Capra, Frank, 100
Cardiff, 12, 40, 170, 171, 193
Carnivàle (TV), 113
Carson, Jack, 100
Cat People (film), 103
catharsis, 11, 149, 153–5, 158–9, 161
CBS (Columbia Broadcasting
    Service), 189
celebrity, 8, 32, 41, 43, 59–60, 64, 67
Celebrity Big Brother (TV), 69n8
Celebrity Juice (TV), 69n3
censorship, 129, 130, 137–8, 140,
    142–3, 211, 212
Chaney Jr, Lon, 9, 91, 102
Channel 4, 8, 17–19, 21–35, 40, 61,
    69n3
Channel 5, 69n9
Chapman, James, 168–9
Charlie Chan in London (film), 94
Chelsea, 39, 45, 56
Cherry, Brigit, 134–5
Chuck (TV), 210
Ciardi, Francesca, 142
Citizen Kane (film), 96
Civil Rights, 83, 218
Colbert, Claudette, 93, 97
collecting, 2, 3, 6, 10, 21, 131, 137–9,
    140, 177, 213, 220
Columbia Pictures, 9, 91
comedy, 3, 4, 93, 94, 116, 119, 158
    screwball, 99, 100
comics, 1, 187, 191, 207

community, 6, 9, 17, 21, 26–7, 30,
    63–4, 73, 78, 80, 83, 84n3, 134–5,
    172, 177, 180, 191, 208, 209,
    211–13, 216–18, 222–3, 225–6
Conan Doyle, Arthur, 12, 186, 190–2,
    198, 201
    estate, 187, 193–7, 199–200, 235
Conan Doyle, Dame Jean, 193
Confessions of a Nazi Spy (film), 103–4
convergence, 1, 7, 11, 34, 41, 62, 64–5
Conway, Tom, 103
Cooper, Kyle, 122
copyright, *see* intellectual property
Corman, Roger, 93
Coronation Street (TV), 40, 69n5
Cotton, Joseph, 9–10, 91–3, 96–9, 106
Cregar, Laird, 105
crime, 92, 94–5, 102, 104, 106, 191
Crime Scene Investigation (TV), 40
CSI Miami (TV), 116
cult, 1, 2, 7, 10, 111, 114, 118, 133,
    135, 160–1, 218
cultural acupuncture, 13, 206–9,
    217–18, 223, 225
Cumberbatch, Benedict, 189
CW (channel), 159

D'Amato, Joe, 135
Dallas (TV), 84n4
Davidson-Houston, Richard, 34
Davies, Russell T., 170
Davila-Irizary, Cesar, 122
Dawson's Creek (TV), 40
Day, Doris, 44
DC Comics, 187, 191
de Certeau, Michel, 73
Denisof, Alexis, 149, 153–5,
    158–9, 161
Dent, Grace, 32
Deodato, Ruggero, 128, 133, 137–8,
    140–2
Derrida, Jacques, 132
Desperate Scousewives (TV), 31, 40, 56
Destination Tokyo (film), 100
Detective Comics, 187
Dexter (TV), 110, 113, 119–21
Digital Britain Report, 18
Digital Kitchen (design company),
    112, 113, 118–19, 124

disability, 80
DIY culture, 207, 215
Doctor Takes a Wife, The (film), 93
Doctor Who (TV), 6, 7, 12, 114,
    166–74, 176, 179–81, 212, 224
Doctor Who Experience, 171–2
Dollhouse (TV), 160
Don't Torture a Duckling (film), 140
Double Indemnity (film), 94
Downey Jr., Robert, 189, 202
drama, 7, 8, 19, 31, 33, 49–54, 78, 79,
    100, 116, 170, 186
  historical, 201
  regional scripted reality, 39–43,
      46–9, 51–5, 58–62, 66–8,
      68n2, 236
  teen, 22, 40, 47, 51–2
Dubai, 56
Duel in the Sun (film), 98
Duffett, Mark, 41, 177
Dumbledore, Albus, 209, 220–1
Dumbledore's Army, 218–19, 225–6
Duncan, Andy, 18
Durbin, Deanna, 97
Dust and Shadow (book), 190–1
DVD, 3, 7, 21, 111–12, 127, 130–1
  Blu-ray, 128
  extras, 33, 234
  marketing, 133, 145
  packaging, 6, 10, 134, 137
Dyer, Richard, 75–80

E4 (channel), 8, 19, 22, 27–9, 31, 33,
    39–40, 68n2, 69n3
EastEnders (TV), 40
Easthope, Anthony, 75
Egan, Kate, 129, 138–40, 142, 144
Elementary (TV), 187, 189, 192, 194,
    203n3
Ellis, John, 127, 132
Embarrassing Bodies (TV), 29
Emmerdale Farm (TV), 40
emotions, 5, 9, 11, 20, 42–3, 50–1, 54,
    73, 84n3, 92, 101, 118–19,
    149–50, 153–8, 161, 178, 180,
    202, 211, 217
Empire Strikes Back, The (film), 4
Engelhardt, Tom, 83

entertainment, 3, 27, 49, 54, 65, 68,
    69n5, 69n8, 75–7, 79–80, 144,
    192, 200
Entertainment Weekly (magazine), 123
ephemera, 1, 3, 4, 7, 8, 10, 18–22, 51,
    64, 116, 201, 236
Essex, 39, 55
Eureka Masters of Cinema (film
    distributor), 134
Everitt, Jace, 110
Everything Happens at Night (film), 93

Facebook (social media), 19, 30, 34–5,
    41, 59, 60, 62–3, 167, 169, 171
Fades, The (TV), 120
Falchuk, Brad, 117
fan fiction, 1, 5, 11, 49, 50, 53, 213,
    214, 226
fans, 1–13, 17, 20, 28, 42–58, 62–8,
    73–8, 80–4, 113, 117, 121–4, 134,
    149–50, 153–62, 164–82, 186,
    189, 190, 210, 212, 216, 219, 221
  as activists, 13, 24, 61, 75, 207–9,
      211, 213–15, 217–20, 223–6,
      236
  and blogs, 155, 176, 178, 179, 213
  as journalists, 164–5, 175–6, 180,
      182
  and letters, 9, 73–8, 80–1, 84, 84n3,
      210, 234
  ordinary, 73, 84n3
  as producers, 8, 11, 22, 27, 29, 73,
      165, 172, 174, 207, 209, 214
  and set reporting, 7, 12, 164–5, 167,
      169, 172–7, 179, 235
fanzines, 173
film, 1, 3–5, 7, 9–10, 23, 54, 75, 91–3,
    95–6, 98–105, 122, 129, 131, 133,
    135–7, 140, 160, 186, 189, 194,
    202, 211, 224, 233
  documentary, 119, 128, 142–3
  exploitation, 10, 93, 127–9, 133,
      136–7, 140, 142–5
  locations, 12, 122, 129
  reviews, 6, 10, 96, 105
  trailers, 21, 140–1, 236
Fincher, David, 122
Firefly (TV), 159, 214, 224, 225

Fiske, John, 63, 165, 174–5, 206–7, 223, 233
Fleming, Dan, 6
Flickr (social media), 169
Fontaine, Joan, 99
Fordism, 66
Foreign Correspondent (film), 103
4Beauty, 26, 34
4Food, 26, 34
4Homes, 26, 34
4Later, 17, 32
4oD, 22
Fox (network), 203*n*4
Fox, Charles, 117
Franklin, H. Bruce, 82
Fray (graphic novel), 149
Freeman, Martin, 189
Friends (TV), 117
Fringe (TV), 115
Fulci, Lucio, 133, 140
FX (channel), 113

Game of Thrones (TV), 112
Garde-Hansen, Joanne, 4, 20
Gaslight (film), 92, 97, 98
Gatiss, Mark, 12, 189, 193
Gelder, Ken, 2
Genette, Gérard, 61, 112–13, 231
genre, 9, 10, 39, 50–1, 53–4, 57, 69*n*5, 75, 76, 91, 93, 102, 110, 112, 118–19, 121–2, 124, 128, 132, 134–6, 144–5, 170, 190, 209, 211, 225, 233, 235
Geordie Shore (TV), 40–1, 46, 49, 57, 67, 68*n*2, 69*n*3
Geraghty, Christine, 77–8, 85*n*9, 85*n*10
Geraghty, Lincoln, 2, 132, 139, 234
Ghost and Mrs. Muir, The (film), 106
giallo, 128, 134–5
Gilded Lily, The (film), 94
Gimbel, Norman, 117
Glass Key, The (film), 94
Glee (TV), 117–18, 225
Gone with the Wind (film), 84*n*4
Gotham (TV), 203*n*4
Grant, Cary, 9–10, 91–3, 99–101
graphic design, 113, 125*n*5
graphic novels, 124, 125*n*5, 149, 191

Gray, Jonathan, 1, 7, 22, 61, 117, 123, 127, 131–3, 164, 169
Grey's Anatomy (TV), 116
Guinness Book of World Records, The (book), 186
Gwenllian-Jones, Sarah, 2, 27

Hangover Square (film), 101, 105
Hannibal (TV), 110, 119–21
Harry Potter, 3, 209, 215, 217–18, 221, 225, 235
  books, 187, 212–13, 218, 220, 226
  fans, 7, 213, 219
  films, 212, 217, 223
Harry Potter Alliance, 13, 206, 223–4
Harry Potter and the Deathly Hallows: Part 1 (film), 224
HBO (channel), 113, 118
Heimat, 64
Her Cardboard Lover (film), 102
Hers to Hold (film), 97
Hill Street Blues (TV), 40
Hills, Matt, 2, 5, 11–12, 41, 57, 63, 159–61, 165–6, 182, 188, 235
Hills, The (TV), 39
His Girl Friday (film), 99
history, 2, 9, 17, 20–1, 24, 42, 53, 75, 77, 81, 127–30, 132–3, 136–7, 140–3, 153, 173, 191, 193, 195, 208–9, 219, 222
Hitchcock, Alfred, 96–100, 103
Hogwarts, 209, 213, 215, 221, 223
Hollyoaks (TV), 69*n*3
Hollywood, 43, 77, 94, 97, 102, 105, 181, 189, 217
  New, 187
Holmes, Sherlock, 7, 12, 178, 186–203
Horowitz, Anthony, 12, 194
Dr. Horrible's Sing-Along Blog (web series), 149
horror, 7, 9, 91–106, 110, 112, 117–19, 121–4, 132–5, 137–8, 143, 233
  gothic, 10, 98, 99, 101, 119–22, 124
  Italian, 128–9, 134, 144–5
Hound of the Baskervilles, The (book), 201
Hound of the Baskervilles, The (comic), 191
House of Silk, The (book), 12, 194, 196

House of the Laughing Windows
    (film), 133
House of the Seven Gables, The (film),
    101, 104
House on the Edge of the Park (film),
    133, 140
How I Met Your Mother (TV), 69*n*3
Hush, Hush, Sweet Charlotte (film), 96
Hussey, Ruth, 94

I Walked with a Zombie (film), 103
I'll Be Seeing You (film), 98
I'm a Celebrity . . . Get Me Out of Here
    (TV), 69*n*8
Inner Sanctum Mysteries (book series),
    102
intellectual property, 12, 22, 186–9,
    190–1, 193, 195–9, 201–3, 212
Internet, 1, 7, 12, 13, 19, 22, 25, 27,
    84*n*3, 114, 134, 153, 173, 177,
    178, 213–14, 225
    archives, 8, 17–23, 34, 177, 234–5
    forums, 17, 28, 134, 164, 167, 177,
        208, 234
    intertextuality, 4, 11, 61, 159, 161,
        188, 191–2, 236
iPlayer, 30
iPod, 19
Irene (film), 94
Iser, Wolfgang, 53–4, 66
It's All About Amy (TV), 69*n*9
ITV (channel), 68*n*2, 69*n*3, 69*n*9
ITV2 (channel), 8, 39, 40
Ivanhoe (film), 106

Jack the Ripper, 105
Jacoby, Russell, 74, 75
Jameson, Fredric, 75
Jancovich, Mark, 9–10, 91, 96, 233
Jenkins, Henry, 6, 13, 25, 27, 29, 51,
    62, 65–6, 73, 134, 165–6, 182,
    187, 191–2, 195, 207, 210–12,
    214, 219, 223, 226, 235–6
Jones, Jennifer, 98
Joseph-Witham, Heather, 73
journalism, 6, 130, 141, 175,
    180–1
    citizen, 12, 164–5, 175–7, 179–80,
        182

grassroots, 165, 176–7
professional, 175, 182
Journey into Fear (film), 96
Jowett, Lorna, 118–19
Jungle Love (film), 93
Jungle Princess (film), 93

Karloff, Boris, 9, 91, 100
Killer Nun (film), 135
kinesthetic empathy, 149–50, 156–8
King Jr., Martin Luther, 210, 221
Klein, Melanie, 44, 48
Klinger, Barbara, 4, 131, 132, 137
Klinger, Leslie, 195–203
Kripke, Eric, 114

Lady has Plans, The (film), 94
Lamour, Dorothy, 93
Lancer Spy (film), 103
Lang, Fritz, 94, 103, 106
Last Tango in Paris (film), 142
Laughton, Charles, 94, 95
Laverne and Shirley (TV), 116–17
Law, Jude, 189
Lego, 2–6
Levine, Peter, 224
Lime Pictures (production
    company), 67
Liu, Lucy, 189
liveness, 29, 30, 169
Liverpool, 40, 56
Livingstone, Sonia, 178
Locke, Matt, 25
Lodger, The (film), 101, 105
London, 7, 13, 39, 43, 55–6, 95, 120,
    167, 180, 181, 189, 193, 202
Lord of the Rings, The (film), 187, 188,
    224, 225
Los Angeles, 39, 150
Lost (TV), 18, 31, 125*n*3, 170
Lost Weekend, The (film), 93, 95
Lotz, Amanda, 23, 24
Loughton, 39, 44
Love Goddess of the Cannibals (film),
    135
Love Letters (film), 98
Lugosi, Bela, 9, 91, 104
Lured (film), 105
Luther (TV), 120

Made in Chelsea (TV), 8, 39, 41, 43–53, 55–6, 59–62, 65, 67, 68*n*2, 69*n*3, 69*n*4, 69*n*5
Madonna, 206, 207
Magnificent Ambersons, The (film), 96
Major and the Minor, The (film), 94
Manhattan Baby (film), 133
Manhunt (film), 103, 105
Mark Wright's Hollywood Nights (TV), 43, 69*n*9
marketing, 6–7, 9, 33, 56, 125*n*4, 133, 135, 137, 141, 187, 189
  ballyhoo, 136, 138, 140
  viral, 26, 32
Marvel Studios, 202
Massey, Raymond, 100
Matrix, The (film), 114
McDonald, Paul, 131, 132
McDonaldisation, 66–8
McNamara, Robert, 83
media conglomeration, 187, 189
media franchises, 2–3, 8, 12–13, 187–8
Medium (TV), 114
melodrama, 50, 51, 94, 100, 103, 117
Menace (film), 94
Mendik, Xavier, 142, 143
Metz, Christian, 131
Midsummer Murders (TV), 40
Milland, Ray, 9, 10, 91–6, 99, 106
Miller, Jonny Lee, 189
Ministry of Fear (film), 93–6
Misfits (TV), 31, 120
Mittell, Jason, 23, 54, 233
Moffat, Steven, 12, 114, 168, 189, 192–3
Momoco (design company), 118, 120, 124
Monkey Kingdom (production company), 67
Moonlighting (TV), 51
moral panics, 129, 234
morality, 2, 50, 77, 80, 101, 112, 119, 129, 221
Mr. Lucky (film), 100
MSN (website), 28, 30, 35, 46
MTV (network), 8, 39, 40, 49, 69*n*3
Much Ado About Nothing (film), 149–50, 153–62, 236

Muppets, The, 191
Murphy, Ryan, 117, 123
music, 1, 41, 61, 98, 112, 122, 207
  filk, 73
  opening sequence, 110–12, 115, 117, 124
  video, 21, 118
  musicals, 76–8
Myspace (social media), 19, 25, 26
myth, 1, 52, 162, 188, 218, 219, 225

narrative, 1–6, 11, 32–3, 40, 47, 49, 51–3, 60–1, 74, 81, 84, 97, 101, 110, 113–17, 119, 122–4, 127–30, 132–5, 137, 141–4, 149, 153–5, 159–61, 168, 170, 186, 192, 199, 234, 236
narrowcasting, 39–41, 43, 57, 59, 64–5, 68
NASA, 210
National Gallery, 180–1
New Girl (TV), 69*n*3
New York, 56, 79, 189, 199
New York Ripper (film), 140
New York Times, 122, 190, 194–5
Newcastle-Upon-Tyne, 40
Newman, Kim, 93, 101, 142
newspapers, 41, 59–60, 105, 124, 167, 173
Newsround (TV), 26, 27
Next on 4 (TV), 18, 24
Next Time We Love, The (film), 94
Nichols, Nichelle, 210
Night and Day (film), 101
Night Gallery, The (TV), 119
A Nightmare on Elm Street (film), 133
9/11, 218
Nine Inch Nails (music group), 122
Nip/Tuck (TV), 117
None But the Lonely Heart (film), 101
Notorious (film), 101

O.C., The (TV), 40
Once Upon a Honeymoon (film), 100
Once Upon a Time (film), 100
Only Way is Essex, The (TV), 8, 39, 41, 43–7, 49–52, 54–7, 59, 61–2, 65, 67, 68*n*2, 69*n*3–5, 69*n*9

Organization of Transformative
  Works, 212
Orientalism, 231

Panic in the Year Zero (film), 93
Paramount Studios, 189
paratextuality, 3, 7–13, 18, 19, 28–9,
  35, 64, 127–30, 135, 137, 140–4,
  174, 187, 190, 231, 234–6
  fan, 2, 6, 173
  theory of, 113, 131–3, 230, 233
Party Wright Around the World (TV),
  69*n*9
Payment Deferred (film), 94
Pearson, Roberta, 2, 12, 188,
  230*n*3, 235
Penley, Constance, 73
Perkins, Hilary, 31
Petley, Julian, 128–30, 139–40,
  142–4, 234
Phantom Lady (film), 106
Picture of Dorian Gray, The (book), 101
Picture of Dorian Gray, The (film),
  102, 105
Pinterest (website), 34
Pirates of the Caribbean (film), 3
Pop Idol (TV), 41
Portrait of Jennie (film), 98
Premature, Burial, The (film), 93
Prisoner, The (TV), 2
Private Eye (magazine), 173–4
Prologue (design company), 118, 124
Psycho (film), 122

Quiet Please: Murder (film), 104

race, 9, 74, 78, 79, 83, 219
Rage in Heaven (film), 104
Real World, The (TV), 39
Rebecca (film), 99, 101, 104
remediation, 10, 127, 133, 138,
  139, 145
Revolution (TV), 125*n*3
Ripper Street (TV), 120
Ritchie, Guy, 189
Ritzer, George, 66–7
Robinson, Edward G., 104
Roddenberry, Gene, 9, 74–5, 78, 81,
  84, 209–11

romance, 39, 49–53, 66, 96, 98, 106
Roosevelt, Theodore, 100
Ross, Andrew, 210
Ross, Jonathan, 32
Rowling, J.K., 187, 208, 212–14, 216,
  218–20, 223

Saint in London, The (film), 103
Saint in Palm Springs, The (film), 104
Saint's Double Trouble, The (film), 104
Samson and Delilah (film), 106
Sanders, George, 9–10, 91–3, 101–6
Sandvoss, Cornel, 8, 41–2, 52, 54, 58,
  59, 63, 64, 66–8, 177, 236
science fiction, 7, 9, 49, 73, 75, 115,
  209–11, 215
ScoobyDoo, Where are You? (TV), 117
Se7en (film), 10, 122–3
second-screen viewing, 8, 17,
  29–30
self-improvement, 73
Serenity (film), 149, 156, 159, 214
Seventh Victim, The (film), 103
sex , 48, 49, 51, 53, 64, 66, 78, 119,
  211
sexuality, 49–50, 136, 138
Shadow of a Doubt (film), 97
Shakespeare, William, 160, 188
Shameless Screen Entertainment, 128,
  133–8, 140, 143–4
Sherlock (TV), 12, 166, 167,
  169, 174, 176, 189, 192, 194, 202,
  203*n*3
Sherlock Holmes (film), 189
Sherlock Holmes: A Game of Shadows
  (film), 189
shipping, *see* fan fiction
Showtime (channel), 113, 121
Silence of the Lambs (film), 121
Since You Went Away (film), 97
Six Feet Under (TV), 112, 113, 118
Skins (TV), 8, 19, 22, 27–31, 33
Skylark (film), 93–4
Slack, Andrew, 13, 206–7, 209,
  213–19, 221, 224
A Slight Trick of the Mind (book), 190
So Evil My Love (film), 93, 95
soap opera, *see* television

social media, 6, 7, 8, 17–19, 24, 27–8,
30, 32–5, 41, 57, 59–60, 62, 64,
164–5, 167, 170–4, 177, 180, 189,
210, 234
social networks, 24, 26, 28, 30–2, 34,
62, 212, 214, 223
spectatorship, 75, 100, 150, 156–7,
158, 172
Spider-Man, 202
spoilers, 7, 166–9, 172, 174–7, 179
spreadable media, 165, 195
Stacey, Jackie, 43–5
Star Trek (TV), 1, 2, 9, 73–84, 187, 188,
189–90, 209–10, 212, 213, 224,
234
Star Trek: The Next Generation (TV), 79,
211
Star Wars (film), 1, 3–6, 75, 224
Starburst (magazine), 167, 176
Stargate SG-1 (TV), 210
Starsky and Hutch (TV), 213
Strand Magazine, The (magazine),
200–1
A Study in Scarlet (book), 198, 199, 200
A Study in Scarlet (comic), 191
Summer Storm (film), 106
Supernatural (TV), 114, 116–17
Suspect, The (film), 106
Suspicion (film), 92, 99

Takeover TV (TV), 17
Tales of the Unexpected (TV), 96
Talk of the Town (film), 100
Tea Party Movement, 214, 225
teenagers, 25–6, 219
telefantasy, 114
telephilia, 21
television, 1–2, 5–12, 18–21, 23, 28,
30, 32, 34, 39, 60, 73, 78, 80, 82,
84n3, 93, 96, 110, 131, 149, 151,
153, 156, 159, 170–1, 186–90,
196, 202, 203n4, 232–3
archives, 8, 21–2
catch-up, 111
crime, 40, 120
documentary, 39, 41, 51, 113, 186
drama, 43, 49–51
idents, 21, 116

locations, 39, 40, 56, 113, 115,
164–7, 169–72, 174, 176–7,
181–2
networks, 189, 209, 211
opening credit sequences, 10, 54,
111–24, 125n2
reality, 39–41, 54, 57, 59, 67, 69n5,
69n8, 69n9
sitcom, 69n3, 116–17
soap opera, 39–41, 51–2, 69n5,
85n9, 170
teen, 22, 29, 33, 39–40, 47, 51–2,
69n3
Texas Chainsaw Massacre, The (film),
122
textual poaching, 11, 73, 165–6, 235,
236
Third Man, The (film), 98
This Land is Mine (film), 106
3D, 114
Three Smart Girls (film), 93
TimeWarner, 187
To Kill a Mockingbird (film), 122
tourism, 56, 164
toys, 1–3, 6
Trafalgar Square, 180–1
transmedia storytelling, 6, 12, 66, 192
transmediality, 6, 8, 31, 60, 64–5,
67–8, 125n4, 188, 236
Tron (film), 115
True Blood (TV), 10, 110, 113, 116,
118, 121–2, 125n4, 225
Tulloch, John, 210–12
Tumblr (social media), 34
Twilight (film), 12, 166, 225
Twilight Zone (TV), 19
Twilight: New Moon (film), 165
Twin Peaks (TV), 112
Twitter (social media), 26, 30–5, 41,
59–62, 167, 169–72, 177

Uncle Harry (film), 102, 105
Under Capricorn (film), 98
Uninvited, The (film), 93, 94
United Kingdom, 17, 39–41, 46, 68n2,
69n8, 128, 129, 130, 133, 139,
143, 167, 170, 173, 179, 180–1,
189, 193, 195
Universal Studios, 9, 91, 102

USA, 9, 73–4, 76, 81–2, 85*n*25, 119, 136, 194–5, 210
Utopia (TV), 6, 8, 19, 28, 31–3
utopianism, 73, 75, 78–9

Valleys, The (TV), 40, 49, 68*n*2, 69*n*3
Vampire Diaries (TV), 125*n*3
vampires, 112–14, 162
Van Dijck, José, 4, 182
van Zoonen, Liesbet, 178, 211
Vancouver, 181
Verbier, 56
VHS, 136, 139, 234
video, 6, 12, 19, 21–2, 25, 31–2, 60, 73, 111, 139, 172, 174, 216
   fan made, 2–4
   Recordings Act, 130
video nasties, 10, 129, 136, 138, 140, 234
video games, 1, 3–4, 6, 186
Vietnam War, 82–3

Walking Dead, The (TV), 121, 124, 125*n*5
Wal-Mart (store), 213
Warner Brothers, 12, 187, 189, 194, 203*n*4, 212, 220, 223
Watson, Dr John, 189–91, 194, 198–9, 201
Web 2.0, 25, 212

Welles, Orson, 96–7, 98
West Wing, The (TV), 112, 114
Whedon, Joss, 7, 11, 113, 149–50, 153–6, 158–62, 236
Wilde, Oscar, 101
Wilder, Billy, 94–5
Wilding, Michael, 98
Wilson, Shaun, 4
Wire, The (TV), 112
Wizard of Oz, The (film), 77
Woman in the Window, 106
Wonderful Wizard of Oz, The (book), 76–7
Wood, Mary, 142–3
World War One, 103
World War Two, 85*n*25

X-Factor, The (TV), 41
X-Files, The (TV), 2, 51, 116
X-The Man with the X-Rays Eyes (film), 93

Yorke, Carl G., 141, 142
YouTube, 1, 3, 4, 8, 18–23, 34–5, 59, 125*n*1, 174

Zeebox (app), 30, 33, 35
Zipes, Jack, 76
zombies, 124, 191
Zucco, George, 9, 91